Captain Boycott
AND
The Irish

Captain Boycott
AND
The Irish

JOYCE MARLOW

Saturday Review Press / E. P. Dutton & Co., Inc.
NEW YORK

First published by Andre Deutsch Ltd., London, 1973
Copyright © 1973 by Joyce Marlow
All rights reserved. Printed in the U.S.A.
First American Edition 1973

10   9   8   7   6   5   4   3   2   1

ISBN: 0-8415-0271-4
Library of Congress Catalog Card Number: 73-78914

FOR PATRICK AND HIS IRISH ANCESTORS

'Perhaps Almighty God reserveth Ireland in this
unquiete state stille, for some secret scourge
which shall by her come unto England.'

Edmund Spenser, 1559.

Contents

photographs follow page 160

Acknowledgements

I should like to thank the following people for their kind assistance during the research and general preparation of this book; the staff of the Reading Room and the Department of MSS at the British Museum; the staff of the National Library of Ireland; the staff of the Public Record Offices in London and Dublin; Mr Mac Giolla Choille, the Keeper of the Manuscripts at the State Paper Office, Dublin Castle, and his staff; Mr and Mrs John Daly of Lough Mask House, County Mayo for their help and hospitality; the Reverend James Gilchrist, of Aldeby, Suffolk, for showing me round Burgh St Peter parish church, allowing me to examine the records and for his hospitality; Mrs Gilian Pope who conducted me over Boycott's birthplace at Burgh St Peter, now her home; John E. Shephard, Q.P.M. of Belfast, particularly for his generous co-operation regarding the photographs of the Relief Expedition in his possession; and Des Wynne for giving me permission to use these photographs which were taken by his grandfather and now form part of the Wynne Collection, Castlebar, County Mayo.

Captain Boycott
AND
The Irish

CHAPTER I

'A Respectable Gentleman, Formerly an Officer in Her Majesty's 39th Regiment'

Charles Cunningham Boycott was born at Burgh St Peter, Norfolk, England, on March 12, 1832, the year of the great Reform Bill. Half a century later he had immortality thrust upon him in County Mayo, Ireland, when his name was appropriated for a method of communal ostracism which proved a weapon of such strength that it helped effect changes comparable with the parliamentary reforms initiated in the year of his birth, and which was subsequently adopted by peoples and languages throughout the world. In neither the background nor the character of the child was there any indication of future notoriety, or enshrinement in the linguistic currency of so many nations.

The Boycotts had been settled in Norfolk for nearly one hundred and fifty years, and in the actual parish of Burgh St Peter for nearly seventy years, before the birth of Charles Cunningham. The family was of French extraction, among the many Huguenots who fled to England in 1685 when Louis XIV revoked the Edict of Nantes which had previously granted civil and religious liberty to French Protestants. When they arrived in England and migrated to Norwich the family spelled their name Boycatt, and after eighty years in Norwich Samuel Boycatt – the spelling remained the same – was granted the patronage and rectorship of the living of St Mary's Church, Burgh St Peter. Samuel's grandson, William, was also vicar and patron of the living and when his second son was christened on March 16, 1832, it was as Charles Cunningham Boycatt. Then, abruptly, in the parish burial register in the middle of 1841 and in the christening register at the end of the same year, the name was Boycott. What prompted the change of one letter remains unknown, the parish registers contain no clue, the alteration appears without explanation – Charles's brother, William, born in 1842, is entered as Boycott – and thereafter remains constant as Boycott. The word that is in such common usage, as both verb and noun, could have been 'to boycatt' or 'the boycatt', but for the whim or the express desire of the Reverend William Boycott or another member of the family in the year 1841, when Charles Cunningham was nine years old.

Burgh St Peter was, and is, an isolated community in a remote corner of rural England. It lies on the north bank of the estuary of the River Waveney, just in the county of Norfolk (across the river is Suffolk), half surrounded by marshes – treacherous, fascinating, unwelcoming to the outsider – and beyond is the cold grey North Sea. The lonely, mysterious physical environment may have sharpened a certain inborn solitariness in the young Boycott, for later in life he was to demonstrate a liking for remote places. However, in the 1830s as he grew up, Burgh St Peter if isolated was reasonably prosperous. It was not primarily an agricultural community, although good farmland lies behind, but a fishing village. The inching recession of the sea along the East Anglian coast had not then stranded Burgh St Peter, the men sailed their fishing boats down the estuary to the open waters, while a ferry operated across the river linking the north bank hamlets and villages to the focal point of Lowestoft on the south bank.

In the general life of this tight-knit, hardy, seafaring community it is doubtful the Boycotts took much part. They were the patrons and vicars, the representatives of the Church of England, one of the immutable pillars of the edifice of English life. The edifice was already starting to crumble in the towns but in the villages the twin pillars of squire and vicar, smiling beneficently (or otherwise) down the well-ordered ladder, remained as firm as ever. In this system it was the exception rather than the rule for the vicar to show interest in his parishioners other than

christening the newborn, preaching a sermon to a packed ch
on Sundays, handing out the occasional bowl of soup to the p
but deserving, and burying the dead. Otherwise their main p
occupation, often performed in the role of magistrate – the
'parson-justices' reviled by the Radicals – was to detect and remove the malcontents so that everybody should continue to know
his proper place for the benefit of all. There is no evidence that
the Boycotts were exceptional for the period; on the contrary they
seem to have fitted firmly into the rule.

Of family characteristics there is some evidence, notably pages
written by Charles's father, the Reverend William Boycott, of
which the following is an extract:

'From 1790 to this period the Register was kept by Mr Page (a curate
to my father) and there were so many mistakes which I, becoming
acquainted with the parish, had it in my power to rectify, that I thought
it better to cut out the page than to transmit the mistakes to posterity.
By comparing my record of the years 1790, 91, 92, 93 and 94 with the
Bills . . . given, it will be found that Mr Page was uniformly mistaken
in the maiden name of Mrs Thurston whom he registered as Westly
but who is the illeg: d. of Martha Lytton bapt March 29, 1707, and also
the maiden name of Mrs Chalker, and also that he registered Father to
illeg. children of the daughter of Elizabeth Holder registered as illeg.
in 1790. I have to observe that the mother was at the time a married
woman and her husband alive, either transported or on board the
hulks, certainly not in cohabitation with her. . . .'

The sense of superiority that permeates the Reverend Boycott's
castigation of Mr Page is a not uncommon human attribute. What
was peculiar to this period, as to earlier ones, was the certainty
that the superiority was not only inborn but divinely and rightly
so. Some men were created to rule, whether over a vast empire
or within their allotted sphere, and this was inevitable and just,
ordained by God. The confidence such certainty gave was imbibed as mother's milk by the young Charles, and it was to help
provide him with the courage and indifference to hostility that he
later showed. If the sense of superiority was common to the upper

strata of English society, the result of class and upbringing, other traits exhibited in the Reverend William's notes were individual, the product of hereditary and personal character development. Some of these traits were inherited by the young Charles, the irritation with the mistakes of inferiors, the pedantic attention to minutiae, the concentration on trivia that tends to lose sight of the whole, or the importance of other factors. These particular attributes are not greatly appreciated by the Irish as a race and were to contribute, in some small measure, to the situation in which Charles Cunningham Boycott found himself half a century later.

The child matured in a secure, comfortable, ordered environment, insulated by class from the harder, harsher life that surrounded him in the fishing community of Burgh St Peter. His father's forebears had been established as patrons and vicars of the parish for seventy years, not a long time-span in rural England, but the Huguenot ancestry was one that had become respectable and honoured, while his mother, born Elizabeth Georgina Beevor, had a minor title in her pedigree, being the grand-daughter of Sir Thomas Beevor. The insulation provided by the family's social position was heightened by a certain physical isolation. The rectory in which Charles Cunningham was born (still standing in the 1970s and, after a period of dereliction, being refurbished) lay apart from the village, on the road to the parish church. At the time of his birth it was a new house, and a most charming and pleasant one. The Reverend William may have been a pedantic gentleman with a high opinion of his personal worth but when he decided to build the new rectory he chose comfortable elegance rather than rambling ostentation, a compact house with bow windows, light airy rooms, without interminable corridors. In the 1830s the grounds of the rectory were spacious and there were numerous outbuildings, including the bakery and stables. It was presumably as a child in his father's stables that the young Charles acquired his love of horses and riding. Until notoriety was thrust upon him in the 1880s his only claim to fame, in a very limited circle, lay in his ability as a horseman, his skill 'over the sticks' being held in particular esteem. Riding may also have appealed to the taciturn – he was never noted for the art of conversation – rather solitary child; and for those who find communication with other human beings difficult, animals sometimes provide a useful substitute.

If the Boycotts were, on the whole, a conformist family who implicitly accepted the values of Church, Monarchy and Constitution, and believed devoutly in the continuance of the established hierarchy, there was a strain of eccentricity to which the parish church of Burgh St Peter still bears witness. The church lies in splendid isolation a good two country miles from the remaining village, and is today an extraordinary sight, rearing out of the desolate marshland on the edge of nowhere; even in the 1830s when Burgh St Peter was more thriving it must have presented an odd aspect. The main body of the church is longish and low, built in grey stone, typical of uninspired rural medieval architecture, and until 1790 it had an accompanying squat, grey stone tower. In that year, under the direction of Charles's grandfather, the Reverend Samuel Boycott, it acquired a bright red brick tower constructed in a series of ascending boxes of diminishing size. Nobody is quite sure why the Reverend Samuel Boycott added this architectural anomaly which snarls at the rest of the building like a dog at a cat, but the result indicates a lack of taste combined with an eccentricity, not to say temerity, of character. One explanation offered for the red brick tower also suggests a very literal mind. Apparently, one of the Reverend Samuel's sons was in Italy when construction of the new tower started and on his arrival home, the red brick tower then being completed, he gazed at it in astonishment and said, 'But where are the cypresses?' The interpretation of this cryptic remark is that from Italy the son sent a sketch, intimating that he wished cypress trees to be planted along the path from the entrance gate to the main door of the church. The Reverend Samuel interpreted the sketch wrongly and the result was the tower which has been described both as a monstrosity, and a joke, but whose originality cannot be denied.

The idea that the church tower was a joke can be dismissed, as none of the Boycotts left evidence of a sense of humour; ironical, perverted or straightforward. If the tower was a manifestation of eccentricity, this trait was inherited by the young Charles, and if the interpretation of a literal mind is accepted, heredity played its part with Charles Cunningham Boycott. Again, such persevering literal-mindedness was not to endear him to the peasantry of County Mayo, and partly accounted for their reaction towards him and his concomitant position in the halls of fame.

The young Charles grew up in his secure background with neither thought of, nor wish for, future fame. The mode and style of living to which he had been born suited him admirably and driving ambition, or even modest ambition, was not a part of him. Decent respectable people lived decent, respectable lives, providing the backbone of England and the British Empire, and if their lives were not as decently respectable as they might have been, they kept the skeletons hidden, leaving fame or notoriety to the higher-born or the charlatans. At an appropriate age, following the tradition of his class, Charles was sent away to boarding schools at Woolwich and Blackheath, then both pleasantly situated outside London. At the age of eighteen he followed another tradition, an unusual one for the Boycotts but common amongst the class to which they belonged, by becoming a soldier. (It was left to his younger brother, William, to uphold family tradition by entering the Church and, on his father's death, he became rector of Burgh St Peter.) A commission was bought for Charles in the 39th Foot, a good regiment of the line though not among the most fashionable (in the reorganisation of the British army in 1881 it became the 1st Battalion the Dorsetshire Regiment, now the Devon and Dorset Regiment). Little is known about Boycott's life as a soldier, and after only three years he bought himself out of the army. Why he decided to return to civilian life after such a brief spell is uncertain, but he had come of age and the amount of money he inherited on reaching his majority gave him sufficient independence to choose his way of life. What he chose to do in 1853 was to sell his commission and to settle in Ireland, taking the lease on a farm between Clonmel and Carrick-on-Suir in the southernmost part of County Tipperary. In the meantime he had married a young lady called Annie Dunne whom he had met while his regiment was stationed in Ireland. She came from Queen's County (now County Laois) and was a member of the Anglo-Irish Protestant Ascendancy. It is possible that she was disinclined to become a soldier's wife, although from the accepted Victorian position of woman as the docile chattel and the lack of comment made about Annie Boycott's character, it would seem more likely that it was Boycott himself who made the decision to leave the army.

With reference to Boycott's military rank, later, at the height of his notoriety it was stated by the American journalist, James Redpath, of whom we shall be hearing more, that it was not genuine: 'by the by, his title of Captain is a fraud; he is not a captain'. By that date it was perhaps true to say 'he *is* not a captain'; but that he had never been one was untrue. Boycott had held the rank in the 39th Foot and having done so was entitled, if he thus desired, to designate himself Captain for the rest of his life. In fact, it should be noted that Boycott personally did not flourish the title, the few printed references to him before 'boycotting' erupted styled him C. Boycott, Esq., and he signed his name Charles C. Boycott with no mention of his military title. The use of 'Captain' was a later device of journalists, both loyalist and nationalist – the former to demonstrate that it was a man of stature who was being subjected to the boycotting treatment, the latter partly to show that he should have known better than to behave as he had, partly to emphasise that even a man of social standing could now be dealt with by the Irish tenant farmers.

At the age of twenty-one, newly married, Boycott embarked upon a fresh chapter in his life as an English landlord in Ireland, (although only as a lessee and in a small way) but it was this new role that was eventually to lead to his becoming headline news throughout the Western world. In 1853 he was a young man of medium height, standing 5 ft 7½ in. but always erect, with the bearing of a soldier, of muscular build with dark hair and grey eyes, of overall feature neither ugly nor handsome, lacking charm of manner. He seemed to be and was an average man, by no means to be listed among the more vicious or evil sections of the human race but not endowed with high intelligence, imagination, wit, compassion or perception. His friends – and if he did not make them easily he made some – liked him because he was not a fool, he was a good horseman, he could be jovial in their company, he was prepared to work hard and he held the right beliefs, in Queen and Country, but not too passionately. He had few if any enemies, and those who disliked him did so because he was brusque and taciturn with all but the selected few, because he was a rigid, limited, rather solitary figure, but both friend and foe regarded him with moderation. The young man, as the child, seemed firmly placed among the middle mass of the human race, unlikely ever to rouse great love or hate. However, Boycott had decided to settle in Ireland, the country in which the fuse of history has implanted one of its more indelible trails, spluttering, erupting, spending itself like a fire cracker, but with each cracker, on a long remembered lead, tied to the previous one. Thus anything was possible, and such an unlikely candidate as Charles Cunningham Boycott, the son of a vicar from Burgh St Peter, Norfolk, was to be enmeshed in the trail and provide another keg of gunpowder for the apparently endless fuse.

In 1853 when Boycott leased the land in County Tipperary, Ireland was in one of its periods of apparent calm, or torpor, according to whether one viewed the situation from an English or militant Irish point of view. However, the three crucial and fundamental problems that had plagued Anglo-Irish relations since the time of Elizabeth I loomed as large as ever. The three problems were: (a) the constitutional relationship between the two countries (*b*) religion – the imposition of the Established Protestant Church on a Catholic population and the failure of the alien religion to gain any foothold in the faith, loyalty or affection of the populace (*c*) the land – the imposition of the English agrarian system. Of these three, the one that concerned Boycott's fate the least was the religious aspect, although the basic disharmony of Catholic population and Protestant overlordship coloured every angle of Anglo-Irish affairs to some degree. The constitutional relationship was at the root of the discord, and Boycott was partially ensnared in the attempts to find a satisfactory solution. When England subdued Ireland in the seventeenth century there was a parliament in Dublin, although it was already a castrated instrument, assembled only if Westminster thought fit, with such laws as it passed subject to Westminster's sanction. But there *was* an Irish Parliament House on College Green, however supine its members, and in 1782 it and they ceased to fill the role of doormats. Grattan's Parliament, which lasted until 1800, fought for and obtained a certain legislative independence, even though the laws it passed remained subject to a veto from Westminster. The taste of independence led to vigorous demands for greater freedom from the domination of England, culminating in Wolfe Tone's rebellion of 1798. To this uprising of the United Irishmen, England reacted strongly, and in 1800 the Act of Union between the two countries was passed whereby the Dublin parliament assisted in voting itself out of existence – partially due to blackmail, partially fear, partially the self-interest of its members – and Ireland became an integral part of the United Kingdom, governed from Westminster, to which it sent a number of MPs. The memory of the Parliament House on College Green remained indelibly etched, if not in the minds of the mass of peasants, in the minds of the Irish patriots, as the symbol of national pride and independence. Daniel O'Connell vowed, as he watched the new flag (the completed Union Jack) being raised over Dublin Castle in 1800, 'that the foul dishonour should not last if I could put an end to it'. Throughout his life

O'Connell veered and tacked, an Irish cutter in English dominated seas, but fundamentally he stayed true to his vow although,
when he died in 1847, 'the foul dishonour' had not been removed,
the Act of Union had not been repealed. In O'Connell's last years
the Young Ireland movement emerged, disenchanted with his
failure to achieve repeal by constitutional methods, querying the
aim itself, reaching back to Wolfe Tone's republican doctrines,
attempting to rouse the Irish soul as much as the body, to establish a sense of nationality through the resurrection of the Gaelic
cultural heritage. In 1848 the Young Ireland movement rose in
rebellion but it was an abortive effort that occasioned England
little panic, and by 1853 the constitutional position was stagnant,
with Ireland governed from Westminster and little overt agitation either for the repeal of the Act of Union or for separatist
aims.

The third of the major problems poisoning the relationship
between England and Ireland was the land. The great land blunder
was made concomitantly with England's conquest of Ireland. It
was partly the result of misunderstanding, partly the conqueror's
failure to enquire into the minds and customs of the conquered,
but it also arose from England's benign conviction of the superiority of her own way of life – as John Stuart Mill wrote: 'There
is no other nation which is so conceited of its own institutions,
and all its modes of public action, as England is.' Apart from the
inclination to pass on to the natives their superior agrarian system, the English conquerors assumed that the Irish chieftains
owned the land under their jurisdiction as the aristocracy and
squirearchy owned the land in England; that there was a defined
relationship between chieftan and peasant as there was in England
between villager and landlord; that one worked for and was paid
by the other, living in a cottage that was the property of the
landlord, with the maintenance of the cottage and the improve-
ment of the land the landlord's responsibility.

In fact, the feudal system that had centuries before spread
through so much of Europe had failed to cross the Irish sea, and

Ireland in the seventeenth and eighteenth centuries remained a *tribal* society in which there was no clear-cut landlord-tenant relationship, in which the tribesmen-tenant farmed a piece of land, making the improvements on the land himself, and regarding himself, therefore, as the possessor of rights in the soil itself. When James I confiscated tracts of Ireland, giving them to his favourites or encouraging outsiders (mainly of Scottish origin) to settle and thus counterbalance the unruly indigenous population, he considered he was exercising the rights of the conqueror by relieving the defeated Irish chieftans of their property. To the peasant who lived on the confiscated land, it was his property and had been since time immemorial. This view was confirmed by the Bessborough Commission as late as 1880: 'There has in general survived to the Irish farmer, through all vicissitudes, in despite of the seeming or real veto of the law, in apparent defiance of political economy, a living tradition of possessory rights, such as belong, in the more primitive ages of society, to the status of the man who tilled the soil.' Over the years many individuals, both English and Irish, had tried to stress this and other points, to emphasise that the Irish land question was not the same as the British; the Devon Commission, had in the 1840s stated: 'We find that widely spread and daily increasing confusion exists; and it is impossible to reject the conclusion that, unless they (tenant rights) be distinctly defined and respected, much social disorder and national inconvenience must inevitably be the consequence.' The conclusion had been rejected, partly because of the feeling that Ireland was now an integral part of the United Kingdom and must therefore learn to comply with the laws and customs of the land. The prevailing nineteenth-century sentiment was pithily expressed by Lord Palmerston in his famous remark: 'Tenant right is landlord wrong.'

The point was that the Irish tenant farmers had no rights. It should be said that the lot of the mid-nineteenth century English agricultural worker was not a happy one, either. Most of his ancient rights had been eroded by the Enclosure Acts; he worked long hours for miserable wages; he could be evicted from his tied cottage which was often damp and rotten, the landlord having failed to effect his responsibility for improvements; but the English village labourers were still protected by a minimum of Common Law rights and, more importantly, there was a defined relationship between master and man, the terms of the contract were clearly understood. But in Ireland year after year, decade after decade, the old customs were allowed to operate both by the peasants who, dispirited, disorganised and desperate, had little option, and by the landlords, whom they suited. The peasant-tenant rented his plot of land; often he built a cottage stone by stone with his own hands, he then tried to scratch a living and, if he fell behind with his rent, was summarily and legally evicted, without compensation for the improvements he might have made on the land or the cottage he might have built, because there was no defined contract. Again the Devon Commission had emphasised this point: 'The importance and absolute necessity of securing to the occupying tenant in Ireland some distinct mode of remuneration for the judicious improvements that he may effect upon his farm is sustained by *a greater weight of concurrent evidence than any other subject* which has been brought under the investigation of the commissioners.' Again nothing was done, and while the confusion proliferated, the crime and disorder arising from the misery of summary evictions grew ever more rampant.

Furthermore, whereas in England the tenant of a good squire could lead a secure, contented life, Ireland was cursed with the absentee landlord. This situation had started with the initial grants of land to Elizabethan and Jamesian favourites, some of whom had no intention of living in Erin's damp island, and therefore left the running of the estates to agents and bailiffs (others did settle, forming the Anglo-Irish Protestant Ascendancy). The drifting away of landlords was given further impetus by the Act of Union, from which time everything centred on London. The Irish upper classes tended to gravitate towards the new centre, once there they were frequently seduced by a higher standard of comfort and civilisation, and if the landlord was an MP, for instance, he had to be at Westminster for at least half the year. More bailiffs and agents were installed to run the estates in Ireland, and how they ran them was left to their own consciences. By 1849 so many estates had, by this process and other factors, run themselves into bankruptcy, that the Encumbered Estates Act was passed. The intention behind the Act was beneficial – Gladstone said it was passed 'with lazy, heedless, uninformed good intentions', but its effect was disastrous. Thousands of estates had become unsaleable because of encumbrances or mortgages, therefore if, on petition from the owners or creditors, the estates were allowed to pass into the hands of a court for free sale, the stagnant Irish agriculture might be given new life and prosperity might return. What happened was that over seven thousand estates were indeed sold, but into the hands of a race of middlemen who bought speculatively. A few actually settled in Ireland but the majority installed more bailiffs and agents, and the object of all was to make a profit. One way of doing this was to clear the land of its uneconomic smallholdings and turn it over to grazing. The smallholders were evicted in their thousands, without compensation, because they had no legal rights, the land being bought and sold over their heads. In the mid and late 1840s the other main factor affecting Irish land was the great famine, when blight struck at 'the ever damned potato ... the curse of Ireland', over a million people died from starvation and, as significantly for the future, another million embittered survivors emigrated to the United States, forming a reservoir of hatred for England and all things English.

Before leaving the land question temporarily, for its emergence as a dominant factor in Anglo-Irish relations was also the dominant reason for Boycott's being thrust into the limelight, it should be noted that, curiously, in the past it had not been used as a major political weapon. Curiously, because in retrospect the land seems to have been the obvious key with which to have released the passions of the peasants – the ideal (Irish ownership of Irish land), and the practicality (the very means of life itself), for which they would stand up and fight. The man who first grasped the key was James Fintan Lalor, who was most grievously handicapped physically, asthmatic, with a curvature of the spine from birth, and, throughout his brief life, increasingly deaf and short-sighted, but with mental capacities undimmed. It was Fintan Lalor who propounded the doctrine that the land belonged basically to the people, that the landlords' interest should be conditional and, vitally, that land was the prime issue on which the peasants could and should be organised. In a letter printed in the *Irish Felon* in 1848 he wrote:

'The land question contains, and the legislative question does *not* contain the materials from which victory is manufactured'.

He then found the imagery that was to grip future generations. To achieve independence, to prevent England from ultimately conquering the Irish spirit, he wrote:

'There is, I am convinced, but one way alone; and that is to link Repeal to some other question, like a railway carriage to the engine; some questions possessing the intrinsic strength which Repeal wants; and strong enough to carry both itself and Repeal together. . . . And such a question there is in the land – ages have been preparing it. An engine ready-made, one too that will generate its own steam without cost or care – a self-acting engine, if once the fire be kindled. . . . Repeal had always to be dragged. This I speak of will carry itself – as the cannon ball carries itself down the hill.'

Fintan Lalor, who died the next year, did not succeed in kindling the fire among his fellow Young Irelanders; it was not on the question of land that they rebelled. But his prophetic belief in the importance of the question was shared by one surviving member of the movement, Charles Gavan Duffy, and he attempted to utilise it as a practical political platform. By the time Boycott decided to settle in Ireland in 1853, Gavan Duffy had already founded the Tenant Right League whose policy was to maintain an independent Irish party at Westminster, fighting for what later became known as 'the three F's'; fixity of tenure, fair rents and free sale of tenancy. But Gavan Duffy was a moderate, it was perhaps too soon after the trauma of the famine years to expect mass peasant involvement, and he failed to obtain it or to kindle the flame that would weld together the disparate elements of Irish nationalism. By 1855 the Tenant Right League had foundered, and Gavan Duffy left Ireland for Australia convinced from his experience of dissension and back-stabbing that there was 'no more hope for the Irish cause than for the corpse on the dissecting table'. With his departure the country relapsed into its calm or torpor, with as little apparent interest in rectifying the land question as in claiming constitutional independence from England.

CHAPTER 2

'Out and Make Way for the Bold Fenian Men'

Before the disenchanted Gavan Duffy sailed from Ireland's shores, Captain and Mrs Boycott, a further inheritance having matured, made a move from their small farm in southern Tipperary to Achill Island, the wild rugged hump of land with towering cliffs and silver strands that juts into the Atlantic Ocean off the Mayo coast, at the westward extremity of the British Isles. It was a friend named Murray McGregor Blacker who persuaded Boycott to settle on this remote island. Blacker was a magistrate who owned an estate on the Mayo mainland near Claremorris, as well as a house and the lease of several thousand acres of land from the Irish Church Mission Society on Achill, and the arrangement he and Boycott made was that he would sub-lease two thousand of these Achill acres to Boycott who would also act as his agent there. With men of Blacker and Boycott's standing there was a legal lease; the confusing lack of definition applied only to the mass of cottiers and small tenant farmers.

Initially life was hard and money not too plentiful, according to Boycott, who later said it was only after 'a long struggle against adverse circumstances' that his means improved and he became prosperous on Achill. The prosperity may have been assisted by a further inheritance, because Boycott's overall record was to show more reliance on inherited money than on his own ability as a farmer or businessman, but, however the money accrued, he was eventually able to build a fine house near Dooagh with a magnificent view overlooking Clew Bay. Originally he settled near Kim strand where physical conditions were indeed adverse, and apart from the inducements offered by Blacker, the decision to take up residence there underlines the solitary, self-contained strain in Boycott's character.

However, life on Achill was not without its excitement or power struggles and in these Boycott played a large part. Two years after his arrival he was sued for assault by one Thomas Clarke. At the Achill Petty Sessions held in January 1856, Clarke said that at the beginning of December 1855 he had gone to Mr Boycott's residence at Kim to ask for repayment of a debt which Boycott denied owing, and consequently told him to go away. This Clarke refused to do and stood on the doorstep for about half an hour after which time Boycott re-emerged, came close to him and said, 'If you do not be off, I will make you,' whereupon Clarke took himself off, and then instigated legal proceedings. However, after telling this tale to the magistrates, Clarke went on to say that Boycott did not in fact owe him any money and had not struck him, the magistrates adjudged 'there was no assault whatever, either threatened or committed' and dismissed the case on merits. Reading the brief account in the local paper one is left with the strong suspicion that Clarke had grounds for bringing the action; that he should, in the first place, have gone to ask Boycott for repayment of a debt when no money was owed seems doubtful, and that he should then bring an action for assault when none had been committed even more doubtful. The references to Boycott as a respectable gentleman and to Clarke's inferior social status would seem to indicate that the latter's mistake was to try and fight the local power structure and that class solidarity played its part in the verdict.

The contretemps with Clarke was as nothing compared to the acrimony which evolved between Boycott and his friend Murray McGregor Blacker on the one side, and a Mr Carr and Mr O'Donnell on the other. Carr was the agent for the Achill Church Mission Estate from which the two men leased their lands, while O'Donnell was Carr's bailiff. Prior to Boycott's arrival, Carr was one of the kings of the island and certainly lord of his immediate area, but Boycott's residence at Kim was only eight miles from Carr's house and an immediate struggle for power and authority developed. It was probably unconscious on Boycott's part, as he was a gentleman accustomed to the rights and prerogatives of the propertied class, and he was never to show a counterbalancing awareness of other people's feelings; whereas Carr was not quite a gentleman though he possessed a defined authority locally, as agent for the Church Mission Estate which he was determined to retain. The first time the two men directly and acrimoniously opposed each other was in 1858 when a new Board of Guardians was due for election; Boycott supported one set of candidates, Carr another, and the former's won the day.

The next dispute was even more crucial, for it was concerned with salvage rights, which meant money. Shipwrecks were frequent off the stormy, rocky coast of Mayo and previously Carr, assisted by O'Donnell, had been the local receiver, which meant he was entitled to collect the salvage from the beaches and wrecks, and guard it for the official Receiver of Wrecks, prior to public auction. In addition, a percentage of the sale went to the local receiver, and anything not sold became his property. There were also the obvious incidental perquisites, for nobody other than those in the vicinity at the time of the wreck could say what had or had not been washed up. Salvage was, therefore, comparatively big business for those who could get their hands on it legally, and it provided an added means of illegal subsistence for Achill natives.

At the beginning of 1859, a large ship was wrecked off Keel strand, and in this instance it was Blacker and Carr who had a heated controversy over the salvage, but Boycott involved himself in the dispute, called Carr 'a consummate blackguard' and had him summonsed for trespass, but the case was dismissed on merits. O'Donnell also managed to get himself involved and he summonsed Boycott for assault, but again the case was dismissed on merits. By the end of 1859 there was a state of simmering warfare between the Gentlemen represented by Boycott and

Blacker and the Players represented by Carr and O'Donnell, with both sides alternately obstructing or utilising the Achill peasants, poised to leap into action to maintain their power at the slightest opportunity. At the beginning of 1860, action presented itself in the form of another large shipwreck off Keel strand, whereupon Mr Carr wrote a letter to the Receiver of Wrecks for that part of the Mayo Coast which read as follows:

ACHILL, 11 JAN, 1860.

Dear Sir,

There must have been a shipwreck not many miles distant from this island.

A great number of staves and planks, together with part of the side of the ship, have been washed ashore and conveyed to private houses etc.

The Coast Guard, on the information of my men, proceeded to the spot, and found the staves, planks, etc, which should have been reported to you on this day week.

I am sorry to say that the Coast Guards have not found a farthing's worth without being publicly informed by my bailiffs of the house and place to where they were removed.

Mr Boycott's men were found this morning early (in his presence) breaking up the wreck, and conveying the iron to his house.

I beg to call your attention to the 450th and 454th sections of the Merchant Shipping Act both of which are grossly neglected in this locality.

(signed) J. Carr,
Agent for the Trustees of the Achill
Mission Estate.

It was not Mr Carr's business, as agent for the Mission, to track down and report on local salvage although he could claim he had held the local rights and that it was his duty as a citizen to report on illegal salvage. This wreck definitely presented an opportunity to attack Boycott and try to re-establish his authority. However,

Boycott retaliated by suing Carr for malicious libel and claiming £500 damages, an action that was heard not at the local Petty Sessions but in the Record Court of the Mayo Spring Assizes in Castlebar in March, 1860.

Boycott's case was that in the spring of 1859, the Receiver of Wrecks had officially appointed him as the local salvage agent, he had consequently converted an old carpenter's shop on his estate for the purpose of storing the portable salvage prior to public auction, and that Carr's written accusations charging him with larceny of the wreckage were a gross impeachment of his good name and character. Mr Carr's defence, conducted by the leading Mayo barrister of the day, Walter Bourke, Q.C., was unfortunately not reported in the local paper – Boycott and his witnesses received two large columns on the Friday and Saturday, but on Monday all the paper said was, 'The defence occupied the greater part of the day.' However, from the evidence of the plaintiff's witnesses it seems obvious that Carr claimed just comment, that he also claimed that Boycott had frequently failed to report wrecks and had stored salvage not in the carpenter's shop but in his own house. It is also clear that what the case was about was not defamation of character, but whether Messrs Carr and O'Donnell or Messrs Boycott and Blacker would possess the local salvage rights and the financial advantages therein entailed. In the event, the jury disagreed, and after this expensive excursion into court the animosity of the two sides appears to have cooled, or at least they managed to keep their differences private as there is no further record of summonses or legal actions between Boycott and Blacker and Carr and O'Donnell. In 1863, Boycott's name again appeared in the local paper when allegations of inhumanity were made against the Achill Poor Law Guardians, but he was merely noted as being among 'the gentlemen who took an interest in the proceedings'.

In 1880, when Boycott was at the height of his world-wide notoriety, the *Connaught Telegraph* levelled the most extraordinary accusation against him about his years on Achill. Refuting the statements of the loyalist newspapers to the effect that Captain Boycott was a decent, honest, upright citizen it said he was 'one of the trio so ably described by Walter Bourke Q.C., as "The three hairy beggars, Boycott, Blacker and McGregor"'. This description, according to the *Telegraph*, was used by Bourke when he had been prosecuting Boycott at the Castlebar Assizes 'for the offence of getting a poor man, who came demanding debts due to him, coiled in a rope and dragged to the beaches or some cliff in Achill'. The *Telegraph* also said that the 'inoffensive Boycott' had been given the alternative of paying £20 fine or going to jail and that he obviously chose the former. This grave charge was laid at Boycott's door and the facts were quoted in an off-hand manner; the accusation appeared in the middle of a long article about the whole Boycott affair and thereafter was never referred to again.

The *Connaught Telegraph* had good reason for being off-hand because its facts do not bear close investigation. The only time Walter Bourke appeared against Boycott was in the libel case in 1860 which was not concerned with a poor man demanding his due debts, but was based on a fight for power between the upper and slightly lower echelons of Achill society, and the man who had demanded payment of debts was Thomas Clarke in 1856, not at the Assizes but at the Achill Petty Sessions. Whether Boycott threatened to have, or actually had, Clarke man-handled over those frightening Achill cliffs one does not know, but it was certainly not brought out in evidence at the Petty Sessions, and Boycott was not given the choice of £20 fine or a sojourn in jail because the case was dismissed. Whether Walter Bourke mentioned Boycott's alleged indulgence in the pastime of dangling people over the Achill cliffs during his defence speech for Mr Carr, one again does not know, and will not unless the actual court records come to light, but that he spoke of 'the three hairy beggars, Boycott, Blacker and McGregor' seems unlikely. It would be stretching the bounds of coincidence too far to suppose that Boycott had two close friends on Achill, one named McGregor Blacker and the other McGregor.

The amount and type of litigation in which Boycott was involved during his early years on Achill casts an interesting light on the roughness and toughness of the island's life and justice, and on his character. From birth and background he had his unquestioning belief in the superiority of an English gentleman, but by deciding to live on Achill where physical circumstances were harsh, where everybody fought and lived equally harshly, where those who had power were able, because of the remoteness, to exercise it harshly, his inborn characteristics were given little chance to mellow. His battle for the salvage rights also emphasises that he was not a man to back down from a fight, and indicates that he was not averse to making money. But this latter trait had its limitations; there were legitimate, frequently unscrupulous ways, in which a gentleman could make money, and into this category salvage rights came, but there were other means which were beyond the pale, as we shall see later.

As Boycott's character matured and hardened on Achill, as he fought his local battles unknown to the world at large, the separate strands were being woven that were later to be drawn together by circumstance and individuals to produce the tapestry on which his name was to be stitched. His interest in political developments on the Irish mainland and, across the Irish sea, in his native land was restricted to the belief that England must continue to govern Ireland firmly for the Irish benefit as much, if not more, than the English. Had a seer or prophet told him that by 1880 he would in any way be directly involved in a crucial stage of Anglo-Irish relations, he would have dismissed the forecast as nonsense; had they further prophesied that he would be at the centre of the struggle, he would have demanded their incarceration in a lunatic asylum, as indeed would anybody supposedly in his right mind in the late 1850s, 1860s and early 1870s.

Even as the Boycotts moved to Achill in 1855, beneath the surface of the apparent calm the genesis of one of the strands already existed – that strand being Fenianism. The new secret movement grew out of the trauma of the famine years – never again must Ireland be in a position where Irishmen lay down and died in their own country, applauded by Catholic Irish bishops who thanked God that they lived in a land where people would die rather than defraud the landlords of their rent, calmly watched by their English governors. (This was not the whole picture of the famine years but it was the light in which many Irishmen viewed them.) A further impetus was provided by the demise of the Tenant Right League; the failure of Gavan Duffy's attempts to gain anything by constitutional means, more particularly the manner in which he had failed – due to internecine warfare, status-seeking and political intervention by the Catholic bishops – left its mark. The lessons to be learned from the famine years and Gavan Duffy's failure were that it was now essential for Ireland to achieve independence, that England would never respond to the pressure of persuasion or reasonable demands, and that a new movement must be organised, dedicated to throwing off the yoke of oppression by armed rebellion, the basis of which should be non-sectarian and anti-clerical (although not anti-Catholic).

In the mid 1850s, the foundations of this new republican movement were laid in Ireland, and by 1859 its oath had been amended by James Stephens, one of its founders, with some optimism to, 'I, in the presence of Almighty God, do solemnly swear allegiance to the Irish Republic, now virtually established; and that I will do my very utmost, at every risk, while life lasts, to defend its independence and integrity; and finally, that I will yield implicit obedience in all things, not contrary to the laws of God, to the commands of my superior officers. So help me God. Amen'. It was several years before the movement gained the initials that were to sound as a tocsin call to future generations – IRB – and even then nobody was certain whether the 'R' stood for Irish *Republican* Brotherhood or Irish *Revolutionary* Brotherhood, but by then it did not much matter as the concept of final independence through force had been established.

The actual word 'Fenian', and the original movement known as Fenianism, did not originate in Ireland, but in the United States – started, more or less simultaneously with the IRB, by Irish exiles there with the declared policy of supplying funds and arms for the IRB and the successful rebellion which must ensue, while organising American public opinion against England. But it was the name Fenian – coined by John O'Mahony, a Gaelic-speaking survivor of the 1848 rebellion, from the ancient heroes of folklore who were the Irish equivalents of the Samurai – that caught the popular imagination, and the agitation that swept through Ireland and England in the 1860s was known as Fenianism. What the IRB did, by founding a movement based on the twin precepts of total independence and armed revolution and by making close contact with the Irish exiles in the United States, was to bring the Irish-Americans into the arena as a force to be reckoned with, and they were the second of the strands that were to affect Boycott's life.

There were already thousands of Irishmen in the States, many of them survivors of the famine years, vowing, as one said, 'Never to forgive the bloody English Government that allowed a man to be treated worse than a dog', and the new Fenian movement gave them a cause into which they could pour their hatred. Fenianism, in its turn, encouraged the bitterness – in pamphlets and deeds, ensuring that the hatred did not die with new generations; later Sir William Harcourt was to say, 'In former Irish rebellions the Irish were in Ireland ... Now there is an Irish nation in the United States, equally hostile, with plenty of money, absolutely beyond our reach and yet within ten days sail of our shores.'

It must be emphasised that although Fenianism was a popular movement, in the sense that it attracted the lower echelons of Irish society in a manner that constitutional efforts for the repeal of the Act of Union had not (at least since the brief great days of Daniel O'Connell's last campaign), it remained a minority movement. The majority of peasants in Ireland – and the majority of immigrants in the United States – were too engrossed in the business of trying to stay alive to lend more than a vague ear to concepts of Irish independence, or whether it was to be achieved by force or not. Further, the secrecy of Fenianism, particularly the taking of the oath, ran contrary to the tenets of the Catholic faith, and therefore aroused the hostility of the bishops and the suspicion of the faithful. (The platform of 'no priests in politics' did not endear the bishops either.) The immediate effects of Fenianism were not startling, and their actual attempts at action were ludicrous, but the shock waves were immense. The idea that English oppression must be overthrown by force of arms took root, and the interest of the Irish-Americans was roused, if not yet organised.

Fenianism was to have a history of splits and more splits; partly because the movement never threw up a really great or decisive leader; partly due to the inherent difficulties of holding together a secret political organisation; partly from the trait in the Irish character which loves plotting for the sake of plotting and thereby lays itself wide open to counterplotting; and partly from its declared aim. England was to be overthrown only by force of arms, no good Fenian must dream of joining a movement not based on this premise, most good Fenians lacked arms in sufficient quantity, therefore the organisation had long periods of inertia, and the more pragmatic, realistic or energetic of members were constantly hiving off into splinter groups. However, by the 1860s the movement was said to have 100,000 members in Ireland and England,* and 1867 was its year of maximum activity.

In the spring of that year there was a badly organised uprising in Ireland itself which the British government had no difficulty in coping with. Simultaneously, there was an attempt to obtain arms from Chester Castle but, as the garrison was forewarned, due to the success of the counteragents in penetrating the move-

* The figures are suspect because (a) the secrecy of the movement made an accurate head-count difficult (b) they come from the memoirs of early Fenians who may well have exaggerated their support.

ment, this too failed dismally. In North America there were armed incursions into Canada, the idea being to rouse the Irish and possibly the French in that country and thus strike at British domination, but these, too, were abortive. The most dramatic act of 1867 was, however, the ill-fated rescue of the 'Chief Organiser' of England and Ireland, Colonel Thomas J. Kelly, from the van which was taking him to prison in Manchester; ill-fated because, although Kelly was successfully rescued, one of the guards was accidentally killed. The result was that five men were arrested and charged with murder and three of them – Allen, Larkin and O'Brien – were hanged, providing Ireland with 'the Manchester Martyrs' and England with the conviction that dark and sinister forces were at work in her very heart, aiming to destroy society itself. This conviction was enhanced by a further attempt to rescue imprisoned Fenians which occurred at the end of the year. The method chosen this time was to blow a hole in the wall of Clerkenwell prison but it succeeded only in killing a number of innocent bystanders.

If the majority of the British people, and the Irish loyalists, regarded Fenianism as an organisation both ludicrous and malevolent which must be firmly suppressed, there were others on whom the outbreaks had a different effect and included among their number was arguably the greatest Englishman of an era not lacking in heroic figures, William Ewart Gladstone. The sobriquet 'Grand Old Man' had not then been bestowed upon him, but Gladstone was approaching his sixtieth birthday when the Fenian eruptions made him consider what lay behind them, teaching him 'the intensity of Irish disaffection', sounding 'the chapel bell to rouse the conscience of England'. The national conscience had not been roused, it had been outraged by the events of 1867, but Mr Gladstone's had been quickened and, once touched, it was one of the most formidable consciences of all time, erupting like a volcano, spewing forth down the paths of righteousness.

The next year, 1868, Gladstone became Prime Minister, assuming supreme power for the first time, and he noted in his diary, 'I ascend a steepening path, with a burden ever gathering weight. The Almighty seems to sustain and spare me for some purpose of His own, deeply unworthy as I know myself to be. Glory to His name!' (Disraeli's equally typical comment on becoming Prime Minister had been, 'Yes! I have climbed to the top of the greasy pole'.) Ireland was to be the greater part of Gladstone's burden, as he himself prophesied in one of the better known anecdotes of history. When the news that the Queen was summoning him to form a government arrived at Hawarden, Gladstone was engaged in his favourite and much-lampooned form of relaxation – chopping down trees on the estate. According to a later account: 'he said "Very significant" – after a few minutes the blows ceased, and Mr Gladstone resting on the handle of his axe, looked up with deep earnestness in his voice and with great intensity in his face, exclaimed, "My mission is to pacify Ireland". He then resumed his task and never said another word till the tree was down.'

By 'pacifying' Ireland Gladstone meant it was his task to rectify the past mistakes of British governments, through reforms which would assuage the disaffection demonstrated by the Fenian outbreaks and thus bring Ireland to play her due part in, and receive her due benefits from, the British Empire. The lesson of Fenianism had not then in any way led him to believe that Ireland might have justification for wishing to loosen its ties with England or demanding any form of self-government. On becoming Prime Minister he began to focus his massive attention, his great physical and mental energy on to Ireland,* reminding the House of Commons that, 'It has only been since ... the appearance of Fenianism that the mind of the country has been greatly turned to the consideration of Irish affairs.' In 1869 he succeeded in removing one heavy thorn from the Irish flesh by introducing a Bill to disestablish and partially disendow the Church of Ireland. At this date the population of Ireland was 5,750,000, of whom some

---

* 'Don't talk to me of Gladstone's wonderful mind – we all know about that – what I envy is his wonderful body', said Lord Granville.

4,500,000 were Catholics, but the established Protestant Church enjoyed enormous privileges not the least of which was its revenue. Gladstone's Bill dissolved the connection with the English Church, abolished ecclesiastical corporations and curtailed the power of their courts, created a new Commission to deal with the old Irish Church revenues and put the surplus to secular purposes for the benefit of all Ireland. The Bill passed through the House of Commons with comparative ease – the large Non-conformist element in Britain, not to mention within the Liberal party, had no more love for the established Church than had the Catholics. Although the Bill met with heavier weather in the Lords, where many of the about-to-be-disestablished Irish Protestant bishops sat, it was not thrown out, and Mr Gladstone duly received the gratitude of the Catholic hierarchy and some of its flock.

Having disestablished the Irish Church and thus cut a swathe through part of the Anglo-Protestant ascendancy, the next year – 1870 – Gladstone turned his attention to the land question. He had absorbed some of the implications of the problems of divided ownership of Irish land and his Bill was an attempt to give legal recognition to the long-standing tenant grievances; specifically, it aimed to legalise what was known as the Ulster Custom. In the earlier picture of Irish peasant-tenant life, mention of Ulster was deliberately omitted because what obtained in that Province was not true of Ireland as a whole.* It had been into Ulster that the Protestant settlers had been introduced and where the 'plantations' had flourished. From the time of James I, Ulster had been the most prosperous, although not always the least rebellious, part of Ireland (many of the United Irishmen and some of the Young Irelanders had been Ulstermen). On the not always reliable premise of prosperity producing stability, the Ulster Custom,

* The province of Ulster consisted of Cavan, Monaghan and Donegal in addition to the six counties of Down, Antrim, Londonderry, Fermanagh, Tyrone and Armagh, which in 1922 remained part of the United Kingdom, since commonly referred to as Ulster.

whereby the outgoing tenant was paid by the incoming tenant for improvements made during the period of his occupancy, had flourished. The snag to the legalisation of this custom in Gladstone's 1870 Land Act was that it became legal only where it was established – mainly in Ulster and a few isolated pockets in the rest of the country.

The 1870 Bill aimed to assist tenant farmers throughout Ireland by (a) giving all outgoing tenants compensation for the improvements effected by them or their forebears and (b) deterring landlords from capricious eviction by creating a 'compensation for disturbance' clause which would mean that the landlord would have to pay the tenant compensation if he did evict capriciously. With regard to the first, what the Bill failed to do was to legally define 'improvements' so that anybody trying to obtain his compensation became enmeshed in legal battles to prove what he or his forebears had effected, and few peasants could either understand or afford such litigation. With regard to the second, the primary and fatal flaw was that compensation for disturbance was to be paid when eviction was due to causes *other than non-payment of rent.* Bailiffs, agents and landlords swiftly found the answer to this, by raising the rent to a level the tenant could not afford and then legally evicting him without compensation. In addition to these declared aims, John Bright introduced amendments which became known as 'the Bright clauses', the intention of which was, again, wholly admirable – to enable more tenants to buy their land and thus solve the problems of dual ownership. Unfortunately the Bright clauses, mainly due to the obstruction of the Opposition and the Lords but partly because no legislation presided over by Gladstone was ever simple, became clogged with so many conditions as to be virtually inoperable.

Gladstone carried the Bill through both Houses, and it duly became law, but the opposition was much fiercer than that which had greeted the Church Act, because this Bill struck at the rights of property and cut a more dramatic swathe through the Protestant Ascendancy in Ireland. In practice, none of the terms of the Act really worked to the benefit of the tenants, chiefly because Gladstone had tried to do the impossible – to improve the lot of the tenant farmer without striking too fundamental a blow at the landlords. However, for the first few years of the 1870s, the Act's failures were obscured because its terms were not put to the test, there were good harvests in these years, and most tenants managed to pay their rents so evictions were comparatively few. Many tenant farmers thought the Act would succeed and, with naïve optimism in financial matters, indulged in a borrowing spree from the 'gombeen men' and the banks, on the strength of the hoped-for stability; and this was to lead to further trouble when bad harvests struck again, and money had to be repaid, thus revealing the fact that the 1870 Land Act had only dented the fundamental problems of divided ownership.

If the 1870 Land Act, in practice, eventually proved to be but a tentative blow at Irish landlords, it was the first one, establishing the new principle that tenants had some legal rights, and because of this far-reaching implication it should be regarded as one of Gladstone's major pieces of legislation. However, in some Irish nationalist circles, Gladstone's own admission that the Fenian outbreaks had focused his attention on the country, reinforced the belief that England would only ever act under severe pressure; and the gap between the two countries' difference of approach to the whole Irish question was not greatly diminished.

CHAPTER 3

'Home Rule Keeps a Little Cauldron Simmering'

After the massive exertions of the Church Act and the Land Act, Gladstone temporarily withdrew his attention from Ireland (and on his next Irish move, the attempt to establish a Catholic University, he was to fall as heavily as his predecessors in the field). The Fenians, after the spectacular failure of the 1867 uprisings, shorn by the arrests that had followed, went into one of their periods of public inertia; the Irish-Americans were similarly lying fallow, as far as Ireland was concerned, fighting between themselves for leadership, beginning to concentrate some of their attention on American politics; while in rural Ireland generally there was a reasonable degree of contentment, brought about by the good harvests and the anticipated stability of the Land Act. But in Dublin there were fresh stirrings of nationalism, and these provided the third strand that was to entangle Charles Cunningham Boycott – the constitutional one.

The origins of what was to become the Home Rule movement were complex and curious. Fenianism was one of its progenitors, although the reaction to the secret revolutionary organisation was obviously not the same in Ireland as in England. Fenianism may have aroused Gladstone's intellect and conscience to the recognition that Ireland's discontent had deep-rooted and justified causes, and he was then able to harness a changing English political climate to a new policy of construction rather than the old one of oppressive inertia. But any Irishmen with the faintest pretensions towards nationalism had known for years that his country's treatment by England had been unjust, thus the

Gladstonian revelation was no flash of lightning for him. What the Fenian outbreak of 1867 did for some Irishmen, including ex-Fenians, was to clear the air. The attempts at violent revolution had failed so ludicrously that the path was re-opened for constitutional agitation in the tradition of Daniel O'Connell; a restatement of possible political aims in the sense that politics is the art of the possible while violence is the self-defeating realisation of the impossible. Fenianism also provided a more concrete base for the new movement, in that an Amnesty Association was formed after the imprisonment of so many Fenians in 1867, and this provided an organised nucleus prepared for fresh fields once the initial objective was within sight.

Fenianism was not the sole source of the new movement. There was a segment of the Irish community for whom the 1870 Land Act provided the spur of disappointment, who saw that it had done little more than prick the surface of the problem. They came to the conclusion that the only body which could solve the land question was an Irish parliament in Dublin, for however sympathetic or well-intentioned a British government might be, it would always be beset by other problems, many with higher national priority. There was yet another segment of the community who arrived at the same conclusion that the reinstatement of the Dublin parliament was now necessary, but from different motives. This section was composed of disenchanted middle-class Protestants who correctly interpreted Gladstone's Church and Land Acts as undermining the Protestant Ascendancy which was the bulwark of their comfort and stability. This section wanted power to remain in Protestant hands and, with the Ascendancy under attack from Westminster, an autonomous government in Dublin presented a possible solution to their new instability. Finally, there were a few upper-class Catholics who, in the light of Gladstone's Acts, considered it their duty to join with the Protestants in presenting moderate, reasoned, constitutional demands, with the emphasis on moderation and reason, if only to prove that not all Irish Catholics were wild men of the hills.

Representatives of this strange assortment of bedfellows met in Dublin on May 19, 1870, and the Home Government Association of Ireland was inaugurated.

The person who brought together this diverse and divergent collection of men and motives, who formulated the policy of the Home Government Association, was Isaac Butt. Irish history has not treated him kindly perhaps because he failed in an undramatic fashion as opposed to, for instance, Parnell who failed with the greatest possible drama. But it was Isaac Butt who started the movement that came so close to success, which might, had Gladstone's Home Rule Bill of 1886 become law, have started to settle the centuries-long acrimony between the two countries, and as an originator he should not be dismissed. He was born in Donegal in 1813, and was therefore an Ulsterman, starting life as: 'the very type of ultra-domineering, narrow-minded, Protestant Ascendancy', studying at the educational bastion of the Ascendancy, Trinity College, Dublin, convinced that the Union between England and Ireland was essential for Ireland's welfare.

After a brilliant academic career, Butt became an equally brilliant lawyer and it was his bar practice that led him to question his traditional beliefs. He defended some of the Young Irelanders after the 1848 rebellion and in the next twenty years, spent mostly as an MP in England, he moved further from the orthodox acceptance of the *status quo*. He was among those who saw clearly that the land question was the fundamental social and economic issue – he wrote some excellent pamphlets on the subject. He began to nurture a dream of federalism as the answer to the relationship between the two countries. It was in 1867 that Butt entered the limelight when he defended the Fenian prisoners, and later founded the Amnesty Association. Unfortunately, the reason that led him to return to the bar stemmed from a fundamental weakness of character. He had a convivial, generous nature which did not know when to cry halt, particularly with regard to wine and women. He spent much of his life hopelessly in debt, some of it actually in debtor's prisons, and it was basically to earn some money that he resumed his law practice. However, the fame he won while defending the Fenians, and the organisation he built for the Amnesty Association, put him into a position where he could attempt to realise his federal dream, and thus he inaugurated the Home Government Association of Ireland.

Butt's proposals broke with the O'Connell tradition, the campaigns for a straightforward repeal of the Act of Union, and for the reinstatement of Grattan's Parliament in Dublin. This idealised Parliament had, as Butt saw, suffered from two major defects; firstly its Acts were subject to a veto from Westminster; secondly the government of Ireland remained in the hands of a Lord Lieutenant appointed by the Crown. Butt therefore proposed the restoration of a Dublin parliament with Crown, Lords and Commons, but without the veto from Westminster; responsible solely to an Irish executive for internal affairs. Butt also pointed out that his proposed parliament would be representative of all Ireland – Catholic and Protestant – whereas Grattan's Parliament had been solely Protestant. To this extent, Butt's proposals were new and went further than the legislative concessions gained by Grattan, but Butt knew it was essential to win the support of Englishmen and members of the Anglo-Irish Ascendancy, and his proposals for internal legislative independence were unlikely to achieve this. What he hoped would win over the members of the English and Irish establishments was his cherished proposition of federalism, as opposed to separatism.

While Ireland would have control over her internal affairs, Westminster would continue to exercise power over Imperial affairs, including foreign policy, defence, war and essential taxation, and Ireland would continue to send members to Westminster to make her voice heard on these wider issues. Butt's proposals were a fresh and gallant attempt to solve the constitutional relationship but it was on the aspect of federalism versus straightforward legislative independence for a Dublin parliament that views quickly diverged, and this division was to plague the movement. Butt had provided a new impetus for Irish nationalism, one that appealed to the majority of moderates rather than the minority who advocated violence, and towards the end of 1873 his movement expanded and changed its name to the Home Rule League;* this title caught the popular imagination in a way that 'Home Government Association' had not. The idea of 'Home Rule' did not by any means take the country by storm, but it was a phrase that could mean most things to most men, and it had come to stay.

Unfortunately, only two months after the foundation of the new Home Rule League, Gladstone's administration fell, and the ensuing general election found the movement ill-prepared. 'There was not a vestige of plan or arrangement; no direction; no discipline; nothing of that generalship which, in great debate, is so essential' said *The Nation* after the election. However, the ill-organised movement had one thing in its favour, the 1872 Ballot Act (another achievement of Gladstone's first term of office), which, for the first time in British electoral history, made voting secret, protected from the eyes and therefore the pressures of the local hierarchies. There was no dramatic change in popular voting habits (by no means all the population possessed the franchise anyway), and in Ireland many continued to put their crosses where landlords or priests dictated, but some of the success of the Home Rule movement is attributable to the secrecy imposed by the Ballot Act. Despite the disorganisation and lack of leadership, the new movement was remarkably successful; fifty-nine Irish members, nominally pledged to Home Rule for Ireland, being returned to Westminster.

The Nation's assessment of the election campaign continued to be sadly true of Butt's movement as a whole (one cannot call it a political party because he himself did not). Apart from the crucial fact that he lacked the qualities of a general, the personal ruthlessness and decision to impose the bit and bridle on the diverse team

---

* The phrase 'Home Rule' had appeared in print in *The Celt* in 1858 and in *The Nation* in 1860 but it was Professor Galbraith of Trinity College who re-coined it in 1873 and made it popular.

he was trying to steer, Butt saw his movement as a pressure group designed only to persuade the British government to review the Irish situation. Furthermore as he believed in moderation (in theory if not in his private life) and in the right of each man to make his individual choice, he could not impose discipline or order on his supporters. Apart from being pledged, although only verbally, to further the cause of Home Rule, the fifty-nine members returned to Westminster in the 1874 elections were otherwise free to do what they liked and vote how they liked. Many of them, following the example of Butt himself, increasingly plagued by debt and the disorganisation of his private life, chose to absent themselves from the business of the House, whether it concerned English or Irish affairs. Generally it was a ramshackle movement whose nationalist fervour can be summed up in the memorable words of one member: 'I think a man should be a gentleman first, and a patriot afterwards.'

However muddy a movement Isaac Butt led into the House of Commons he had charted a new course, continuing to stress the fundamental nature of the land question, and if he personally was not capable of providing the necessary leadership, the constitutional approach had been sufficiently re-activated for others to follow.

From the start, the Home Rule idea attracted the attention of the more realistic, or less intransigent Fenians, and for a time there was an alliance of a kind between the Fenian upholders of the principle of separation from England to be achieved by physical force, and the Home Rule believers in the principle of internal legislative independence to be achieved by moral suasion. How precise this alliance was has since been a subject for debate, but it existed to the extent that Fenians were not barred from becoming MPs, which was a considerable concession since MPs had to take the oath of allegiance to the Crown. Among the Fenians who took advantage of the alliance and became MPs were John O'Connor Power and Joseph Biggar. O'Connor Power was a 'character', an ugly pock-marked man from a poor background, self-educated, an early Fenian, a great fighter, full of courage but the possessor of a foul temper. Joseph Biggar was born in Belfast, the Protestant son of a prosperous merchant (he became a Catholic later, not from religious conviction but because he thought it would further his political aims). He was short and squat, almost a hunchback, with the self-confidence that sometimes accompanies that physical deformity. He was described as 'the Belfast Quasimodo to the Irish Esmerelda'; the possessor of 'the true Ulster nature, uncompromising, downright, self-controlled, narrow'; these latter attributes he turned towards the Irish nationalist, not the loyalist, cause.

The tentative alliance between Fenianism and constitutionalism did not last long; orthodox Fenians soon became convinced that there was no possibility of the Home Rule movement achieving success, that Fenianism would be contaminated by continued co-operation, and they returned to their former stance of upholding the purity of the revolutionary ideal (both Biggar and O'Connor Power were expelled from the Supreme Council of the IRB in 1878 for refusing to abandon their open political activities). The importance of this alliance, however vague it may have been, was that it had occurred at all, and, as a result of the contact with the constitutionalists, a number of Fenians became convinced that somehow the two strands of Irish nationalism must be brought together, since their aim was basically the same: independence for Ireland. Only a united front could hope to achieve this objective. (Orthodox Fenians did not, of course, accept that the aim was the same; there was a vital difference in the interpretation of the word 'independence'.) In the early 1870s, even the more moderate and optimistic of the Fenians were defeated in trying to find some common ground on which a merger of the two opposing viewpoints might be achieved. However, the idea of future co-operation between the two forces of nationalism had been sown. From the other side of the fence the introduction of Fenians into the parliamentary movement meant that a more dynamic element stiffened Isaac Butt's gentlemanly association.

In England, the Home Rule movement was at first viewed with alarm – 'If we do not cleanse the parliamentary bosom of this perilous stuff,' said Disraeli, 'we shall bring about the disintegration of the Kingdom and the destruction of the Empire' – while slightly less dramatically, or less presciently, Gladstone had said, 'Can any sensible man, can any rational man, suppose that at this time of the day, in this condition of the world we are going to disintegrate the great capital institutions of the country for the purpose of making ourselves ridiculous in the sight of all mankind, and crippling any power we possess for bestowing benefits, through legislation, on the country to which we belong?' After a short while, during which the movement did not appear to be making much impact, alarm changed to patronising amusement, of which the comment 'Home Rule still keeps a little cauldron simmering' was typical. From 1875 onwards, however, the attitude started to change again.

The man who initiated the change, who stirred the simmering cauldron, was Joseph Biggar. One way in which it might be stirred had already been enunciated by another Home Ruler, Joe Ronayne, thus: 'Let us interfere with English Legislation; let us show them that, if we are not strong enough to get our own work done, we are strong enough to prevent them getting theirs'. The policy of obstructing the business of the Commons, of utilising the rules and customs of the House in such a manner as to bring procedure to a standstill, was not new. Various groups of British members had at times used it to press a minority view, and the House was wide open to anybody who chose to employ this method because there was then no check on debate; once a motion or Bill had been proposed or introduced, it could, in theory, be discussed endlessly. The open-endedness of debate stemmed from the nature of the British parliament. It had been created as a counter bulwark to the Crown, a place where grievances could be heard, a guardian of the people's rights – not as a legislature. Up till 1875 the obstruction policy had been used within limits. Once the threat had been implemented, the point had been made and both users and government adhered to the rules of the game because both sides appreciated that the rules represented more than a game, they were the essence of British parliamentary life. When Joseph Biggar decided to implement Ronayne's advice, to embark upon a policy of obstruction, it was limited in concept. Biggar and the few Home Rulers who supported him intended to make as bloody a nuisance of themselves as they could to focus attention on Ireland, but none of them had really bothered to study the rules of the House, none of them really appreciated how formidable a weapon obstruction could be if raised to the level of a fine art. In their hands it was a ponderous instrument, and although it did indeed upset the business of the House, it was nowhere regarded as a lethal weapon, and in some quarters was viewed with amusement. It was on April 22, 1875, that Biggar first staggered into the House of Commons, weighed down under a mass of Blue Books, and proceeded to read every passage down to the vital words, 'Printed for Her Majesty's stationery office by Eyre and Spottiswoode, printers to the Queen's Most Excellent Majesty'. On that same day, in one of the coincidences that are supposed to occur only in fiction but happen in life, Charles Stewart Parnell took his seat in the House as MP for Meath.

The man who was arguably the greatest politician, tactician and nationalist leader Ireland has produced – he certainly remains one of its most fascinating, complex, and analysed of leaders – was twenty-nine years old when he first took his seat at Westminster. He was born at Avondale, County Wicklow, in 1846, the seventh of eleven children, a member of the Anglo-Irish Protestant land-lord class, the original settler having come from Congleton in Cheshire as a Cromwellian supporter. However, the Parnells had a more nationalist tradition than the family origin would indicate; Thomas Parnell had been a friend of Dean Swift's, Sir John Parnell a Chancellor of the Exchequer in Grattan's Parliament and one of the few members to vote against the Act of Union in 1800, one of the latter's sons had been a nationalist member of the

House of Commons, while another was a friend of Tom Moore. Charles's father, John Henry Parnell, who died in 1859, left no particular imprint on the world, nor apparently on his family, but his mother was a most formidable lady. Born Delia Tudor Stewart, she was American although descended from Ulster Protestant stock, and her father, a Commodore in the United States Navy, had fought vigorously and successfully against Britain in 1812 and earned the sobriquet 'Old Ironsides'. Some of the iron and the anti-British sentiments were bequeathed to his daughter and it was later said that Parnell's hatred of England, which many regarded as the mainspring of his political life, was a pathological inheritance from his mother (although others doubted that he really hated England, and the amount of time he voluntarily spent in the country he was supposed to detest does make it a moot point).

His mother may have been an anglophobe but she was also a snob and acquiesced in the tradition of an English education for her sons, Charles included, and he duly went to various English private schools and on to Cambridge University. From the larger of the two off-shore European islands he acquired a clipped, upper-class English accent and a reserved, aloof English exterior. Beneath this was a core of passion, burning like white-hot steel, and had Parnell been born into the upper class in England the passion could well have taken him to the top of the tree, made him a great reforming Prime Minister, perhaps Tory because he had some inbred conservatism. But he was born in County Wicklow, Ireland, and the passion was turned against those who treated him as a second-class citizen, a member of a violent, maddening, quaint, backward race who could only be dealt with as refractory children. Also included in Parnell's armoury was a mind that ran on a railway track, narrow-gauge some said, lacking intellectual breadth, but it possessed the priceless ability to see the line ahead clearly, to ignore peripheral distractions and to seize any opportunity presented. At the root of his character was an arrogant pride to match that which he so disliked in the English, an absolute belief in himself. Michael Davitt (whom we shall shortly be meeting) once said that Parnell 'frequently quoted two lines of Shakespeare which inculcated fidelity to oneself as the rule of existence'.* The background that allowed such pride ironically came from the inborn, inbred, unquestioning self-confidence of the Anglo-Irish Protestant Ascendancy which Parnell was to try and smash.

The child and the young man showed no more signs of writing his name deep into history than did Charles Cunningham Boycott of acquiring nominal immortality; the pride was apparent and Parnell was liable, as a child, to indulge in startling tantrums if he did not get his own way, but he was more often reserved and well-mannered; he had a methodical mind with a scientific bent, but its singular powers of concentration were not apparent; and in politics, or Irish history, he had apparently no interest. When he returned from Cambridge (which he left without taking a degree), he followed the life of the Anglo-Irish landlord, hunting, shooting, playing cricket – at the English national game he was extremely good, being a batsman of repute and captain of the Wicklow team.

With the physical attributes of a future leader, nature had been lavish; Parnell looked the part, he was ideal casting. Tall and slim, with dark auburn hair and delicate features, his bearing was described as proud and resolute, fine and pleasing, 'the very picture of manly strength', while his most striking feature, it was generally agreed, was his eyes – 'especially remarkable', said a fellow nationalist, 'I have not seen others like them. Their light was peculiar and penetrating and, to use aptly a somewhat hackneyed term, magnetic.' With only one of the attributes required by a popular political leader had nature been miserly – the vocal chords. Parnell's voice had neither resonance nor range, the best that could be said of it was that it was clear, and at the start of

---

* Davitt's lack of knowledge of 'To thine ownself be true' was unsurprising. Polonius's injunctions to Laertes were not then amongst the most widely quoted of Shakespearian lines.

his career it was not even that; he was described as being 'barely able to utter three consecutive sentences'. Nor did he have any of the natural orator's instincts, the love of applause, the intoxication of manipulating an audience, of hearing the response swelling from murmur to roar until a thousand voices became one; on the contrary he loathed crowds and had always to steel himself to address a meeting.

Later he was to say it was Fenianism that had focused his attention on the condition of Ireland – one of the few reasons he himself ever gave for entering politics – but it was not until 1874, seven years after the major Fenian eruptions, that he took the first step on the road to fame and power. When he informed the Home Rule movement that he intended to enter the political arena he was, as a Protestant landlord, High Sheriff of Wicklow, sufficiently rich to pay his own election expenses, welcomed with open arms.* 'We have got a splendid recruit,' said Isaac Butt enthusiastically, 'an historic name, my friend, young Parnell of Wicklow,' adding presciently, 'unless I am much mistaken, the Saxon will find him an ugly customer, though he is a good-looking fellow.' In general, with his reserved and distant manner, his halting speech, his poor performance on the public platform, the Home Rule movement regarded him more as just another member to swell the ranks than as a candidate of potential, let alone a future leader.

One nationalist thought he was 'a frightful duffer' while another considered the clipped upper-class English accent 'a serious disqualification for an Irish patriot', but it wasn't particularly. There was a long tradition of the Protestant Anglo-Irish in the forefront of rebellious movements, the malcontent aristocrat than whom, it has been said, there is no fiercer revolutionary. Along with Isaac Butt, Joe Ronayne also showed foresight when he said, 'Keep your eye on Parnell. He's as meek as a Methodist

---

* MPs were not then paid, of course, and new political parties whether Irish or English were plagued by lack of funds, and consequently welcomed anybody who could pay their own expenses.

minister, but he'll tread on John Bull's corns harder than ever Boney did.' Parnell was not returned at his first attempt to become an MP, being defeated in the Cork county elections in 1874, but when the electors of Meath voted him into Parliament in an 1875 by-election, to tread on John Bull's corns was what he soon proceeded to do.

CHAPTER 4

'Long Life and Good Health to Bowld Parnell'

While the Home Rule movement was being inaugurated, before Parnell embarked upon the obstructionist tactics in Parliament which were to bring him into the limelight, Boycott finally left Achill Island and took a step nearer his surprising destiny. As he himself later said, 'family circumstances placed me in possession of further capital', and for some reason he decided not to invest it on Achill so he and his wife moved, not far, but back on to the mainland of Mayo. Boycott was by now forty-one years old, well into middle-age by Victorian standards, and twenty years married but without children. Why the Boycotts were childless, an unusual occurrence in Victorian days, remains unknown. In the coming years of notoriety he was to be accompanied by a faithful male friend considerably younger than himself, but imputing homosexuality to him, whether active or latent, is probably unjustified and certainly not based on concrete evidence. Indeed, if he were of a homosexual nature he would, in the prevailing climate, have been likely to have had a brood of children to allay suspicion. The explanation for the lack of children is probably the obvious one, that either Annie Boycott was physically incapable of bearing them or Boycott himself was sterile, and as he had nephews and nieces to care for, there was no need to adopt; while the explanation for his young friend is probably that he preferred male company, finding women tiresome.

It was at Lough Mask House, four miles from the small garrison town of Ballinrobe, that the Boycotts settled, a residence that exactly fits George Moore's description of a real Irish country house: 'A square box-like structure approached by stone steps.' But Lough Mask House was (and remains) a nice box, compact, with light airy rooms, not dissimilar to the house in which Boycott was born at Burgh St Peter. It is beautifully situated, lying a mile back from the Ballinrobe to Cong road through the parkland of the estate, on the edge of Lough Mask itself, possessing private access to the clear, cold waters with their mosaic of stones, the reflected reeds, the humping islands, and, across the Lough, a romantic view of the hills of Maam Turk. To complete the idyllic picture, in the grounds, past the extensive stables, lie the ruins of a medieval castle which is graced by a door with stone hinges – such hinges being extremely rare – and the remains of a fine fireplace bearing the inscription 'Thomas Burke 1618'.

Prior to 1873, when Boycott took up residence, Lough Mask House and its three hundred acres of land had been acquired by Lord Erne from whom he obtained his lease but not, as he insisted, as the result of an eviction. He later testified that the former tenant had been a sub-sheriff, not of the ordinary farming class, and although the latter had got into difficulties and the estate had been sold through the Encumbered Estates Court, Boycott said 'there was an amicable arrangement'. He took a thirty-one year lease on the house and land, but the part of the deal that proved to be vital was not the acquisition of the lease but his agreeing to become agent for his lordship's other property in the area. Lord Erne, who was seventy-one years old in 1873, lived at Crom Castle in Fermanagh in which Ulster county he owned 31,389 acres of land whereas in Mayo he had only 2,184 acres. It was for 1,500 of these Mayo acres, in the vicinity of Lough Mask and Castlebar, that Boycott agreed to become agent and collect the rents from thirty-eight small tenant farmers. The total value of the rents was under £500 – Boycott himself paid Lord Erne £500 rent per annum – of which he earned 10 per cent for acting as agent. It was this undertaking, worth £50 a year to him, that was the principal cause of his future trouble.

The man who took up residence at Lough Mask, who directly

employed local people to act as house-servants, grooms, coachmen and labourers on his own estate, and supervised the lives of other Mayo families in his role of agent for Lord Erne, had become set in manner and mode of thought. By temperament he had an orderly mind and he expected other people to be orderly, too. Twenty years on Achill had convinced him that the Irish were a disorderly lot on whom discipline had to be impressed, while the island's remoteness and rough justice had strengthened his innate belief in the divine right of the masters, and the tendency to behave as he thought fit, without regard to other people's point of view or feelings. This is not to say he was one of nature's born tyrants – although he was later accused of being 'the height of a great tyrant' – but his character had become more rigid; life had not knocked him in a way that might have smoothed the edges; and the rigidity did not, from the day of his arrival at Lough Mask, endear him to the tenantry. However, in 1873, as the Boycotts settled into their new home, sinking some though not all their capital into what they hoped would prove a profitable farming venture, surrounded by excellent riding country and with a race-course near by so that the Captain could indulge his chief passion in life, there was no thought of future difficulties. In the parliamentary tactics initiated by Joseph Biggar and soon taken over by Charles Stewart Parnell, their interest was undoubtedly minimal, and that these tactics would in any way impinge on their future never occurred to either Charles Cunningham or Annie Boycott.

Parnell's introduction to the House of Commons coincided, as we noted, with the first serious Irish attempt to obstruct the business of Parliament, and he duly took note of Biggar's tactics, notably the historic occasion, later, in 1875, when the latter espied strangers in the House which then, according to custom, had to be cleared, the stranger in question being the Prince of Wales. Parnell's maiden speech included the trenchant sentences which bore omens for the future – 'Why should Ireland be treated as a geographical fragment of England . . . Ireland is not a geographical fragment but a nation.' In 1876 he made a passionate intervention about 'the Manchester Martyrs'; 'I wish to say as publicly and as directly as I can that I do not believe, and never shall believe, that any murder was committed at Manchester.' Later in the same year he was selected, with John O'Connor Power, to travel to the United States and present a loyal (i.e. nationalist) Irish address to President Grant on the hundredth anniversary of the American Declaration of Independence, but the selection was occasioned more by virtue of his being Master of Avondale, the possessor of a historic name in Ireland, and notable Stewart connections in the United States, than because people had become convinced that he himself possessed tremendous qualities.

It was not until 1877 that Parnell, not rushing, giving himself time to learn every detail of the rules of the House of Commons, took control of Biggar's blundering tactics and coolly, without losing his temper, seldom raising his voice, started to turn it into a weapon that could not be ignored. Soon Henry Lucy, among the most entertaining if not the most profound of parliamentary correspondents, was increasingly mentioning Parnell in his articles. He was writing of 'the newly formed Irish party of which Biggar is the head, Parnell, the tail'; asking the question, 'Why isn't Parnell the biggest bore in the House? *Answer* Because there's Biggar'; and printing the poem:

> Oh! Parnell Mavourneen! Oh! Biggar go bragh!
> It's the pride and the joy of your country you are!
> Sustained by O'Donnell and the might of O'Gorman,
> You have broken the might of both Saxon and Norman.
>
> A light o'er the darkness of Erin now breaks,
> You have bullied the Speaker and trampled on Raikes,
> And the House, dispossessed of its prestige and vigour,
> Lies low at the feet of Parnell and Biggar.
>
> Oh! Parnell mavourneen! Oh! Biggar go bragh!
> The noblest your country has sent us by far;

Through the lobby you march with a conqueror's stride
When you've summoned your host to the cry of 'Divide'.

Oh! Keep us not here in this terrible weather,
While the grouse-cocks are calling us off to the heather,
While the yacht, with its sails flapping out to the breeze,
Invite us away to the smooth summer seas
(and the final plea was)
Sweet Biggar – kind Parnell – please let us away!

The O'Donnell referred to was Frank Hugh O'Donnell, an extraordinary man of good intelligence but overweening conceit, who claimed that everything inaugurated in these years was his brainchild, purloined and ruined by others. Later he was to claim the Indian Congress party as his brainchild, and to play a catalystic role in the setting up of the Parnell Special Commission.

It was precisely the patronising attitude reflected in the poem that Parnell, not in any case noted for a sense of humour, certainly not the English variety, was out to quash. He meant Ireland to be taken seriously and obstruction was a means, a publicity-attracting means, towards that end. In some respects the poem exaggerated the effects of his obstruction tactics. The majority of Home Rulers might, by now, have swung from the view that the Master of Avondale was a duffer to regarding him as a force to be reckoned with, but he was not a force they welcomed, many of them believing his policy would alienate the English rather than persuade them to support the Irish cause. By the British public he was, when noticed, looked upon as merely another Irish irritant, while even in Ireland his name did not resound among the mass of peasants. As one observer wrote, 'Mr Parnell was little known ... except among political experts, the names of O'Donnell and Biggar being more often in men's mouths'. The same observer also commented that the obstruction policy was of interest only to a minority of the farming community, as it was too esoteric a tactic, seemingly too far removed from the problems of the peasants to capture their attention. However, the poem did not over-exaggerate Parnell's growing stature among the 'political experts', and it was his cool handling of obstruction that first focused their attention on him.

This attention was further held by his cogent utterances outside parliament, and by 1878 Parnell had mastered the technique of public speaking, his will-power had overcome his natural reticence and disdain. Gladstone was later to say, 'No man, as far as I can judge, is more successful than the Hon. Member in doing that which it is commonly supposed that all speakers do, but which few in my opinion really do – and I do not include myself among those few – namely, in saying what he means to say'. Among the utterances that attracted attention was, 'I care not for this English Parliament and its outcries. I care nothing for its existence if that existence is to continue a source of tyranny and destruction to my country.' Here, for the increasing number of nationalists who were accepting the view that a link between the revolutionary and constitutional forces was required, was the man who might be able to forge the link; a man who patently did not give a damn for English sentiments and more importantly, for this much was true of other obstructionists, was as patently a man of breeding and inborn authority, capable of fighting the English on a level footing. In the growing focus on Parnell, there was apparent the ambivalence of the Irish hatred for England, its mingling with a certain admiration for the most hated qualities, the ruthlessness, decision, discipline and singlemindedness the English were supposed to possess, an element of 'set a thief to catch a thief'; and Parnell was described as 'an Englishman of the strongest type, moulded for an Irish purpose'. One nationalist section demonstrated its belief in his potentiality for leadership of the right kind as early as 1877. This was the Home Rule Confederation of Great Britain, founded shortly after the Home Rule League in Ireland but from the start a more Fenian-dominated, stronger, better-organised body than the parent League. In 1877, the British Confederation ousted Isaac Butt from its presidency and elected Parnell in his stead, although Butt retained the leadership of the Irish Home Rule League.

Parnell was a born leader, there was never any question in his mind of taking second place to anybody (and in his letters to Katharine O'Shea it is revealing that she was Queenie while he was 'your own King'; prince or princess or any other subordinate role would not have done). By 1878 he undoubtedly knew what he wanted, to be the leader of an independent Ireland, although how complete the independence should be was less certain. While keeping his eye fixed on the goal of a high degree of autonomy for his country, which he would control, he proceeded to demonstrate that he was a supreme tactician, as flexible in detail as he was rigid in aim, cautious or daring, cool or passionate as the situation demanded, capable of walking the tightrope between violence and constitutionalism so that the upholders of both views were kept reasonably happy – and behind him. But in 1878, apart from being elected President of the Home Rule Confederation of Great Britain, Parnell was merely the Member of Parliament for Meath, and what he did was to continue to consolidate his position by obstruction in Parliament and succinct nationalist speeches outside, and wait for circumstance and other strands of Irish Nationalism to approach him.

By 1878 the Irish-American strand had re-emerged as a potent force, with John Devoy as a leading figure. Devoy had been born near Naas, County Kildare, in 1842 but had spent most of his early life in Dublin. He was involved in early Fenian activities, then for a spell served in the Foreign Legion (because he wanted to learn how to fight and organise an army), returning to Ireland to be conspicuous in the abortive Fenian uprising of 1865, after which he was arrested and imprisoned. In 1871 he was among those released, as a result of the efforts of Isaac Butt and the Amnesty Association, on condition he never set foot in Ireland again. With remarkable lack of foresight the British government duly allowed him to sail for the United States to provide leadership for 'the sore-hearted Irish exiles ... the missionaries of hatred' already settled in their millions across the Atlantic. Devoy found employment on the *New York Herald* and became a trenchant, not to say scurrilous journalist, obviously violently anti-British.

Before his arrival in the United States there had been a split in the American Fenian movement, as a result of which James Stephens and the older exile brigade were ousted from power and the Clan na Gael was formed. The Clan na Gael had a dual purpose; the old Fenian aim of subscribing to armed rebellion in Ireland by moral and practical assistance was heavily endorsed, but its members also wanted to make the Irish-Americans a force within American domestic politics. Apart from the emotional ties and impulses that drove them to support the concept of an armed rebellion in Ireland the members of the Clan na Gael also felt that an independent Ireland would help them achieve their aim of becoming powerful within American politics. Many members of the Irish-American community suffered from a sense of national inferiority, and the Clan na Gael considered that, as sons and grandsons of the sovereign state of Ireland, they would be able to exert greater influence on the American domestic scene. They were therefore as interested in American politics as Irish, and indeed, until the late 1870s, there was no direct link between the Clan na Gael and the IRB. By this period Devoy, through the strength of his will and personality, had become a leading figure within the Clan and helped turn it into the dominant, but by no means only, Irish-American political organisation, and Devoy had one obsessive idea, the severing of each and every tie that bound Ireland to England. To this idea he dedicated his life with maximum embittered effort and efficiency, and he was a very efficient, if unlovable, man – 'Forbidding of aspect, with a perpetual scowl on his face ... his friendships were few and far between'.

If Devoy was obsessive about Ireland, he was also a realist, and it became clear to him, as it had to others, that some new approach to the tortuous issues of Irish land ownership, Fenianism and constitutionalism, all of which were entangled in the paramount issue of independence, was essential. He had never had much faith in Isaac Butt's Home Rule movement and by the end of 1877 he had dismissed it – 'as it now stands it is a heart-sickening picture, a miserable caricature of the movement of Grattan without a scintilla of its fire and spirit'. But in the same letter to Doctor Carroll, another leading member of the Clan na Gael, he also wrote, 'I hope for nothing from the Home Rule conference except that some young men of spirit who may by some oversight of the managers be admitted will show their spirit by manly protest against such drivelling senility'. He was shortly to come to the conclusion that Charles Stewart Parnell might be just such a young man.

In fact, contact between the Clan na Gael and Parnell had already been made, in the August of 1877, when J. J. O'Kelly, one of its members, met Parnell in Paris, France being a favourite Irish meeting place, neutral but with emotional ties from the past, outside British jurisdiction. O'Kelly then reported to John Devoy that Parnell considered some link between the conservative and radical elements of nationalism was required, that he had many of the qualities of leadership, that he was cool and resolute, adding, 'I am not sure he knows exactly where he is going. However, he is the best of the parliamentary lot'. At that juncture in time, Parnell was not the only person who could be accused of uncertainty of immediate direction; the air might be filled with the idea that a link was necessary, but nobody could put his finger clearly on the subject matter that would provide the common ground between the moral and physical force sides and, as importantly, would rouse the mass of apathetic peasants in Ireland and the embittered but directionless immigrants in the United States. It was abundantly clear that neither Fenianism nor Home Rule was currently performing either of these tasks – both were still minority movements.

However, one thing had been established by the August 1877 contact, namely that Parnell was a man of the constitutional side, with qualities of leadership, who favoured a more defined *rap-prochement*. In January 1878, Doctor Carroll had an interview with Parnell, this time in London, in order to explore the possibilities of a more direct link between him and Fenianism, of a new joint movement that would be able to draw on the strength of both sides. Nothing definite resulted, but Doctor Carroll emerged from the interview convinced that Parnell was willing to work with the Fenians and, as vitally, that they could work with him because he was in favour of absolute independence for Ireland. At this interview Parnell demonstrated another of his outstanding qualities, the ability to convey the impression of saying what the negotiator wanted to hear without actually committing himself. This ability, which he utilised in all the meetings that followed, was partly achieved by the use of another of his qualities – 'His silence. It was extraordinary', said a biographer, 'All Irish agitators talked. He didn't.'

Two months later, towards the end of March 1878, Doctor Carroll arranged a further meeting in London which he hoped might have a dramatic and far-reaching conclusion. He had persuaded leading members of the IRB, including John O'Leary, a revered founder member, to meet Parnell, but the hoped-for result of the personal confrontation – a tacit or more binding agreement between the two home-based forces of nationalism to pursue together the objective of Irish independence – did not materialise. Having once been tentatively bitten by Isaac Butt's dream, the members of the Supreme Council of the IRB were twice shy, or one could say they were less impressed than was Doctor Carroll with the revolutionary side of Parnell's nature. They refused to participate in any constitutional programme led by him, and restated the Fenian view that Irish independence could only be achieved by armed rebellion and that any other course would be deleterious to their movement. If Carroll failed in his endeavour to weld together the two sides, he personally remained convinced that a merger was necessary and that Parnell was the man who might effect it, while Parnell himself retired in the knowledge that the American Fenians were less rigid in tactical matters even if they did adhere to the principle of independence-through-revolution.

Personal contact between John Devoy and Parnell was yet to come, but in the meantime circumstances in Ireland were changing fast, in part propelled by nature, in part by man. Following several good years, 1876 had produced a poor harvest, and 1877 was worse; the value of the potato crop, still Ireland's staple food, falling from £12,000,000 in 1876 to £5,000,000 in 1877. The peasants and tenant farmers who had borrowed so optimistically from gombeen men and banks found they could not repay the interest or loans, but the gombeen men and banks, needing money themselves, demanded instant repayment or refused further credit. Thousands, consequently, fell behind with their rents and evictions started to increase, while the situation was worsened by a general agricultural depression arising mainly, if ironically, from the growing American competition and the import of cheap American produce. As this depression also affected England, where many of the Irish farm labourers normally migrated in the summer, this source of extra income was severely curtailed, too. In many parts of rural Ireland, notably Connaught, always the poorest of areas where the peasants depended almost wholly on the potato crop, the threat of famine loomed again. The failure of the 1870 Land Act to stabilise or remedy the situation for the tenant farmers was revealed, and the Irish land question yet again began to take on a very real and desperate significance.

The political front, too, was in a state of flux. Isaac Butt's star was waning, partly assisted by his own disorganisation, partly by increasing ill-health, but mainly by the pressure of mounting opposition within the Home Rule movement. The older Fenian element and a younger, fiercer group whose leading light was John Dillon, were demanding that the parliamentary members act as a cohesive, independent party, dedicated solely to Ireland's interest, determined to harass the government on every occasion.

Butt insisted on the right of individual members to vote as they thought fit, except when the national interest was at stake, when they should support the government. By the 'national interest' Butt meant that of the United Kingdom as a whole, but for the opposition his interpretation meant the English interest, and when England was in external difficulties (as she was during this period) it seemed to them the ideal moment to attack, not to provide gentlemanly support. At stormy Home Rule conferences Butt managed to carry a sufficient majority of the members of the Home Rule League, parliamentary and grass-root, but it was obvious his authority was declining, his way of tackling the problem of Irish independence was failing, and control of the movement was becoming ripe for the picking.

Parnell had his eyes firmly fixed on the leadership, but they were also focused on the Fenian and Irish-American support which could propel him towards it. In general, the attention of Ireland's major figures was on the political power struggle, although they were aware of the worsening agricultural situation. At the end of 1877, the man who more than any other reacted to the fast deteriorating agrarian circumstances, and provided the vital missing, or neglected, link, for which so many had been searching, emerged on to the national scene. He was Michael Davitt.

CHAPTER 5

'It Is Time We Came Out of the Rat-holes of Conspiracy'

Michael Davitt was born in the same year as Parnell, 1846, so the time parallels of the two men whose lives were to converge to form one of the vital movements of Irish history – and the one that immortalised Boycott's name – are conveniently exact, serving to emphasise their total dissimilarity of background and circumstance. Davitt was born a Catholic in a dismal shack in the tiny village of Straide in the wilds of County Mayo, with the mountain of Nephin dominating the landscape. The year 1846 was also a famine year when the potato crop failed, nowhere more disastrously than in Mayo. In 1852 the Davitts fell behind with their rent, and in the clearances after the famine, were evicted like thousands of peasant families before and after them. And, like thousands of other Irish families before and since, they made their way to Lancashire, the birthplace of the Industrial Revolution, whose machines supposedly provided an endless supply of work.

It was in Haslingden, one of the many small cotton towns that served the heart of King Cotton in Manchester nineteen miles to the south, with its rows of back-to-back houses cramped into the valleys and clinging to the sides of the bleak Pennine Hills, that the Davitts settled and tried to eke out a living. The young Michael was partly tutored by his Gaelic-speaking mother, and from his father he imbibed the lessons of Irish history and the famine, which spelled nationalism, but he also obtained some education at the local Wesleyan Methodist school (Methodism was the main source of education for the poor in the north of England).

The influence of the nonconformist teaching was to have a profound effect on the adult Davitt, and he matured with a fine religious tolerance, not common among working-class Christians of whichever order, particularly the Irish. The tolerance also stemmed from inherent qualities, for while Davitt was passionate, depressive and emotional, he was also idealistic, a believer in the potentiality for good in the human race, and his passion and compassion were allied to a high natural intelligence which gave him a rare breadth of vision.

The formative years in Lancashire included a particularly malign stroke of fate which was to test Davitt's courage and character. At the age of eleven he went to work in a cotton mill, as was then common practice among working-class Lancastrian children whether of Irish or English descent. A year later, his right arm was trapped in the machinery, also far too common an occurrence, and was so badly crushed it had to be amputated at the shoulder. But he proved his innate qualities, overcame the pain, and readjusted to the loss of a vital limb, slowly learning to do everything with his left hand, including writing. After he had recovered from the accident, he was taken on by Mr Cockcroft who ran the Post Office in Haslingden, and at the age of sixteen was promoted to assistant letter-carrier, which was a comparatively important and responsible task, infrequently entrusted to Irish immigrants, and shows the respect he had earned. Tramping the mean streets in the valley, over the windswept moors with their jutting black rocks and low stone walls, delivering letters to the isolated farmhouses, brought him into contact with native Lancastrians and undoubtedly influenced his later socialistic beliefs that the basic desires of working men were the same: the right to work, sufficient food to eat, a house to live in, hope for the children's future; and that it should therefore be the aim of all thinking, caring men to blur rather than to emphasise national differences.

But in the 1860s, Davitt was first and foremost an Irishman, his passionate nature led him into Fenian circles and by 1867, when he was twenty-one, he was already a committed Fenian and was among those ordered to seize arms from Chester Castle. He escaped without arrest from that fiasco, and by the next year was 'Centre' of the Rossendale Fenian circle (Haslingden lies in the old Forest of Rossendale by which name the area is still known). One of the tasks of any Fenian leader was to obtain arms for the uprising that they believed must shortly occur, and Davitt threw himself into the job with enthusiasm, organising ability and unusual dependability. However, in May 1870, when he was waiting for a case-load of revolvers to arrive by train from Birmingham, he was arrested on Paddington station. The police commissioner who ordered his arrest said of him, 'the Fenian conspiracy can boast of no more interesting personality', but in 1870 few people showed interest. His trial in London opened on the day the Franco-Prussian war broke out, and consequently received scant attention, even in Ireland. Davitt was charged with conspiracy to rebellion, to deprive Her Majesty of her royal style, to levy war upon Her Majesty by procuring arms and ammunition and by divers other overt acts. Mr Cockcroft travelled from Haslingden Post Office to give evidence of good character, but it was to no avail, the evidence provided by the Crown more than upheld the charges and Davitt, found guilty of treason/felony, was sentenced to fifteen years penal servitude.

His treatment while in prison was appalling. A belief in due retribution and the redemptive value of harsh punishment was prevalent; for few prisoners in Britain was life easy and for political prisoners even less so, but Davitt seems to have been singled out for particularly ferocious treatment. He was imprisoned in London, principally at Millbank, where he was kept in solitary confinement, was compelled to sit upright on a small bucket picking oakum ten hours a day ('it was very distressing on the chest', he said), and where, in winter, the cold was so intense that many prisoners suffered from frostbite. The food was filthy and inadequate and the sanitary conditions disgusting, the bedding was never washed and fifteen men bathed in the same water once a fortnight. After ten months in Millbank he was moved to Dartmoor, where conditions were even worse and where he was subjected to yet harsher treatment. His initial job on Dartmoor was stone-breaking, wielding a heavy pick-axe with his one good arm, out in all weathers on the bleak moor; he was later transferred to the job of cart-labourer for which eight men were harnessed together, acting as beasts of burden, pulling trucks of coal and manure. The collar that was daily yoked across his chest caught the stump of Davitt's amputated right arm and rubbed it off and, with some reluctance, he was then transferred from this task, and assigned to the less arduous, but more revolting, one of pounding putrid bones into manure.

Throughout his years as a convict, although his conduct was good and he was therefore legally entitled to receive visitors, all his applications were refused. Eventually he managed to establish communication with the outside world, notably with John O'Connor Power, whom he had known as a boy in Lancashire. It was O'Connor Power's revelations to the House of Commons regarding Davitt's treatment on Dartmoor that helped effect his release in December, 1877, when he was given a ticket-of-leave, with his freedom conditional on his good behaviour. Even though the fifteen-year sentence was cut, Davitt had already served seven hideous years, and his strength of will, sheer force of spirit, and the grip he kept on his emotional and depressive nature, demand the utmost admiration.

Incidentally, Davitt was materially to assist future prisoners in British jails, both by the evidence he gave to the Commission appointed to enquire into the working of the Penal Servitude Acts in 1878, and by a pamphlet he published on his prison life which had a wide circulation. He recommended that: (1) a proper medical authority be appointed to inspect prisoners, their sanitary and ventilation arrangements; (2) that the question of the work assigned to physically disabled prisoners be examined; (3) that the number of prisoners committing suicide be similarly examined; (4) the number of self-inflicted injuries likewise; (5) that the

Governor's minutes and orders on prisoners be examined by an independent body; (6) that the fitness of ex-soldiers and sailors to be prison officers be enquired into. Not all his recommendations were implemented, but the evidence of such a man as Davitt – intelligent, sincere, honest and quite remarkably objective in his judgements, considering he had only just been released from the horror – was respected and did bear fruit in penal reform.

If nature had endowed Charles Stewart Parnell with the physique and looks of an heroic leader of men, it had not been unkind to Michael Davitt in his role of visionary revolutionary. He was 6 ft tall, with raven black hair, and dark luminous eyes burning from a gaunt, swarthy face. Some said he looked more Spanish than Irish, and a Spanish ancestor was possible as survivors of the Armada had been washed up on the Mayo coast; others said he was the very image of the Connaught Celt, the ideal Connaught Celt, that is, in the same way that the blue-eyed, fair-haired, Anglo-Saxon is supposedly the English image. The overall impression of a melancholy, mystic romantic figure was enhanced by the absence of the right arm, the symbol of a life maimed by hostile forces, or of Ireland maimed by English domination. As an orator Davitt was in a different class from Parnell, with a deep resonant voice and the ability to sway crowds with his rhetoric. Like Parnell he had an English accent, although Davitt's was compounded of the burring 'r's' and the slow broad vowels of Lancashire.

When Davitt emerged from prison at the end of 1877, he was in poor physical condition – he weighed only 8 stone 10 lbs, not, as he said, 'the proper weight for a man 6 ft in height and at the age of thirty-one' – but his mental capacities were remarkably unscathed, and his lack of bitterness about the English was particularly remarkable, for if ever an Irishman had reason to hate the English, it was he. During the seven long years in Millbank and on Dartmoor he had had ample time in which to consider the state of Ireland and its future, and he later said that when he came out of prison he had reached the same conclusion as some nationalists in the outside world, namely that a link between the secret revolutionary movement and the open constitutional one was long overdue. He also claimed that he had arrived at a precise definition of what could and should provide the vital initial bridging point and engage the apathetic peasantry – the land question. The social discontent and economic evils arising from this unsolved problem, allied to the violent, deep-rooted hatred of landlords, provided, as he said, 'a vast, untilled field of popular force'. Davitt had in fact reached Fintan Lalor's conclusion, that the land was the ready-made engine that would generate its own steam once the fire was kindled, although he said he had not then read the writings of Fintan Lalor.

Immediately on his release Davitt, together with other Fenians, was entertained at a celebration breakfast in London, and among those who attended was Parnell, an attendance that indicated the latter's independent stance, and that he was prepared to meet the Fenians at least half-way. This was the first time the paths of Davitt and Parnell crossed and it was later said by some that they disliked each other from the start. However, the few utterances Parnell made on the subject of Davitt show a sympathetic if amused respect, while Davitt was generous to Parnell in his later published assessments. It would seem more accurate to say that if they had no instinctive accord, because their backgrounds and temperaments were so dissimilar, equally they did not dislike each other and there was a mutual respect. This first encounter produced no cataclysmic effect, and Davitt crossed to Ireland, setting foot in his native land for the first time in more than twenty-five years which must have been an overwhelmingly emotional moment in the life of such an emotional man. In Dublin he was entertained at another celebration breakfast, again attended by Parnell, but after this the two men temporarily went their separate ways. From Dublin Davitt travelled to Mayo, the county of his birth, where he was given a hero's welcome, bonfires being lit on the hill-sides, a further emotional occasion for him, and shortly afterwards he was back in England, addressing Fenian meetings.

It has been pointed out that after his release from prison Davitt did not act as if he had become convinced of the necessity of a Fenian constitutional merger, but continued to act on the straight Fenian line. It is probably fair to say that his head was seething with ideas he had not then clarified, and retrospect made the clarification seem quicker and more decisive than it had been. One notable Fenian meeting, over which Davitt presided, at St Helens in Lancashire in May 1878, was attended by Parnell who, during the course of his speech, suggested that if the Home Rulers were expelled from the House of Commons for their obstructionist tactics, they might secede and form a provisional government in Dublin. The suggestion was not new, Gavan Duffy had expounded the idea, Joseph Biggar and the early obstructionists had toyed with it, and John Dillon had recently elaborated on it at the stormy Home Rule Conference in Dublin in January, 1878. Parnell's decison to restate it, at a Fenian meeting, at that moment in time, in clear, unrhetorical language, demonstrates how brilliantly he could walk the tight-rope. It was a declaration of revolutionary aim calculated to warm and capture Fenian hearts, particularly American Fenian hearts, as they had been urging such action, and it further marked him out as a different breed from the milk-and-water run of Isaac Butt's Home Rulers, the man who might prove to be the leader Ireland had been waiting for. A speech Parnell made at another meeting in Manchester in July, strengthened these impressions: 'I do not believe in a policy of conciliation of English feelings or prejudices – what did we ever gain in the past by trying to conciliate them? . . . We will never gain anything from England unless we tread upon her toes; we will never gain a single 6d worth from her by conciliation.'

Such speeches, while focusing the vital attention of the politically-minded on Parnell, remained part of the power struggle, and failed to attract the interest of the mass of peasants who, as the agrarian situation worsened, were increasingly involved in a fight for survival. However, Davitt later said it was at the time of the St Helens meeting that he had a long conversation with Parnell in which he proposed that a new party be formed, or the existing Home Rule movement be reorganised by Parnell, composed of parliamentarians of separatist sympathies, whose policy should be based on 'a war against landlordism for a root settlement of the land question'. Davitt said that such a policy would bring in the Fenians, the maximum support of the peasants, and would lead to Home Rule because it would attack the most hated, and therefore the weakest, part of the English domination, the landlords. This policy and plan of campaign was more or less what happened, but if Davitt did advocate it in May 1878, the time and circumstances were not ripe for implementation. All he received from Parnell, on his own admission, was a vague agreement that a stronger platform should be put before the public, especially in relation to the land question, and that Parnell could see no reason why men who took opposing views as to the best way of liberating Ireland could not work in harmony on minor reforms. Thereafter, he and Parnell again went their separate ways.

The strands of a tripartite alliance between constitutionalism, Fenianism and the Irish-Americans were all the time pulling, or being pulled, closer together, and Michael Davitt further assisted the process by a visit to the United States. He had come out of prison penniless and jobless, and he also wanted to see his mother, who had emigrated from Haslingden to the United States several years earlier. The solution to these problems emerged as a visit to the States, during which he would earn his living as a lecturer propagating the Irish cause, and in July 1878, Davitt duly sailed for New York. He was fortunate in that Doctor Carroll, whom he had met in London, recommended that the Clan na Gael should sponsor his tour for, as John Devoy later pointed out, without this sponsorship, Davitt would not have obtained wide audiences, and without audiences he would not have earned the money which enabled him to devote his time to the foundation of the Land League (although Davitt, true to his nature, insisted on giving part of the proceeds to an English gunsmith who had helped in his early Fenian days and had suffered as a result of the association). The Clan na Gael gained from the sponsorship, too. Davitt was the first Fenian to give public lectures – Fenianism was, after all, supposed to be a secret organisation – and there was therefore the attraction of novelty; his oratory, his gaunt face, emaciated body and armless right sleeve did no disservice to the tale of Irish grievance and English injustice. The audience consequently came in good numbers, and interest in the Irish question quickened.

Davitt's lecture tour officially opened in Philadelphia in mid-September, 1878, and his platform remained the general Fenian one of total separation from English domination to be achieved by armed rebellion (and American aid), with some extra emphasis on the land question as possibly providing the key which would unlock the door to independence. From personal contact with leading Irish-Americans he had learned that they too, and John Devoy in particular, were moving towards the idea of a more overt link between Fenianism and constitutionalism, and he had also learned that he was not alone in thinking the land question might be the vital key. One person who had been thinking on these lines, for months insisting that to talk of Irish independence without first solving the basic land dilemma was ridiculous, was Patrick Ford, with whom Davitt struck an immediate rapport. Ford, described by one Irish nationalist as 'a small, dingy, silent man', was yet another exile and editor of a newspaper called the *Irish World*. It was a weekly paper devoted to Irish affairs, the front page featured 'Irish News from London', the events of each Irish county had a column, and what was happening in America received scant attention. It had no clear practical policy other than being endlessly pro-Irish and vitriolically anti-British, its style was, to put it mildly, lurid, but it reached the mass of working-class Irish immigrants in a manner that John Devoy's middle class dominated Clan na Gael or the middle class papers such as the *Boston Pilot* did not.* Patrick Ford and the *Irish World* therefore represented a further potentially highly influential section of the Irish-American scene, and from the first contact in mid-1878 Davitt had Ford's whole-hearted support which was to be of great importance in the success of the Land League.

By early October Davitt was openly urging co-operation between the radical and conservative elements of Irish nationalism with a view to, as he said, 'bringing an advanced nationalist spirit and revolutionary purpose into Irish politics'. He was also pushing the land question to the forefront of his arguments, although he did not then go as far as a recent Clan na Gael statement that 'the only final solution of the Irish land question is the *abolition of landlordism* and the substitution of a system by which no one should stand between the State and the tiller of the soil'. Davitt contented himself with suggesting co-partnership between landlords and tenants. Generally, in those autumnal days of 1878, as news of the worsening agrarian situation arrived from Ireland, there was a sense of urgency among the Irish-Americans, a feeling of excitement; the expectation that something dramatic and far-reaching must soon occur, with the added zest that whatever did occur would in part be dictated by them. Much remained intangible – an air, a feeling, a sense – with the additional unreality imposed by distance; what was happening was in Ireland, and the scene on which the Irish-Americans would impose their new-found strength was thousands of miles away across the Atlantic.

It was left to John Devoy to take the initiative, which he did on October 24, 1878, by sending a telegram to Parnell announcing a new Fenian departure. The telegram promised Parnell American Fenian aid and support, if he agreed to the following terms: (1) the abandonment of federal Home Rule and the substitution of a general declaration in favour of Irish self-government; (2) vigorous agitation on the land question, based on peasant

* The Clan na Gael had some working-class members but they were the more articulate, politically minded Fenians which was *not* the mass of immigrants.

proprietary; (3) exclusion of all sectarian issues from the platform; (4) Irish MPs to vote together as a party on all issues whether Irish or Imperial, and to adopt a more aggressive policy; (5) advocacy for struggling nationalities throughout the British Empire and elsewhere. It was a brilliant, pragmatic telegram. What the substitution of a general declaration in favour of Irish self-government meant was deliberately left vague so as not to hamper Parnell. The clause on peasant proprietary was qualified by the acceptance of temporarily less revolutionary measures which would restrict eviction; the non-sectarian issue was an old Fenian principle but cleared Parnell the Protestant; the formation of a genuine Irish party, as opposed to the loose Butt association, was practical and had already been mooted; while the final clause, advocating support for all struggling nationalities, was addressed to world opinion, and was not one of which Parnell or many Irish nationalists were likely to take notice.

Unfortunately, the effect of this crucial and dramatic telegram – it was both those things, the first public commitment to any form of alliance with constitutionalism made by any Fenian body – was anti-climactic. In the first place the telegram was sent, not direct to Parnell, but to Charles Kickham, a revered leader of the IRB, which gave Parnell a splendid opportunity not to commit himself by the simple method of saying he had not received it. In the second place, whether he had received it or not, Parnell was in no position to accept American Fenian aid as he was not the leader of the Home Rule movement. However, the offer had been made and the next day Devoy ensured it would receive maximum attention by publishing it in the *New York Herald*, and two days later he had himself interviewed by the paper (together with other leading Irish-American political figures) on the subject of 'The Irish New Departure'. Incidentally, the phrase 'new departure' which was to resound so loudly, was used from the moment Devoy sent the telegram. In the interview Devoy explained the whole new idea, saying a combined effort between the advocates of physical force and those who believed in constitutional methods was long overdue, an obvious, necessary measure to achieve the goal of Irish freedom from English domination. He also said his side was not abandoning the concept of physical force, they were merely abandoning the idea of ill-organised rebellion – 'We simply don't believe in little insurrections that England can crush in a few weeks.' Interestingly, in the interview, he derided the Fenian movement, saying it had been a ghost for years and had breathed its last gasp with the death of John O'Mahony (the man who had donated the name Fenian). However, the world continued to classify him as a Fenian (the label was useful, indicating a physical force man) and he continued to act like one; working hard to obtain Irish Fenian support for the new departure; subsequently emphasising that although a new departure had been launched it only entailed a shift of emphasis and method, the end remained the same – complete independence for Ireland – and this would still be obtained by armed revolution if necessary, i.e. if the constitutionalists, notwithstanding the support of the Fenians, failed to gain independence. In the actual interview he demonstrated other basic Fenian tenets, by his fierce attacks upon the Catholic hierarchy and its reactionary interference in politics, and by his insistence on the necessity for non-sectarian education in Ireland. The vital factor was that the telegram had been sent and the way was open for a Fenian-constitutional merger, even if at that moment in time the pragmatic Devoy chose not to regard himself as a Fenian, or, perhaps more accurately, had chosen to abandon sterile Fenianism.

Davitt, who knew nothing of the telegram until after it had been sent – he was in Missouri on his lecture tour – considered it both premature and injudicious. It was indeed premature, principally because Parnell was not the Home Rule leader, Devoy having been misled on this score into believing that Isaac Butt had already been ousted. The injudiciousness was a more debatable point; Davitt considered an open offer from known revolutionaries would hamper rather than assist Parnell the parliamentarian, and would certainly alienate the moderates; but

Devoy was not interested in moderate opinion, he thought it could be trusted to swim with the successful tide. If Davitt considered the Fenian support should be less publicly overt, he quickly accepted the concept of the New Departure, realising that Devoy's telegram had opened the way – even if in his view in the wrong way – for a merger of the two forces, and that joint action should now be pushed ahead.

The New Departure might have been fact as far as public utterances were concerned, and that was an important factor coming from such a secret, suspicious, inbred movement as Fenianism, but the grand new alliance still had to be translated into action and nobody was taking any particular action. Parnell, whom Devoy had marked as the pivot of the New Departure, as the man who could implement it by making him the nominal recipient of the telegram, had made no comment whatsoever on its contents, while the IRB was making a great deal of comment, none of it favourable, and moderate Home Rulers were – as Davitt had predicted – appalled at the thought of an alliance with the proponents of violence. The next obvious steps were to win the support of the IRB and to get Parnell to commit himself; to obtain these results, Devoy, influenced by Michael Davitt, sailed for Europe. The first aim was to enlist IRB support because this seemed vital from the Fenian angle (and Devoy could say it was only American Fenianism he considered a dead movement), and it also seemed desirable to present Parnell with an offer from a united front. Consequently Devoy and Davitt attended a meeting of the Supreme Council in Paris in January, 1879. The encounter was not a success, only Devoy and Davitt themselves favoured the alliance with Parnell and the constitutional movement, while Charles Kickham, who took the chair, proved an unbrookable adversary. Kickham, as revered a founder member of the IRB as John O'Leary, was by then almost totally deaf, and cut short any argument he disapproved of by the simple expedient of removing his ear-trumpet. Davitt was outraged by this behaviour and railed against 'the fate of Ireland dependent on the impression conveyed to a physically helpless man through the deaf and dumb alphabet'. At one point in the proceedings, according to Devoy, Davitt's frustration and rage released themselves in a passionate flood of tears, although the tears could have been partially induced by physical exhaustion. For a man who had spent seven years in prison, appallingly undernourished and overworked, Davitt's programme since his release had been onerous, and there were signs of severe strain at the end of his American lecture tour, some of his letters betraying the weariness and irritation of a man physically at the end of his tether. Whatever caused Davitt's tears, they had no effect on the members of the Supreme Council of the IRB and the only concession gained was the agreement that the officers of the organisation should be left free to participate in the open movement if they felt so disposed (this was rescinded the next year).

Davitt himself was by now committed to the idea of an alliance based on a programme of land agitation and having decided, as a result of the abortive Paris meeting with the Supreme Council, that the concept of the New Departure was too revolutionary for men who could only comprehend the secret society, he proceeded to work for an agreement between those who could grasp the ideal and the necessity. He helped arrange a personal meeting between Parnell and John Devoy which again took place in France, this time in Boulogne, on March 7, 1879. At this moment in time, neither Parnell nor Devoy was similarly convinced that a movement based on the land question was the answer to the problems – nature and Davitt had yet to lead them to this conclusion – and the discussions in Boulogne centred on what sort of practical alliance Fenianism and constitutionalism could make. Parnell was nowhere near as intransigent in his attitude as Kickham had been, but he remained non-committal about a formal alliance; meeting the Fenians half-way was one matter, placing himself at the head of the Fenian inspired New Departure was another, and he continued to perform his brilliant tight-rope act, alienating neither the moderates nor the Fenians. As usual, he succeeded in creating the desired impression, and Devoy was convinced that 'he was prepared to go more than half-way to meet us', and that he had backed the right man in Parnell. Interestingly, one of the reasons Devoy gave for not selecting Davitt as the leader of the New Departure underlines the Catholic-bred respect for authority which helped make the Protestant Parnell an acceptable candidate. Later, when reviewing the possibility of Davitt's candidacy, Devoy wrote, 'His impetuous temperament and lack of tact, *to say nothing of his social standing*, made him impossible'. (The italics are mine.)

By the terms of his amnesty Devoy was not supposed to set foot in Ireland but this did not deter him, and he made several visits to his native land by various back-door entrances. In the first week of April, 1879, he re-met Parnell in Dublin but the results were negative, relations remained cordial but Parnell still refused to commit himself to any definite merger or plan of action. In the meantime the agrarian situation was worsening, and it was Michael Davitt who proceeded to take the step that set the ready-made engine of the land question into motion.

CHAPTER 6

'The Only Issue upon which Ireland can be United is the Land Question'

Davitt returned to Ireland after the meeting with the Supreme Council of the IRB in Paris, which had thrown him into such a depression and occasioned his disenchantment with Irish Fenianism. By the spring of 1879 he was in Mayo, where the conditions aroused his emotional nature to fever pitch. The conditions were not new, they had merely been exacerbated by two bad harvests. Mayo lies in the province of Connaught – Sligo, Galway, Roscommon and Leitrim comprise its other counties – and over the whole area the soil is mostly poor, much of it stony and bogridden, while the climate is harsh and fickle, subject to frequent storm and mist, particularly on the beautiful Atlantic coastlines of Mayo, Galway and Sligo. In Connaught there were then nearly 105,000 farms with less than thirty acres of land, and of these over 22,000 had under five acres, and in some Mayo villages two hundred acres of land were supporting two hundred and fifty people, less than an acre per person, whereas to obtain a reasonable life from the soil several acres per person would have been necessary.

Superimposed on the adverse physical conditions was the English agrarian system, the outstanding defect of which was, as already outlined, that the landlords more often than not did nothing other than let the land, but had the legal power to evict without compensation for whatever improvements might have been made. This basic defect was tied in with rack-renting, which can mean the payment of the fullest possible rent, but which, in Ireland, always meant the payment of excessive rents because the soil was the principle means of livelihood, and all landlords knew that as fast as they evicted one family another set of hopefuls would take its place. A further constant grievance arising from the tangle of dual ownership and instability was the question of the abatement of rents – their adjustment when harvest and times generally were bad – which again more often than not the landlords refused to allow, and tenants were accordingly evicted when they could not meet the demanded rent.

This was the land problem as Davitt saw it on his return to Mayo, the tenants squeezed, cheated, lacking security of tenure, given no incentive or encouragement to effect the real improvements that might have made their holdings viable, with the threat of eviction always dangling over them. It was these questions of rack-renting, land-grabbing (i.e. taking a farm from an evicted tenant), insecurity of tenure, lack of legal contracts, that he set out to remedy. He was confronted by a fierce, powerful, entrenched opposition, and those who viewed the Irish land question unsympathetically, or, as they would have said, realistically, asserted that the trouble lay not in the imposed English system (which in their view was superior anyway), nor in the admitted complications that had arisen over the centuries, but from the basic fact that far too many peasants were engaged in the hopeless task of trying to extract a living by primitive and inadequate methods from unsuitable and unviable land with a rotten farming climate, in small uneconomic holdings. The answer, in their view, lay not in further repeal of the land laws but in the clearing of uneconomic land for grazing, letting the fittest survive on larger holdings, and the rest take other jobs or emigrate.

One notably unsympathetic landlord, William Bence Jones, an Englishman who had farmed near Cork for fifty years and who was to hit the headlines immediately after Charles Cunningham Boycott as another victim of the new 'boycotting' weapon, said, 'a patch of bog and rock Connaught really is, to which such patriotic sentiment is supposed . . . in preference to the magnificent land of Manitoba and N.W. America where splendid crops of corn grow in succession without manure'. Bence Jones stressed that conditions were nowhere near as bad in the rest of Ireland as they were in Connaught (which was on the whole true), and had a good deal to say about the Irish character, at whose door he considered the major part of the blame for the agrarian situation should be laid. According to Bence Jones the faults of the Irish tenants and not the situation in which they were placed were the cause of all the trouble, and their faults included 'drink, indolence, debt and scheming, with ignorance and want of self reliance as consequence'; that far from being unable to contract freely with their landlords because there was no legal definition, the Irish were 'the keenest and best bargainers in Europe ... Jews cannot live in Ireland. They have no chance'; that, overall, Ireland was 'a barbarous and backward country totally different from England in principle and thought'; that improving its character (up to English standards) would be the work of centuries; that the only hope for the country was to treat farming as commerce on sound business principles, and there was absolutely no point in encouraging successive generations to farm as badly and live as dismally as had their forebears.

Bence Jones's was an extremist view, but to a degree it was shared by many others, and, less racially or arrogantly expressed, it was held by many intelligent Englishmen and Anglo-Irishmen. However, the more sympathetic observers also asserted that if the Irish peasant could not be counted amongst the most lovable or civilised section of the human race, it was circumstance that had made him cling so tenaciously to the one thing he knew and the one thing left open to him – the land – and had therefore turned him into what he was; that the fault lay with the centuries of agrarian instability and the unsolved problem of divided land ownership, and that it could, at root, only be blamed on England, because for centuries she had been the dominating and legislating power. Almost all English observers who actually went to Connaught returned horrified, irrespective of whether they had a solution to offer (and most of them had). The descriptions of life in Connaught abounded: 'The cabins of the peasantry seemed to be about the very worst dwellings for human beings I had ever viewed. I noted that many of the cottages boasted no windows, that they all had mud floors, and most of them mud walls'; and again: 'Men, women and children sleep under a roof and within walls dripping with wet, while the floor is saturated with damp. The construction and dimensions of their hovels are, as the abodes of human beings, probably unique ... Their dimensions ... varying from 12 ft × 15 ft down to one half that limited space'. General Gordon's famous letter to *The Times* said that the Bulgarians, Anatolians, Chinese and Indians were better off than the Irish peasants, and the comparison with supposedly wretched and inferior races was notable, even among the horrified and sympathetic observers. Another officer who had lately served with honour in Zululand told a reporter that 'not even in the worst parts of Cetewayo's dominions did he come across anything so bad as here' – here in this instance being Davitt's home county and Boycott's adopted county of Mayo.

When Davitt came face to face with the situation early in 1879, which was the first time he had really faced it as an adult, when he saw the hungry children crying in the mud shacks or the evicted families huddled by the roadside, his initial reaction was emotional, for these were his people and questions of whether they were lovable or unlovable, civilised or uncivilised, and why, did not enter his mind. He identified with them, for had he not once, twenty-seven years ago, been in the same situation, a hungry, destitute, evicted child? He became absolutely convinced that the land question was the basic problem in Ireland, that on this issue the peasants could be made to stand up and fight, and then their enthusiasm could be harnessed to the wider issue of independence. But he knew something had to be done now, not next year by Charles Stewart Parnell in Parliament or in the next decade when the Fenians might be ready for an armed insurrection, but now, to arrest the tide of human suffering in Connaught.

The incident that triggered off the ideas seething in his brain was the action of a clerical landlord, Canon Geoffrey Burke, the parish priest of Irishtown in Mayo. Burke had recently inherited an estate near by and when he found that his tenants were in arrears with their rents, he threatened them all with eviction. Outraged, Davitt decided to call a meeting in Irishtown, specifically to protest against the action of Burke, generally to condemn the whole landlord system. An announcement in the local *Connaught Telegraph*, owned by an ardent nationalist, James Daly, stated that 'a mass meeting of the tenant farmers of Mayo, Galway and Roscommon will be held at Irishtown, a few miles outside Claremorris for the purpose of representing to the world the many and trying ordeals and grievances the tenant farmers labour under'. The meeting took place on Sunday, April 20, 1879, and despite the pouring rain the *Connaught Telegraph* estimated that 13,000 tenant farmers attended (probably an exaggeration, such figures usually were, but as no other newspaper covered the meeting one cannot argue with the *Telegraph*). Among the speakers were editor Daly and John O'Connor Power, Davitt's old Fenian friend and the only MP to appear, and resolutions were passed urging the small tenant farmers to unite against the iniquitous extortions of landlords and to demand an abatement of rent. As a result of the meeting Burke withdrew the eviction notices and reduced his tenants' rents by 25 per cent, so the immediate aim was achieved. Davitt himself failed to attend – it was later maliciously said that he would have been 'the Father of the Land League had he not missed the train' – but the impetus for the meeting was his, the emphasis on the need for the tenant farmers to unite and organise for the final, root settlement of the land question was his. In fact, James Daly claimed he organised the meeting but there was agreement that Davitt had drafted the resolutions; one resolution had a typical, orotund, emotional Davitt ring, namely that the tenant farmers were determined 'to resort to every lawful means compatible with an outraged civilised people, whereby our inalienable rights – political and social – can be regained from their enemies'.

The formation of the Land League still lay ahead but this meeting in the obscure village of Irishtown – 'a neat little hamlet on the borders of Mayo, Roscommon and Galway' according to the *Connaught Telegraph* – was the first organised 'Tenant Right' meeting in decades and proved that the peasants were finally in a mood to be roused from their supineness, for 13,000 of them had congregated in foul weather to provide the largest public demonstration since the days of Daniel O'Connell. It had further proved that combined action was effective, to wit the withdrawal of the eviction notices and the abatement of rent granted by Burke. What was now needed was leadership and organisation, and Davitt quickly announced a further Tenant Right meeting for June 7, to be held at Westport, a much larger and more important Mayo town, with its wide streets climbing up the hills, situated by the sacred mountain of Croagh Patrick.

Before the grand public demonstration in Westport, there was a further private meeting in Dublin on June 1 between Davitt, Parnell and John Devoy, and this proved to be the crucial encounter between the three men. To an extent, outside circumstances precipitated the meeting for the weather had been foul, the prospect of another dreadful harvest loomed, and Devoy himself stressed the importance of the elements, making it essential that a move be made, as the alternative was a recurrence of the famine conditions of the 1840s. At this vital meeting no minutes were kept, and the precise nature of the agreement reached between the three men has since been a source of endless debate and doubtless will continue to be so. John Devoy was the only one of the three who later gave a detailed account of what transpired, and he was adamant that a firm understanding was reached, that Parnell verbally committed himself to the New Departure as dictated by the Clan na Gael. This meant that, while on the one hand the Clan agreed to support Parnell in his attempts to gain independence by constitutional methods, Parnell on the other hand agreed not only to support Davitt's plan for land agitation, which could be linked to Home Rule and was heavily endorsed by the Clan, but committed himself to the underlying Fenian precept that armed revolution might yet prove to be the only solution to Ireland's problems. Devoy himself patently believed that Parnell made such a commitment, indeed he had to be convinced, otherwise he could not and would not, being the man he was, have thrown his weight behind Parnell, however much he might have considered a concerted effort desirable.

Parnell and Davitt were as adamant, if in less vehement detail, that no explicit agreement was reached. Davitt considered that any binding agreement between Fenianism and constitutionalism was impossible, that the most that could be expected was 'a commonsense plan of semi-revolutionary action', and that this was achieved at the June meeting in Dublin. He further stated that Parnell did not commit himself to the possibility of armed revolution but only to participation in an agrarian-based agitation. It has been pointed out that Davitt made his comments years later when he had embraced international socialism and wanted to disassociate himself from his Fenian past, and that in June 1879 he had accepted the New Departure as outlined by the Clan na Gael, whereas Parnell had not. This is true, but does not fully explain why he should wish to exonerate Parnell, as opposed to himself, from the taint of violence. Parnell himself merely said later that he had never entered into any compact with the Fenians, and the consensus of opinion had since accepted the Parnell-Davitt interpretation. That Parnell, the born leader, should subordinate himself to anybody is unlikely, and by explicitly agreeing to the New Departure he would have submitted to the Fenians; that Parnell, the master tactician, should at this fast-flowing moment of Irish history have committed himself to any ultimate plan of action is even more unlikely. The explanation would seem to be that Parnell once again performed his famous silent illusion act and convinced John Devoy – not an easy man to convince – that he was totally in favour of the New Departure and all it entailed, without actually saying so.

Whether Parnell had allied himself with the Fenian proponents of violence and explicitly agreed to a programme based on violence, was to be of the utmost importance in the years to come, and was greatly to influence British reaction to the whole question of Irish Home Rule. But the immediate relevance of the meeting was that as from June 1, 1879, the New Departure started to be a practical rather than a verbal fact, an alliance (however tacit) between the constitutional movement and the previously underground Fenian impulse, tied to the new Irish-American power, producing the most formidable Irish force with which England had yet had to contend. The previously missing link which formed the basis of the merger, which it was now accepted could probably provide the essential social and economic convulsion to involve both the mass of peasants at home and the embittered immigrants in the United States, was land agitation. If various Irish nationalists had been moving towards the conclusion that the land problem was the key to the whole Irish situation, it was Michael Davitt who first showed how it could be used, with the Irishtown meeting and then proceeded to unlock the door with an organised programme of land agitation.

A new land movement needed as much outside weight and influence as it could obtain, and before the Dublin agreement of June 1, 1879, Davitt had asked Parnell to attend the meeting in Westport on June 7, and the latter had accepted. The Irishtown meeting had been ignored by the press, other than the *Connaught Telegraph*, but Parnell publicised his decision to attend at Westport by sending a telegram – his favourite form of communication, brief and to the point – and the news was widely reported. On June 5, John McHale, the Archbishop of Tuam, sent an open letter to the *Freeman's Journal*, the leading moderate nationalist newspaper, in which he denounced the proposed meeting. In the letter he said that an Irish Member of Parliament had 'unwittingly expressed his readiness to attend a meeting convened in a mysterious and disorderly manner', and while no body could be more sympathetic towards the rack-rented tenants or more willing to redress their genuine grievances than the Catholic clergy, equally he and the clergy could not but condemn the proposed meeting because it was organised by men who were promoting only their own personal interests and who were of lawless nature and occult association. (The taint of the occult had frequently been directed against the Fenians by the Catholic hierarchy.) He and the faithful clergy must therefore raise their voices to point out to the people that unhallowed combinations led only to disaster and to a firmer riveting of the chains which bound the unhappy Irish nation.

The redoubtable John McHale, the most venerable and revered member of the Irish hierarchy, had turned his thumbs down on the meeting, its organisers and its aims – what would Parnell the Protestant do in the face of this Catholic veto? His Grace had presented Parnell with an escape route by his use of the word 'unwittingly'; now that the true nature of the meeting and its organisers had been revealed by John of Tuam, Parnell could plead that he had been misled and gracefully withdraw. Immediately after the publication of this strong denunciation, Michael Davitt hurried round to see Parnell in Dublin, and in a state of considerable anxiety asked him what his reaction was and would he attend the Westport meeting? Parnell replied with his customary succinctness, 'Will I attend? Certainly. Why not? I have promised to be there, and you can count on my keeping that promise.' Davitt said of Parnell's decision that it was 'the most courageously wise act of his whole political career'. It *was* a courageous decision – John McHale was not to be brooked lightly – and it certainly proved to be wise in the context of Irish nationalism and leadership, although Parnell could not know this for certain when he took it. He was probably prompted by his fine tactical sense which told him that the passionate, emotional Davitt was almost certainly right and the land issue was the ready-made engine he could later drive, and partly by his own character, the confidence to stick to a decision and to be undismayed by the strictures of Catholic bishops.

June 7 in Westport dawned another foul day, with the rain pouring down, the hills wrapped in mist and Croagh Patrick blotted from sight, but Davitt had publicised and organised his meeting well and the elements did not deter thousands of Connaught farmers from crowding into the town. A central procession marched to the meeting place consisting of five hundred young men 'all wearing green scarfs, beautifully embroidered with the heart and the shamrock', and carrying banners bearing the legends: *Ireland for the Irish – Serfs no longer – The Land for the People – Down with the Land Jobbers.* Behind the main procession marched and rode contingents from virtually every Mayo town, village and hamlet; from Ballinrobe, the nearest small town to Boycott's residence at Lough Mask, came a brass band and seventeen carts crammed to bursting point. There were several speakers, including Connaught nationalists who were to be prominent in the Land League, but the two main ones were Michael Davitt and Charles Stewart Parnell, and their speeches provide an interesting contrast in style and reveal much about the characters of the two men.

Davitt's speech was long, passionate, rhetorical and involved.* He proposed the general resolution: 'Whereas all political power comes from the people, and the people of Ireland have never ceased to proclaim their right to autonomy, we hereby re-assert the right of our country to self-government', having, characteristically, previously made it clear that he would not commit Mr Parnell or other gentlemen present to his definition of the word 'self-government', which was total independence, although, as characteristically, he did not actually say so. He mentioned the Zulus whom he called 'a race of savages in South Africa' as a splendid example of how unrighteous conquest could be resisted and the sublime principles of national independence defended, and this reference to the Zulus earned one of the biggest cheers of the

* Parnell, referring to the intricate flow of words and the socialistic visions, later said, 'Davitt would get stoned by the farmers, only he talks Greek to them'.

meeting and was singled out for much editorial comment in London as evidence of the subversive, revolutionary, anti-British nature of the new land agitation. Interestingly, as he was later to urge co-operation between the British and Irish working classes, he warned his audience not to expect any assistance from the English farmers or farm labourers, and he also warned them not to anticipate any success from the parliamentary party with their legislative tinkering at Westminster. In orotund phrases he urged the audience never 'to forego their hereditary and inalienable right to the possession of the soil, until the land unrighteously taken from our forebears, shall be given back to the people who cultivate and improve it', and to teach their children 'that if their fidelity to their country's imperishable cause goes hand in hand with a firm resolve to win back the soil of Ireland from the land-robbers who seized it, no power on earth can stand in the path of victory and keep them enslaved'.

Parnell's speech was briefer, more colloquial and infinitely more concrete, upholding Gladstone's contention that he said what he meant in phrases that only the most obtuse could fail to understand. Not shirking an important issue he started by referring to his Grace the Archbishop of Tuam's letter. He said it would ill-become him to treat anything coming from his Grace with anything but respect, but the meeting had been placarded throughout Mayo for the last six weeks, during which time nobody had spoken against it or intimated that his Grace was opposed to it. Indeed, it was only yesterday morning, as he was leaving home, that he had read of the opposition and he was sure his Grace would not have wished him at that late stage in the proceedings to have dishonoured his promise and failed to have attended the meeting. This firm taking of the Catholic bull by the horns was well received – 'It was never him wrote the letter' – shouted a voice from the crowd – and Parnell proceeded to propose his resolution, which demanded an immediate readjustment of land tenure in Ireland.

Parnell continued by saying he did not believe that landlords were a natural institution in any country, that of all countries Ireland had perhaps suffered the most from this class whereas England had perhaps assimilated herself better than any other. He dealt briefly with France, Russia, Belgium and Prussia, where the land had been given to its occupiers, and with the methods by which this had been achieved – revolution or purchase by the state. He said he now sought a method whereby, without injuring the landlord, the tenant could own his land, and in the meantime it was necessary to ensure that as long as the tenant paid a fair rent he should be left to enjoy the fruits of his industry. He defined a fair rent as 'a rent the tenant can reasonably pay according to the times', and if the landlords failed to accept the proposition that the tenants could not pay as much in bad times as in good, what must be done? He answered his question thus: 'You must show the landlords that you intend to keep a firm grip of your homesteads and lands. You must not allow yourself to be dispossessed as you were dispossessed in 1847. You must not allow your small-holdings to be turned into larger ones'. It was the simple phrase 'Keep a firm grip of your homesteads' that became the clarion cry of the Land League, and resounded round the Western world as evidence of a new-found Irish peasant determination.

After Parnell's speech, further resolutions were passed pledging the meeting to resist landlord oppression, then it was over – 'a magnificent success, a glorious triumph', according to the *Connaught Telegraph*; 'Communism in Connaught', according to the Dublin *Evening Mail*. It had indeed been a significant occasion, although few at the time on either side, particularly the loyalist side, realised how significant. But the Catholic tenant farmers of Connaught had responded to Michael Davitt's call and Charles Stewart Parnell, Protestant landlord and Member of Parliament, had given his blessing to a movement whose aim was to abrogate the power of the landlords.

CHAPTER 7

'Communism in Connaught'

Parnell's attendance at the Westport meeting had occasioned its wide reporting, despite the fact that, although Isaac Butt was by now dead (he died in May, 1879), Parnell was still not the leader of the Home Rule movement. Butt's supporters had just succeeded in voting into power one William Shaw, but that Parnell was a fast-rising star was apparent to most people, a circumstance underlined by the press coverage he was receiving. In addition, Parnell had donated a vital slogan – throughout Mayo people were soon heard saying, 'We'll keep a firm grip of our homesteads' – and the flame had been lit. Tenant right meetings were quickly held in other Mayo towns, and on July 13 John Devoy attended one in Claremorris, telling the suspicious constabulary that he was the correspondent of *The Times* which they believed. But the demonstrable enthusiasm and determination of the tenant farmers was, in the appalling wet summer of 1879, confined mainly to Mayo, and even here the enthusiasm needed to be harnessed and organised to prevent its dissipation. It was Michael Davitt who continued to throw himself mind and soul, to the limits of his physical endurance, into the task of creating a unified, disciplined agrarian movement which, he hoped, would for the first time in Irish history be non-violent in its approach because of its unity and discipline.

On August 16, 1879, Davitt called a convention at Castlebar in Mayo, a typical Connaught town with its rows of squat grey houses opening on to the pavements, mainly treeless, but possessing an immaculately verdant English-type village green. This was the first convention to be held in Ireland for nearly a century, for the good reason that the Convention Act which had forbidden such gatherings of delegates had only just been repealed. Davitt and his fellow-organisers kept a wary eye upon the reaction of the British government, but in the event they did not intervene or threaten re-introduction of the ban. Davitt read a lengthy declaration of principles to the assembled delegates, in which he reviewed Irish land history – the original failure to assimilate feudalism, the imposition of the alien English system based on feudalism, and the trauma of the famine years; he quoted John Stuart Mill – 'The right to hold the land goes as it did in the beginning with the right to till it'; appealed to the farmers of Ireland to organise themselves to their full strength in order to ameliorate and redress their social and political wrongs. He followed this address with the practical methods by which amelioration and redress could be obtained. He proposed the inauguration of the National Land League of Mayo whose aims would be (1) to watch over the interests of the peasants and protect them from capricious or unjust exercise of power; (2) to resort to every means compatible with justice for the abolition of the present land laws of Ireland; (3) to expose the injustices inflicted on the farmers of Mayo by rack-renting and eviction; (4) to undertake the defence of any members forced to go to court; (5) to assist the evicted financially; (6) to undertake the organisation of local clubs, public meetings and the printing of informative literature; (7) to act as a vigilance committee throughout Mayo.

Davitt later said his dual overall aims were the obvious ones of obtaining a root settlement of the land question, and the equally important one of teaching the peasants not to be subservient to the gentry. He said 'the gospel of manhood' was as vital a lesson as the cry 'the land for the people', for without the former the people were unlikely to obtain the latter, or when they obtained it to be able to utilise it properly.

The Land League was in being, although only locally, in

Mayo, and its officers proceeded to propagate its aims by means of public meetings, and to try and effect its objectives by concerted opposition to rack-renting, land grabbing and evictions. In practical terms they did not at first meet with great success but in propaganda terms, in instilling the will to resist into the local populace, they were much more successful.

In 1879, although his world-wide notoriety lay a year ahead, Charles Cunningham Boycott, in residence at Lough Mask in the heart of the Land League country, was not unaffected by the ferment. In the six years since he had lived at Lough Mask House, Boycott had managed to make himself thoroughly unpopular with the local tenantry. He had become a magistrate, a pillar of the establishment, although this would not necessarily have made him disliked, and that he was an Englishman was not the sole cause either; many landlords and a good proportion of agents were. His unpopularity was more a question of personal temperament and failure of comprehension. In fact Boycott himself insisted that in the early days, indeed almost up to the time of his 'boycotting', he was on friendly terms with the tenantry, that he met many of them socially through his participation in events at Ballinrobe Races, that they were interested in his training and running of horses at the Curragh. (This latter activity was part hobby, part business venture.) The tenants themselves told a different tale, failing to mention the popular sporting figure, swearing that from the day of his appointment as agent to Lord Erne he had played 'the part of tyrant in every shape or form'; that he never had a civil word for anybody but that his greeting was a curse or blasphemy; that he laid down numerous penal laws – no gates to be left open, no hens to trespass on his property, nobody to arrive late for work, and the like; that he fined anybody who transgressed these petty restrictions; that he refused to allow the tenants to collect wood from the Lough Mask estate or to use short cuts across the farm – privileges they had previously enjoyed.

Boycott was not a perceptive man, nor was he a sociable one, but he was an Englishman, and the explanation for the divergence of views perhaps lies in the amalgam of these three facts. Even when he met the tenants socially, they were not of his class and he would take little notice of them, so that their dislike would genuinely not be apparent to him. The curses and blasphemies he was accused of hurling at the tenants were probably an exaggeration of his naturally curt manner, with a strong dash of English exasperation with Irish behaviour thrown in. The imposition of the petty rules and regulations and the withdrawal of earlier privileges stemmed partly from character, and partly, almost certainly, from a common English reaction to the Irish. From personal character Boycott believed in the value of discipline in minor matters, while his Englishness led him to find the peasants a maddeningly vague and idle lot, for whom truth meant little and time meant nothing, full of promises they had no intention of keeping, and, who, given an inch, would take a mile. For their own benefit they needed discipline, they needed to be made to understand the English values of punctuality, keeping a bargain, honouring an agreement, so that they could more profitably run their dismal farms and lives. Upholding this attitude, Boycott later said that he only fined the owners of hens that had been wrecking the corn in his meadows, that he only stopped the indiscriminate cutting down of Lord Erne's timber, not that required for legitimate purposes, that he only forbade the use of paths that were his private property, not those that were a right of way.

Despite Boycott's insistence on discipline and efficiency among the tenant farmers and those labourers who were directly employed by him at Lough Mask House, there was current local comment that he was not particularly brilliant at managing his own estate. The belief that Boycott was a bad farmer and that one of the reasons he created such a stir in 1880 was because he wanted the government to bail him out of an unprofitable venture, persists in the Lough Mask area today. Although one should take such information with a pinch of salt, because much of the evidence the raconteur's father or grandfather knew for fact is palpably inaccurate when laid against proven fact, this particular belief could be true. The disarray in which Boycott left his affairs, and with which his widow had to cope, does not reveal him to have been a good manager or businessman. However, in 1879 Boycott was not in poor financial straits because, in the April of that year, he bought the estate of Kildarra which consisted of '95 acres, one wood and 11 perches statute or thereabouts'. Kildarra, which lies on the borders of Mayo, on the road from Claremorris to Ballinlough, cost him £1,125, £525 of which he paid cash into the Bank of Ireland, taking out a mortgage of £600 for the balance. It is possible that the purchase of the Kildarra estate stretched him financially, that the mortgage repayments were a burden so that when eighteen months later he became the first victim of the Land League and financial ruin stared him in the face, the knowledge of the Kildarra commitments (about which he kept very quiet) added extra incentive to his reactions.

It was on August 1, 1879, that Boycott received the first intimation of a more militant expression of discontent among Lord Erne's tenants, and personally realised that the role of land agent in Ireland was not necessarily a pleasant one. On that morning a notice was pinned to the wrought-iron gates of the Lough Mask estate warning him not to collect the rents unless an abatement of 20 per cent or 25 per cent was allowed, and underneath was the familiar drawing of a coffin (familiar from earlier land agitations). Of this particular demand for abatement, Boycott said it was not made because Lord Erne was an illiberal landlord; on the contrary he had always made allowances for tenant improvements and had been among the first in the area to grant reductions in bad years. Boycott insisted it had been made partly because of the malign influence of the Land League in Mayo, sowing discontent among the peasants, and partly because the tenant farmers were feeling the pinch of their previous heavy and improvident borrowing from the gombeen men and the stopping of credit by tradesmen. In the event, he ignored the threatening notice, and in 1879 no further direct or concerted action was taken by the tenants. However, three of them refused to pay the rent unless the abatement was granted, and against them eviction decrees were obtained at the Ballinrobe Quarter Sessions. The incident did nothing to improve the relationship between Lord Erne's Lough Mask tenantry and his appointed agent. Indeed, as a result of the affair, Boycott deemed it advisable to apply for police protection, and Lough Mask House remained under the surveillance of the Royal Irish Constabulary from November 1879 to May 1880.

The idea of the Land League – of an organised, combined tenant movement to fight the power of the landlords – was gaining ground in Mayo, as an incident such as the tenants' demands to Boycott indicates. But Michael Davitt realised only too clearly that if it were to succeed, either in its immediate aim of forcing radical land legislation from Westminster, or in its longer-term aim of providing the springboard for Irish self-government, it would need to be a national movement involving national figures, and the key national figure in his (and others) estimation was now Parnell. At this moment in the late summer of 1879 Parnell himself, with Parliament in recess, was touring Ireland addressing meetings, but not only about the land question; his attention being as much fixed upon the leadership of the Home Rule party, which involved other issues. Parnell might have agreed to support an agrarian-based agitation at the June meeting in Dublin, and he had undeniably given his blessing by his attendance at Westport, but support and blessing were a different matter from leading the enterprise, and he was still not convinced that the land was the crucial factor behind which he should throw his entire weight. As Davitt wrote to John Devoy in August: 'The Home Rulers are alarmed at a movement independent of theirs ... Parnell is afraid to lead it, too, but wishes it success'. However, a week later, at Limerick on August 31, Parnell made an important speech which can be regarded as a further step towards commitment to the Land League. At Limerick he said, 'It is the duty of the Irish tenant farmers to combine among themselves, and ask for a reduction of rent where a reduction is necessary, and if they get no reduction, then I say it is their duty to pay no rent, and if they combine in that way, if they stand together, keep a firm grip of their homesteads ... no power on earth can prevail against the hundreds of thousands of tenant farmers of the country'. Again the non-payment of rent was not a novel idea, it had been one of the weapons Charles Gavan Duffy had suggested long ago in the days of the Tenant Right League, but its reiteration by Parnell at this moment in time was an affirmation of faith in the Land League's programme.

Partly as a result of this strong speech, Davitt went up to Dublin where he had a long conversation with Parnell about, in his own words, 'the desirability of forming a Land League for Ireland'. According to Davitt, Parnell at first objected strongly, saying he considered local leagues, as the one already established in Mayo, would serve the purpose admirably. But Davitt persisted in his passionate explanations of why he considered a National Land League was essential, why it must succeed if properly organised and led. As John Devoy later wrote, 'Davitt was always very confident of success if we could only get the leader and, at that time, he had full faith in Parnell. I do not think he had then any notion that he could himself be the titular leader'. However, Devoy added, 'I saw very close and convincing evidence that in a short time he developed the belief that he was the power behind the throne – the driving force that kept the movement going – and that at a very early stage he resented Parnell's quiet and silent, but very emphatic, refusal to be a mere figurehead'.

Davitt's belief that his was the driving force behind the Land League was not unjustified, and if he did come to resent Parnell's taking control of the movement, which he himself denied – he said it was on the matter of policy rather than quality of leadership that he diverged from Parnell – in the autumn of 1879 he was more than delighted when Parnell finally accepted the invitation to become President of a National Land League of Ireland. His acceptance of nomination to the leadership was on the clear understanding that the platform to be put forward was a parliamentary one – that land reform and Home Rule were to be achieved by constitutional methods; to this Davitt and his fellow committee members acceded. Davitt considered this a reasonable compromise on both sides, the concession by the Land Leaguers being necessary 'owing to the refusal of the extremist leaders in Ireland to have anything to do with the new departure', while Parnell, by accepting the presidency, gained the support of the more radical (mostly ex-Fenian) Land League, and of the Irish-Americans.

On September 29, 1879, Parnell publicly cast his lot when he issued a letter from his ancestral home at Avondale, stating that he now considered it necessary to form a committee for the purpose of appealing to Irishmen abroad, especially in America, for assistance in forwarding the new programme of land agitation in favour of tenant ownership, and to support the tenants in their hour of crisis by further promoting the Land League organisation. On October 21, at the Imperial Hotel in Dublin, the National Land League of Ireland was inaugurated, with the declared short-term aim of obtaining a reduction in rack-rents and evictions, and the long-term aim of achieving tenant ownership of the land. Parnell was elected president of the new League, Davitt was appointed one of the honorary secretaries, with Joseph Biggar as one of the treasurers (Patrick Egan was the main treasurer, and a very good one he proved to be). The New Departure had become practical from the time of the agreement between Devoy, Parnell and Davitt at the Dublin meeting in June but from October 21, 1879, it became a reality, with the organisation Michael Davitt had forged – the Land League – as its prime attacking weapon. After the resolutions outlining the objects of the League, there were further resolutions stating that Parnell, as president, be required to journey to the United States to obtain support for the League, and that its funds should not be used for furthering the interests of parliamentary candidates. Davitt considered this latter resolution hard on Parnell, particularly as the League had agreed to support his parliamentary platform, but said it was a necessary concession to the extremists whose attitude had in the first place forced the concessions to Parnell's parliamentary strategy.

Parnell did not immediately set sail for the United States, although he accepted the committee's suggestion that he should go there and laid plans for a visit in the near future. In the meantime he returned to addressing meetings and consolidating his position in Ireland, while Davitt spent his time between the offices of the National Land League at 62 Middle Abbey Street, Dublin, and attending League-organised meetings, mainly in Connaught, which remained the stronghold of the movement. By early October *The Times* was commenting that in Ireland, 'The latest novelty in the way of Sunday afternoon amusement, appears to be the land meetings'. The slightly patronising, amused tone of *The Times* article reflected the general establishment attitude in the autumn of 1879, certainly in England, where even the most right-wing newspapers, although appalled by the evidence of 'communism' in Connaught, failed to take the movement seriously. It was bound to collapse soon because the Irish peasants were incapable of sustaining anything for long, and the traditional internecine squabbles would inevitably erupt before long between the leaders. That Parnell was now officially president of the League was regarded as an act of political folly on his part.

Captain Boycott doubtless shared the view that the movement would soon collapse, although there may have been less amusement in his attitude, viewed from close quarters rather than from London, several hundred miles away. He cannot have failed to have been aware of the Land League's activities in Mayo; for example, on October 5, there was a massive tenant right meeting in Ballinrobe, only four miles from Lough Mask House, attended, according to local sources, by between 20,000 and 30,000 people. Among the notables present were James Daly of the *Connaught Telegraph*, John O'Connor Power and Davitt himself, while the meeting was chaired by Father John O'Malley, the parish priest of the near-by Neale, who had already thrown himself heart and soul into the Land League and who was to play such an important part in Boycott's future. At the meeting the banners proliferated, and their mottoes were growing fiercer and more demanding: *Defend your God-given rights, the Land is our Birthright, Fight for Reductions*, and the gospel according to Parnell, *Stick to your Homesteads*. There was a banner from Partry which had an Irish wolf-hound surrounded by the words, *Gentle when stroked, fierce when provoked*, and one which paid tribute to Father O'Malley's participation, *The Priests and the People for ever*. The resolution demanding that the landlords grant abatements of rent was passed, and Michael Davitt spoke emotionally of 'this magnificent demonstration, the greatest honour I have ever received from my native county of Mayo', and said he hurled back with scorn and contempt the accusation that he had ever directly or indirectly sanctioned or encouraged the commission of violence.

However, at the beginning of November Davitt chose to make a particularly inflammatory speech on the subject of rents at Gurteen in Sligo – he himself later said, 'it was a very violent and not very wise speech'. As a result he, together with James Daly and another Land Leaguer, was arrested and charged with the use of seditious language. It should be remembered that Davitt was officially 'a convict at large on a ticket-of-leave', to quote a statement made about him in the House of Commons, and loyalist papers generally had not been slow to enlarge upon the theme of the dubious background of the Land League's leaders. If the British government had truly wanted to silence Davitt it had a simple remedy at its fingertips, the withdrawal of the ticket-of-leave on the justifiable grounds that he had failed to comply with the conditions of his parole, namely to be of good behaviour. With the curious English liberality that sometimes allows its political opponents an enormous amount of rope, Davitt was merely arrested on a straightforward seditious language charge. That he would not be convicted in an area where he was currently regarded as a compound of Robin Hood, Sir Galahad, Jesus Christ and every Irish hero who had ever existed, the government was also aware.

When the hearing opened in Sligo on November 24, Davitt was quickly released on bail, the whole area seethed with excitement, he was serenaded at the house where he was staying, tar barrels were lit in the streets, and the opportunity was taken to address the crowds and further the aims of the Land League. Davitt paid tribute to Parnell's attendance at the hearing which underlined his commitment to the Land League, helped give maximum publicity – twenty-seven reporters covered the hearing – and almost certainly assisted his release. The venue of the trial by jury was changed to Carrick-on-Shannon but it never took place, as the charges were quietly dropped.

The League had already succeeded in arousing Connaught to a degree that no previous land agitation had achieved, indeed it had aroused the peasants in a manner and quantity that no Irish movement since Daniel O'Connell's last great Repeal of the Act of Union campaign had managed. But the main activity remained in the west, remote from the centres of Irish life and particularly of English life, and if various newspapers and individuals were loud in their denunciations of the League and its ruffianly leaders, the general attitude at the end of 1879 was not one of real alarm as the belief that the movement would soon collapse persisted. If the government and establishment failed to recognise the strength and deep-rootedness of the grievances that were driving people into the Land League fold, they did not deny that the succession of bad harvests – and 1879 had been as dire as had been predicted – had led to genuine distress in rural Ireland, notably the always-impoverished province of Connaught.

At the end of 1879, the Duchess of Marlborough, wife of the current Lord Lieutenant of Ireland, and incidentally Lord Randolph Churchill's mother and Sir Winston's grandmother, opened a Famine Relief Fund. Shortly afterwards another fund was opened in Dublin by Edmund Dwyer Gray, the new Lord Mayor and proprietor of the influential *Freeman's Journal*. Gray fell out with Dublin Castle when the Duke of Marlborough refused to attend a banquet at Mansion House because Gray had attended a meeting in the City Hall opposing the government's measures in Connaught. On a tit-for-tat basis Gray opened his fund, so that the money subscribed could be used in a manner he and his supporters considered more appropriate. (The incident also helped swing the *Freeman's Journal* away from its previous moderate nationalist stance towards Parnell's more intransigent nationalism, although it did not immediately come out in wholehearted support for him.) The competition provided by the two funds assisted the victims for whom they were intended – the Duchess of Marlborough's Fund eventually raised £135,000, £500 donated by Queen Victoria, £250 by the Prince of Wales; and Gray's Fund £181,000, much of it from Irish emigrants in Australia, and food and sacks of seed were duly sent westwards. But they were drops in an ocean of misery, and in no way solved or affected the fundamental problems which the Land League was aiming to rectify radically.

CHAPTER 8

'Forty Million Welcomes to the Irish People's Champion!'

As the disastrous year of 1879 ended, the League was gaining strength and spreading its tentacles into other parts of rural Ireland, but as Davitt wrote frequently, 'What we want is money – money – money. Without it the movement must fail – with it success is certain.' Some money was already coming into the coffers of the League from Ireland itself, and from the Irish-American 'Skirmishing Fund',* but it was a trickle rather than a flow. It was principally to obtain the necessary 'money – money – money' that the National Land League had suggested that Parnell visit the United States, and at the end of December 1879 he duly sailed for New York.

He was accompanied by the young John Dillon, as it was considered inadvisable for both him and Davitt to absent themselves from Ireland at the same crucial time. Dillon was selected as travelling companion because of his personality and background; he was born in 1851, the son of John Blake Dillon, a leading member of the Young Ireland movement, and although he had studied for a medical degree, politics were his life-blood. He had the further advantage of looking the part of the wild Irish revolutionary (as did Parnell and Davitt their respective roles), being tall and slender, with dark eyes and raven black hair, and a

* The Skirmishing Fund had been established by the extremist Irish-American element as a means of supplying money for terrorist activities which would keep the pot boiling while the actual revolution brewed. By 1879 John Devoy and the Clan na Gael had gained control of the fund, and used it to send immediate financial aid to Davitt and the Land League. Characteristically, Davitt later insisted on repaying every penny.

melancholy romantic air. The two men, Parnell and Dillon, provided an admirable complement in style and personality, the
former cool, reserved, apparently emotionless, the latter full of
public emotion, fire and passion; they were the personification of
the two sides of the new Irish movement.

In the United States, Patrick Ford's *Irish World* devoted its
space to Parnell's arrival with maximum enthusiasm. Ford had
obviously thrown the power and influence of his newspaper
behind Davitt's Land League from the moment it was inaugurated in Castlebar, but when Parnell accepted the presidency of the
National Land League there was uncertainty about whether he
would throw an equal amount of weight behind him, because
Parnell remained the parliamentarian, the constitutionalist, roles
that were anathema to the working-class readership Ford
addressed. However, Ford had shifted gear to support Parnell,
although remaining loyal to his first hero, Davitt, and the effect
he had in transforming the disorganised bitterness of the working
class Irish-Americans into a viable force which supported Parnell,
was undoubted.

Parnell and Dillon arrived in New York on New Year's Day,
1880, having been delayed by violent storms in the Atlantic (the
former, an excellent sailor, survived the worst crossing in years
unperturbed, but the latter suffered badly from sea-sickness). The
next morning, at the unearthly hour of 7 a.m. Parnell replied to
an address of welcome on the dockside 'in a brief and appropriate
manner', according to the *Irish World*, but the *New York Herald*
managed to obtain a much less brief interview with 'Young
Ironsides'. (His American grandfather, it will be recalled, had
been known as 'Old Ironsides'.) To the *Herald* reporter Parnell
stated unequivocally that his primary object in coming to the
United States was to raise money for the Land League. From the
dockside he and Dillon proceeded to the Fifth Avenue Hotel
where they were greeted, again according to the *Irish World*, by
'multitudinous *cead mille failthes*', and after a brief respite they
plunged into the serious business of their American visit.

At a massive rally in Madison Square Gardens, Parnell restated the primary reason for his presence, to raise funds for the Land League, but he also announced another fund for famine relief, and it was partly on account of this latter fund that he fell foul of the influential *New York Herald.* Prior to his arrival the *Herald* had mentioned the necessity for starting an Irish Famine Relief Fund but had taken no concrete steps to set one up. However, after Parnell had inaugurated his fund in January and after the contributions had started pouring in, early in February the *Herald* started its fund, and thus in the early spring of 1880 there were four separate Irish Famine Relief Funds in existence, two Dublin-based, two American-based. The reason the *Herald* gave for a separate fund was political; the paper said money subscribed to Parnell's fund would inevitably find its way into the coffers of the Land League, a most dubious and probably revolutionary organisation which respectable Americans would do well to steer clear of and subscribe only to a straightforward humanitarian fund such as its own. Parnell's answer was that their supposedly apolitical fund would merely bolster up the evils of Irish landlordism, which was a highly political matter.

Even though Parnell ran foul of the *Herald,* he had the vociferous backing of the Clan na Gael and the *Irish World* for his whistle-stop tour of the United States on which he covered 11,000 miles and sixty-two towns and cities in two months. Undoubtedly the pinnacle of the visit was an invitation to address the House of Representatives, an honour previously only extended to Lafayette, Bishop England of South Carolina and Louis Kossuth. On February 2, 1880, he spoke to the crowded House for half an hour on the subject of Ireland's grievances. The *Daily News* (of London) said that the compliment was 'incredible, inconceivable – ordinary imagination is hardly able to bear the strain which would be required to form a mental picture of the House of Commons handed over for a night to some foreign gentleman, in order that he might denounce his own government there, and the members of the House invited to come in a body and listen to him'. This view was upheld by the *New York Herald* when it accused Parnell of 'stalking around this country preaching treason against the Government of his native land', and told him his proper place was in Ireland, that he should return home forthwith and endeavour to re-establish himself in the good opinion of the world. Parnell retorted by telling the *Herald* that in choosing to support Irish landlordism it had embarked upon 'a very much harder task than the discovery of Livingstone'.

The *Herald*'s accusation that Parnell was preaching treason against his native government was not invalid, that is if one considered the Act of Union as beneficial, which many people did. All of his speeches contained sentences that could be called treasonable; they were calculated appeals to the Fenian instinct, as for example, 'As an Irishman I am bound to say that every Irishman should be prepared to shed the last drop of his blood'; to obtain independence, that was, and only if necessary of course. On February 23, 1880, he made a speech in Cincinnati which could be, and later was, designated highly treasonable – 'With your help in keeping our people alive this winter, I feel confident we shall kill the Irish landlord system. . . . The feudal tenure and the rule of the minority have been the corner-stone of English misrule. Pull out that corner-stone, break it up, destroy it, and you have undermined English misgovernment. When we have undermined English misgovernment, we have paved the way for Ireland to take her place among the nations of the earth . . . None of us – whether we be in America or Ireland, or wherever we may be – will be satisfied until we have destroyed the last link which keeps us bound to England'. The 'last link' phrase was later to resound as much as 'keep a firm grip of your homesteads', although, interestingly, at the time no English, Irish or American newspaper picked it up. They mainly carried only a brief resumé of the speech, concentrating on Parnell's injunctions to the American labouring classes not to allow themselves to be put in the same position as the English and Irish. The *Irish World* was one of the few newspapers to carry the full text of the speech, and even it failed to comment upon the 'last link' phrase and its implications. Later, however, the reverberations were to echo loudly, and if Parnell said what he meant, the meaning was unequivocal. Whether he meant what he said was a different matter and the limits to which he was prepared to go in severing the last link, or whether there was a limit, remained as inscrutable as ever.

The strain of dealing with the organisation of the tour, and the correspondence involved, proved too much for Parnell and Dillon – the former was not interested in such chores and the latter unable to cope with them – and Tim Healy was urgently summoned from England to undertake the secretarial duties. Born in Bantry in 1856 to poor though not destitute parents, at the age of sixteen Healy went to work in Newcastle-on-Tyne where he quickly became the secretary of the local Home Rule Association (he was among those who organised the conference of 1877 that ousted Isaac Butt and elected Parnell chairman of the Home Rule Confederation of Great Britain). By the age of twenty-three he was in London and through family connections had started to contribute to the Irish nationalist paper, *The Nation*, and to be involved in nationalist politics. Tiny, sardonic, with a highly intelligent mind and mordant wit, Healy had a phenomenal capacity for work but his many sterling qualities, which were to take him to the forefront of Irish politics, had to be balanced against an uncertain, volatile temper and a chauvinistic suspicion of outsiders.

However, Healy performed the task for which he had been summoned with maximum efficiency, and it was he who donated to Parnell perhaps the most famous of his descriptive titles – 'the uncrowned King of Ireland'. On March 9 Parnell made his last speech on the North American continent at Montreal, during a brief foray into Canada where he was not particularly well-received, at least according to the *New York Herald*. (His press coverage in Canada was not enthusiastic.) At Montreal, Healy wound up the meeting by saying that Parnell, 'the uncrowned King of Ireland', was going away but would come back with victory shining on his banners. At this precise moment 'the un-crowned King of Ireland' was a premature description, but it quickly took the public fancy and within a short while was used by both Parnell's supporters and opponents, if for different reasons.

It was also Healy who submitted a draft plan for an American Land League, with Parnell's approval. He proposed that branches be organised in every State, with each branch to be independent and *responsible to the executive in Dublin*, but Devoy and the Clan na Gael fought this usurpation of their authority and it was eventually agreed that the American Land League should have an American executive. Over the function of the American League there was less argument, it was to render moral and particularly material assistance to the movement in Ireland which would enable the Irish League to fight the landlords to the death. The inauguration of the American League was a hurried affair, because news of the dissolution of Parliament had arrived from England. Parnell had to cut short his tour in order to return home to fight the general election, and consequently left the States in early March – to a rousing send off from the mainly Fenian 69th Regiment – with little more than an outline agreement on the necessity of forming an American Land League.

Overall, despite the opposition of the *New York Herald*, representing a section of middle-class American opinion, the tour had been a success. Parnell raised some £30,000 (£50,000 according to Davitt) and, as importantly for the future, he had roused Irish-American and general American interest, both working and middle class, to a new pitch of enthusiasm. The working-class support was engendered by the *Irish World*'s whole-hearted approval and by Parnell's own appeals to their Fenian instincts; the middle-class support (other than the section represented by the *Herald*) by Parnell himself. Whatever he might say, he was obviously a gentleman, he remained a parliamentarian and in his hands the expected Land League convulsion might prove to be the long-sought key to ultimate independence. Off the platform

Parnell had not been a great success – the English accent, the reserved, frosty manner, the disdain for social chit-chat, came as an unpleasant surprise. John Devoy said he evoked no warmth of feeling but despite this he also commented that Parnell won the confidence of the Irish-Americans to a degree not attained by any delegate sent from Ireland in the last twenty years. Devoy partly ascribed the success to Parnell's apparent Englishness; he said the Irish-Americans were looking for the qualities of mind and leadership 'to cope with the hard-hearted, stolid, persevering Englishman', and they thought they espied just those qualities in Parnell.

Mrs Delia Parnell was also in the States during her son's tour (they tended, and could afford, to be a wandering family), as were two other members of the family who played such active roles in the Irish agitation, Anna and Fanny. The latter was three years younger than her illustrious brother, being born in 1849, and was generally reckoned to be his favourite sister. She was small, vivacious, clever, as pretty as her brother was handsome, with the passion that lay under his cool exterior more obviously apparent in her. Fanny had been living in the States for some time and was already a published authoress on the subject of Ireland's grievances, although the poems that turned her into the bard of the Land League were yet to come. Anna, younger still, being born in 1852, had not inherited the family looks; she was plain, bony and short-sighted; in manner and words she was as cold and abrupt as her brother but lacked his counter-balancing charm and magnetism, and when her passion erupted it was a wild volcano. They formed a formidable trio, Charles, Anna and Fanny – a quartet when their mother was in attendance – and Tim Healy who had the opportunity of viewing them at close quarters in combined action considered them 'the most extraordinary family I ever came across'. Although he paid tribute to both sisters' capacity for work and the interest they took in Irish affairs – Anna was employed at the Irish Central Relief Bureau in New York while Fanny was occupied with her literary output –

he thought Mrs Delia Parnell was definitely 'a little off her nut' and so, to a lesser degree, were her sons and daughters. It was their apparent indifference towards each other, their lack of demonstrated affection that amazed Healy – 'one set of them doesn't seem to know where the other set is, or is living – or to care'. The outward appearances, very English in manner even if Mrs Parnell was American and her children Irish, probably astonished Healy, given as he was to great shows of family affection – not to say nepotism – more than it would have most other observers. Healy also commented that the only religion Parnell had was 'to believe that Friday is an unlucky day, although he smilingly informed me that he was a synodsman of the "Disestablished Church"' and that his mothers and sisters shared his religious condition. Again, a fierce Catholic such as Healy would have been more surprised by the casualness of such Protestant affirmation than most observers.

When the boat bringing Parnell back from the United States docked at Queenstown (now Cobh) in the early hours of a cold March morning in 1880, Healy had some further revealing comments to make upon Parnell's character. There was no sign of a welcoming party and Parnell appeared to be both hurt and angry at this apparent slight, although Healy considered that it would be noble of anybody to turn up at such an hour in such weather with so much happening in Ireland. In fact, Davitt, Thomas Sexton (another rising member of the Parnell group), and T. D. Sullivan, the famous nationalist poet and MP, were there to greet Parnell. Once he realised that they had not failed him, according to Healy, Parnell's manner changed and he displayed no apparent interest in their loyalty nor showed any sign that he had wanted them to be there.

During Parnell's absence in the United States the Land League had gained considerable ground in rural Ireland. Davitt and his fellow organisers had formulated a more precise plan of campaign. This consisted of obstructing the process of eviction, for once a decree had been obtained by the landlord or his agent the notice had to be served within a specified time, otherwise it became invalid. Moreover the process server, a paid functionary, had officially to deliver the document to the head of the household in question – although it was accepted that his wife could receive it – and he had then either to leave it inside the dwelling or, if the door were shut in his face, to nail it thereon. The Land Leaguers set to work to stop the process servers delivering the eviction notices within the duly authorised period; in Connemara there was a pitched battle between a crowd of some four hundred people, the police and a process server; while in Claremorris, not far from Boycott's house at Lough Mask, a process server was stripped and dumped in the fields. However, Davitt himself admitted that in the early months of 1880 the League not only failed to stop the majority of evictions but actually increased them, particularly in Connaught where the landlords reacted strongly to the pressures and intimidations – and Gladstone had already made his famous remark about the eviction notices falling like snowflakes in Connaught. By their resistance the League was focusing attention on evictions, less and less were families being thrown out of their homes without anybody noticing.

But a far greater success in the early months of 1880 came from another part of the Land League's plan, and this was the attempt to grapple with the internal Irish problem of the land-grabber and land-grabbing; for much of the strength of the landlords' hold had always lain in the fact that as fast as one family was evicted from a farm, another took its place, and this had been a grave weakness of previous land agitations. Now for the first time on a large, organised scale a serious attempt was being made to put embargoes on farms from which the tenant had just been evicted, to turn land-grabbing into a socially unacceptable proposition and the land-grabber into a social leper. It was this attempt to try and ostracise the land-grabber and thus strengthen the position of the Land League and the peasants themselves which, by a peculiar set of circumstances, engulfed Captain Boycott. The shape of the new policy was enunciated in embryo by Michael Davitt at Knockaroo in January, 1880, when he referred to a specific holding from which the occupier had just been evicted thus: 'This farm I trust will not be tenanted by any man . . . If such a traitor to your cause enters this part of the country, why, keep your eyes fixed upon him – point him out – and if a pig of his falls into a boghole let it lie there'.

In the winter of 1880, although Lough Mask House remained under the surveillance of the RIC and the atmosphere between Boycott and the tenantry was potentially more explosive than it had been in previous years, the actual explosion that was to catapult him into the headlines still seemed an unlikely event. The Dublin *Evening Mail*, an ultra-conservative organ, scented signs of trouble, general that is, not for Captain Boycott of whom it had then not heard, when it wrote of 'the wild waves of democracy' surging around Ireland's shores, and said it was time for respectable citizens to stand shoulder to shoulder to stem the tide of revolutionary feeling. In general, however, despite the spread of agitation, the establishment was still not over-worried by the activities of the Land League, and remained hopeful that the movement might soon disintegrate.

CHAPTER 9

'Civil War and Anarchy Will End the Drama'

When Parnell returned to Ireland in the middle of March, 1880, the general election campaign was already under way. In Britain the fight was dominated by the personalities and policies of those two remarkable old men, William Ewart Gladstone, then in his seventy-first year, and Benjamin Disraeli, by now Earl of Beaconsfield, in his seventy-sixth. Prior to the dissolution of Parliament, Gladstone had stormed through his Midlothian campaign, the never-to-be-forgotten fortnight when the speeches rolled out of him and he set the country alight with his attacks on 'Beaconsfieldism' – the concept of chauvinistic glory in foreign fields, the aggrandisement of the Empire at the cost of the people – offering instead his concept of Liberalism, the belief in the human power for good and the strength of individual responsibility which, encouraged by the right mood and circumstances, could revolutionise not only the United Kingdom but the whole world. Once Parliament had unwisely been dissolved by Beaconsfield, his rival continued to fire the citizens of the United Kingdom (Ireland excepted) with the idea that the ideal was obtainable.

On Irish affairs Gladstone had little to say. His first administration might have been dominated by Irish affairs but, by 1880, he had forgotten that his mission was 'to pacify Ireland' and, as he later confessed: 'I did not know, no one knew, the severity of the crisis that was already on the horizon, and that shortly after rushed upon us like a flood.' Beaconsfield had more to say about Ireland, although he mainly campaigned on the record Gladstone was so loudly denigrating, the increase of Imperial power by the purchase of the Suez Canal shares, the creation of Queen Victoria as Empress of India, and his diplomatic skill in re-balancing European power at the Congress of Berlin (although this particular see-saw was already showing signs of imbalance). However, he demonstrated more awareness of the potentially explosive nature of the Irish situation than did Gladstone, and his election manifesto contained a direct attack upon that portion of the Irish population which was attempting to sever the constitutional ties which united it to Great Britain, a policy of decomposition scarcely less disastrous than pestilence or famine and which, if successful, would lead to the ruination of Ireland and the dismemberment of the Empire.

Generally, Irish affairs did not loom large in the electoral campaign for the majority of British voters, while in Ireland considerations of Disraeli's foreign adventures or Gladstone's concept of Christian Liberalism held as little interest. For Ireland it was a crucial election, the future of the nationalist movement was at stake, whether it would move towards Parnell's militant, more intransigent leadership, or whether it would stay on an undefined, moderate path. The dominant issue had become the land, for which the weather, the bad harvests and the consequent deterioration of conditions, could claim some responsibility, with the Land League and the attention it had refocused on the problem claiming the rest. For most supporters of the Land League it was a question of whether sufficient Irish members could be returned to Westminster prepared to fight on this issue and force from the British government a major Land Act overwhelmingly favourable to the tenants; for a minority it was the wider question of land agitation providing the key to unlock the door to Home Rule. For those opposed to the Land League and Parnell, it was a question of keeping him out for the very reason that the issue might indeed unleash lawlessness and terror, perhaps even revolution.

Even though the land was the dominant feature of the election, it was nevertheless a confused affair. For a start, although Parnell had committed himself to the Land League's campaign for tenant right, he was still not the leader of the Home Rule movement. William Shaw retained that position and the agitation was not part of his or the movement's policy, on the contrary many Home Rulers were violently opposed to the Land League. But it was his participation in the League activities that had brought Parnell to the attention of the mass of peasants, and he adhered to the concept of using the land question as the means to achieve Home Rule. But if the movement officially remained committed only to Isaac Butt's federal dream being obtained by moral suasion at Westminster, it was still not a political party as such, it lacked the necessary machinery, discipline and money. To an extent Parnell took advantage of this disarray, although finance, or lack of it, loomed as large in his calculations and manoeuvring ability as it did in the movement as a whole. The Land League had officially vetoed the use of its funds to support parliamentary candidates, but in the event Davitt, with the support of Joseph Biggar, treasurer Patrick Egan, and some others, managed to persuade the League to loan Parnell the money to fight the election. (Davitt said £3,000, others put it at less, while one set of figures later produced by an anti-nationalist pamphleteer stated that £10,000 was loaned.) With the assistance of this vital money Parnell, following his arduous American tour, undertook an equally arduous election campaign, addressing meetings throughout the length and breadth of Ireland. He did not storm through the country in the same manner as Gladstone had rampaged through the Scottish burghs because storming was not part of his nature, but one pamphleteer wrote of his 'phenomenal flight among the Irish constituencies previous to the general election of 1880'. However confused the battle – and in some constituencies pro- and anti-Parnell candidates stood, in addition to anti-Home Rulers – the result was a resounding personal triumph for the Master of Avondale, greater than the personal triumph achieved by Gladstone for the Liberal party in England, Wales and Scotland.

Parnell himself was returned for three seats,* a further acco-
lade, and of the three he chose to represent Cork, to which
constituency he was to remain faithful until his death, and its
constituents likewise to him. The band of Home Rulers who had
given him outright support were all returned, often with handsome majorities, while overall the Home Rule League had
managed to secure approximately sixty seats. One says 'approximately' because the views of some candidates were so vague it
was difficult to ascertain what their politics were or where their
commitment lay, and the figures given by contemporary sources
do not tally. For example, an Irish chronicler of the movement
stated that fifty-nine Home Rulers were returned, while an English
politician, John Morley, gave the number as sixty-one plus four
dubious, most newspapers classified sixty-three of the newly
elected MPs as Home Rulers, and the *Annual Register* said sixty.
Despite the confusion, that the result was remarkable, and that the
personality of Charles Stewart Parnell had greatly contributed
towards it, was never in doubt. On May 17, 1880, Parnell's
status was confirmed when he was elected chairman of the Irish
parliamentary party by forty-three votes to eighteen. The defeated William Shaw said, 'I have not the slightest intention of
competing in popularity with Mr Parnell. Mr Parnell is a good-
looking young man'. It was obviously not a popularity or beauty
contest in which Parnell was involved, it was a fight to create and
control a viable political party dedicated to the pursuit of Irish
self-government.

The combination of these two election results helped consolidate his leadership but he could still only count on the undivided
support of twenty-six Parnellites (it was at a somewhat later date
that this term came into use, but it provides a useful description

---

* Candidates being returned for more than one constituency was then not
an uncommon occurrence. It was made possible by the time-span of the
voting process. This could cover a period of several weeks, and instances
were known of a candidate, usually a prominent one, defeated in one
constituency, promptly standing for another and being returned.

for his outright supporters, and was applicable even then). It remained clear to Parnell that the land agitation was his current passport to success, backed as it was by much of the Fenian impulse in Ireland, by the mass of peasants and by the all-important Irish-Americans with their money. He duly devoted a good proportion of his time and energy to furthering the policy of land agitation; at the end of April he attended the Land League conference in Dublin, at which constructive proposals for a land settlement were put forward. These included the suspension of the power of eviction for two years, a permanent reform involving peasant proprietary, the landlords to be bought out, (probably by the State), and establishment of a department for land administration in Ireland, and the provision of cheap and simple transfer of properties. Three days later on May 2, he was at Irishtown with Michael Davitt, to celebrate the first anniversary (slightly late) of the inaugural tenant right demonstration, an occasion that was already assuming historic proportions.

Davitt himself still regarded the Land League, rightly, as his off-spring, and his time and energy were devoted to furthering its success, to formulating the practical plans of campaign and constructive policies for the future, to keeping in harness the disparate elements that had backed the League, to trying to ensure that it remained a disciplined, non-violent movement. Even had he wanted to stand for Parliament in 1880 he would not have been able to do so, because he remained a convict on a ticket-of-leave which disbarred him from any such aspirations.

On the other side of the Irish Sea the omens looked propitious for a considerable move forward for Ireland. Gladstone was Prime Minister for the second time, known to be sympathetic to Irish affairs (if currently unaware of their overwhelming quality). As Chief Secretary for Ireland he appointed William Edward Forster, the man who had fought for and obtained elementary education as a right for the children of England and Wales, the man who was by some looked upon as Gladstone's heir-apparent, the man whose Irish references were of the highest order (Forster's father had been a noted Quaker, prominent in relief activities during the famine years). The appointment was greeted with general nationalist approval, as an indication of Gladstone's goodwill and intent, for it was the first occasion in a long time that Irish affairs had been entrusted to a minister of such ability and standing.*

Goodwill was one matter, action was another, and the immediate, burning question was: would the new Liberal administration take steps to prevent the eviction notices falling like snowflakes? Temporarily the nationalist forces held their fire to see how Gladstone would deal with the issue. But if they refrained from militant speeches to rouse the peasantry to more militant action, they did not cease from furthering the organisation of the Land League in Ireland, or in America. In May, 1880, Davitt was sent to the United States to see what was happening to the American Land League which Parnell had, of necessity, left in an embryonic state; Davitt went this time because with the new Parliament in session Parnell was required at Westminster. He arrived in the States in time to attend the first national convention of the movement whose official title was 'The Irish National Land and Industrial League of the United States', whose registered headquarters were in the University Building, Washington Square, New York, and of which he was appointed secretary. Despite the inauguration of a national American League pledged to abolish the present English land system in Ireland and to establish peasant proprietary, generally Davitt found that the movement had not progressed greatly, and consequently he embarked on a

---

* Forster's Tory predecessor, James Lowther, had been a notable fiasco. It was said he had a mind 'of mediaeval and impenetrable ignorance', and that his remarks about conditions in Connaught – 'neither so prevalent nor so acute as the depression existing in other parts of the United Kingdom', and about the land laws – 'Much has been said of the present state of the land laws. But I have no hesitation in saying they have nothing to do with the present state of Ireland' – entitled him to be called the real Father of the Land League.

nation-wide tour to encourage the setting-up of branches and the active participation of the Irish-Americans.

While Davitt was heavily engaged in his American tour, in England Gladstone's administration made a move on Ireland – an encouraging one it seemed to be. On June 18 a Compensation for Disturbance Bill was presented to the House, in fact the Bill followed an initiative taken by John O'Connor Power who had previously introduced a Bill on similar lines. The aim of the Liberal-backed enterprise, as of O'Connor Power's, was to plug the gaping hole in the 1870 Land Act whereby tenants had been unable to claim compensation if they were evicted for non-payment of rent and which had led to so many landlords increasing the rent. The new Bill proposed that tenants who were evicted for arrears should receive due compensation from the Irish church surplus, as long as their distress was genuine. The provisions were a step forward and would have deterred landlords from capricious eviction and provided a little more stability for the tenants, but they were not spectacular. The terms covered only those tenants whose holdings were valued at under £50; it made no provision for compensation for tenants whose landlords had granted permission to sell; it was applicable only in certain districts of Ireland and introduced only as a temporary measure, to be reviewed at the end of 1881. Nevertheless, its modest terms were bitterly fought over in the House of Commons. While Gladstone pleaded for its safe passage: 'It is no exaggeration to say in a country where the agricultural pursuit is the only pursuit, and where the means of payment of rent are entirely destroyed for a time by the visitation of Providence, that the poor occupier may under these circumstances regard a sentence of eviction as coming for him very near a sentence of death', Lord Randolph Churchill denounced it as 'the first step in a social war ... an attempt to raise the masses against the propertied classes'.

While the battle raged in the House of Commons along these opposing lines, within the Liberal party itself – more importantly within the cabinet – there was by no means unanimity of opinion upon the wisdom or justice of the Bill. The Whig element with which Gladstone had overburdened his cabinet was as disturbed as were the Tories by an attack upon the privileges of the propertied classes. On June 25, after a particularly fierce session in the House, Forster wrote to Gladstone, 'Flesh and blood can hardly stand a repetition of last night – I hope you will be large and free today in showing the necessity of *doing something*'. In this instance Gladstone managed to do something by proving to his cabinet and party that action was necessary in Ireland, and on July 5 the Second Reading of the Bill took place. Parnell then put his spoke in by deciding to abstain on the motion to go into committee, because of the omissions in the Bill; this was a gesture of Irish nationalist disapproval of its limitations for home consumption rather than a genuine act of intransigence, and the Home Rulers voted in force for the Third Reading on July 26. But on August 3 the Lords threw it out by an overwhelming majority, 278 votes to 51. A delighted Queen Victoria, who disliked her Irish subjects almost as much as she disliked Mr Gladstone, wrote to the Earl of Beaconsfield, 'Do you *ever* remember so many voting against the government in whose party they belong? I *do not*.' However, John Bright said, 'It appeared that while the House of Commons was endeavouring to conciliate Ireland the House of Lords was determined to make a declaration of war on the Irish people'; while Joseph Chamberlain commented, 'The Bill is rejected, the civil war is begun'; and his biographer synthesised his feelings by writing, 'No more foolish vote is recorded in the annals of the Upper House, nor upon them rests a deeper stain'.

It was a foolish vote because the terms were so moderate, the distress so real, but then the 'House of Landlords', as Davitt called them, did not see that there was a need to placate Ireland; what they saw were forces at work within the country whose immediate aim was to erode the power of the propertied classes and whose long-term aim was to loosen the ties with England. They did not believe in the flame of Irish nationalism and therefore in the inevitability of greater independence for Ireland; they believed the canker must be removed at once, and if a few thousand Irish peasants were in a sorry predicament, that was unfortunate, but the situation would sort itself out given time and a few good harvests. It was therefore unlikely that, without great pressure, they would pass a Bill that could have alleviated the lot of the Irish peasants and smoothed the relationship between England and the nationalists. If the House of Lords had not thrown out the Compensation for Disturbance Bill, Charles Cunningham Boycott may well not have added a new word to so many languages or helped create such a universally applied weapon.

The Bill had been thrown out, and the effect in Ireland was immediate. The *Connaught Telegraph* echoed Chamberlain's words when it urged its readers to gird their armour and prepare for civil war if necessary, and throughout the country there was a series of riots at evictions, mounting assaults on land-grabbers, and a general spread of the old trail of agrarian disorder. The reaction of some of Parnell's followers was almost as violent, that of John Dillon in particular, and the inflammatory speeches denouncing the British government and urging greater militancy spewed forth from them. But Parnell himself remained cool, refrained from passionate outbursts, giving himself time to assess the feelings of his countrymen at large and to consider which way he should move next.

Apart from the Irish, one person badly affected by the rejection of the Bill was the new Chief Secretary. Forster had not accepted the post enthusiastically – nobody in his right mind would – but more, as his biographer said, 'in the spirit of the soldier who is sent to the front by his chief'. However, Lord Randolph Churchill made a penetrating if malicious assessment of another side of the spirit in which Forster undertook the job when he said that he 'somewhat rashly accepted the popular verdict that in so doing he conferred a great honour on Ireland. He seemed to be under the impression that his acceptance of the post would change the face of the country and the nature of the people; that from the mere fact of his disembarkation at Kingstown would result a state of things in which the inhabitants of the country would be contented, and that law, order, property and life would become immediately secure.' Forster was not as naïvely or smugly optimistic as that, but he did embark for Ireland believing that his father's record as one of the few Englishmen who had materially assisted the peasants during the famine years, and his own record as a liberal and administrator – his skill in piloting the bitterly opposed Education Act through parliament was generally admitted – would be the passport to Irish favour and success.

Forster was something of a *poseur*, if an unconscious one. He was born in Dorset in 1818 and did not arrive in Yorkshire until he was twenty-one, but it was as 'the best stage Yorkshireman, whether in the parliamentary or any other theatre, of his day' that he was known throughout the United Kingdom. He had welded into his own character the attributes Yorkshiremen were supposed to possess – bluntness, honesty, independence, calling a spade a spade, with no time for frills and fancies. These attributes were now a part of him, but because they had been donned in the way an actor searches for the external mannerisms of a character, he tended to overplay them, once committed to a certain path he had to follow it with dogged persistence and his tactless-ness – otherwise known as calling a spade a spade – was notorious. Moreover, this acquired character rendered him vulnerable if its qualities were challenged and came under attack. By Parnell, whose background gave him the confidence not to play a role, Forster's performance was not appreciated, and he was soon to attack it venomously. Apart from the vulnerability of a stage Yorkshireman, Forster was to suffer from the more general human vulnerability of those whose good intentions are spurned. He arrived in Ireland genuinely believing that he could be the man to find the final, peaceful solution, but he also arrived expecting co-operation from the nationalists, which briefly and always with reservations he obtained. When the Compensation for Disturbance Bill was rejected by the Lords, nobody could say it was his fault, and he continued to expect support because his logic told him it was to the nationalists' benefit to continue to work with a friendly Liberal Chief Secretary. He did not, however, get further co-operation because English and Irish logic did not operate on the same plane, and by the end of August it was apparent that the brief honeymoon period between the new Chief Secretary and the nationalists was over. Forster was replying to questions in the House of Commons about the use of buckshot by the Royal Irish Constabulary in the dispersal of rioters (this particular riot had no connection with the Land League, it had occurred after the traditional Orange parades in Belfast and was strictly sectarian, Catholic v. Protestant, in origin). Buckshot had only recently been issued to the RIC – previously they had had bullets at their command – and Forster was asked whether, as a result of the incident in which a man had been killed and several wounded, he would order the buckshot to be withdrawn. In reply he said that although there was greater possibility of wounding than with bullets, there was not the same probability of killing, and that he was convinced it was 'more humane that buckshot be used'. The nationalists seized upon this unfortunate definition of humaneness, symbolic as they saw it of the whole English attitude towards Ireland, and as 'Buckshot' Forster the Chief Secretary was henceforth known. The relationship between him and the nationalists unfortunately continued to deteriorate, with the mounting outrage of rejected goodwill on Forster's side and alternatively venomous attack and cool disinterest on the part of the nationalists.

When Parliament was prorogued on September 7, 1880, the Parnellites had succeeded in forcing the House into several all-night sittings, and nobody could fail to be aware that Parnell now had the nucleus of a genuine party whose aspect was Irish-dominated, not English-submerged, and which could if it chose wreck the business of the House by obstruction and which, outside Parliament, was prepared to embark upon an all-out land war. However, earlier in the session Gladstone had announced his intention of appointing a commission, headed by Lord Bessborough, to enquire into the current land situation in Ireland as a result of whose findings a new Land Bill would be introduced into the next session of Parliament. Thus far Parnell had made no comment upon the commission, which had already begun to take evidence, nobody knew whether he would support it or block it, or indeed what he intended to do with or against Gladstone's administration. Keeping his thoughts to himself he crossed to Dublin on September 9, and proceeded to go shooting in the Wicklow hills. When the anticipated statement on the Bessborough Commission and the future strategy of the Land League came, it was the one that decisively affected Charles Cunningham Boycott's fate and helped give the League a formidable, virtually unbeatable weapon.

CHAPTER 10

'What Mr Parnell Meekly Designates Social Ostracism'

It was on Sunday, September 19, 1880, in Ennis, that Parnell made the speech that proved of such historic importance and had such far-reaching, if unexpected, results. He arrived in Ennis, as was his non-time-wasting custom, via the night mail from Dublin at 4 a.m. but even at this early hour a large crowd carrying torches and headed by a band was waiting to greet him, and the town was decorated with bunting and banners bearing such inscriptions as: *Tis near the Dawn, The harvest belongs to America, Parnell gave the praties, not the landlords, The two P's, Parnell and the People.* It was in fine weather to an immense crowd, from the Munster town that fifty-odd years previously had returned Daniel O'Connell to Westminster as the first Catholic MP in centuries, that Parnell delivered his address, appropriately, and with the touch of theatricality that distinguished his aloof character, from the foot of O'Connell's statue.

The speech revealed much, if not all, of Parnell the politician and leader. His belief in constitutional methods was there, but so was his equally firm belief that the House of Commons was not filled with fair-minded English gentlemen, and that one could anticipate no concessions from England unless they were prompted by self-interest or the English could be made to see that a peaceful, constitutional but nationalist Irish settlement was in their interest. He stated clearly his belief that such a settlement could be obtained by a united Irish parliamentary party, totally independent, attacking Tory or Liberal with equal impartiality, aligning itself with either party if the circumstances were favourable. But it was his shorter-term instructions to the crowd, and to the Irish people at large, that made the speech historic. He dealt with the Bessborough Commission – should tenants give evidence before it? Would their doing so have any effect upon the findings? He said that personally he had grave doubts about the impartiality or usefulness of the Commission, and was convinced that the measure of any Land Bill introduced by the Liberals in the next parliamentary session would be the measure of the people's energy and activity during the coming winter; the measure of their determination to keep a firm grip of their homesteads and not to pay unjust rents; the measure of their determination not to allow anybody to bid for a farm from which others had been evicted.

If Parnell, rightly and wisely, put the onus for a land settlement on the tenant farmers themselves – because organised determination on their part had been what was previously lacking – and thereby re-emphasised his belief in the Land League, he proceeded to give them the clearest possible directive on how they were to deal with one aspect of the question – the vexed problem of the land-grabbers. He asked his audience directly what they would do if they encountered such a character? Several people shouted, 'Shoot him', whereupon Parnell said he wished to point out a very much better way, a more Christian and charitable way, which would give the sinner time to repent. He enunciated the better, more charitable way thus: 'When a man takes a farm from which another has been evicted you must shun him on the road-side when you meet him, you must shun him in the streets of the town, you must shun him in the shop, you must shun him in the fair green and in the market place, and even in the place of worship. By leaving him severely alone, by putting him into a moral convent, by isolating him from the rest of his countrymen as if he were a leper of old, you must show him your detestation of the crime he has committed.'

These instructions, stated in the clearest, simplest, coldest

Parnell language, were deliberate, but their application was un-planned, for it was not against an Irish land-grabber they were so effectively put into practice but against an English land agent, Charles Cunningham Boycott. Thus, although in one way – and a most important way – Parnell initiated 'boycotting' in his Ennis speech, in another way the policy was inaugurated by a group of men in the area of Lough Mask, County Mayo. Indeed there were some who denied that Parnell had initiated the policy at all; Frank Hugh O'Donnell insisted that it was 'the invention or adaptation of Michael Davitt' from his Knockaroo speech in January, 1880; Davitt himself said it had been foreshadowed by Gavan Duffy and more immediately by the speech of the American journalist, James Redpath, at Claremorris; Redpath himself heartily endorsed this verdict; while the Parnell Special Com-mission of 1888/89 which was to delve at great length into the origins of boycotting, said it had been foreshadowed in the speeches of Davitt, Joseph Biggar, John Dillon and many other Land League leaders but agreed it had been most clearly enun-ciated during Parnell's Ennis speech.

In a sense most human activity has been foreshadowed by earlier generations; sending people 'to Coventry' is as old as Lady Godiva, and various forms of individual or group ostracism have existed almost since the dawn of humanity; but an old policy can be given a new twist or be reiterated at a specific moment in time by a specific person in a specific manner, and genuinely be called new. With his systematic instructions at Ennis on how a land-grabber should be treated, Parnell un-doubtedly outlined a new form of social and moral excommuni-cation. As the man on the receiving end of the effects of the new boycotting weapon, as it developed, Mr Forster strongly con-curred with this verdict thus: 'From the time of that speech dates the beginning of the deliberate, merciless, and scientific boycotting in Ireland'.

Parnell had given the clear lead but it was the combination of place, circumstance and individual character that led to Boycott's being selected as the first victim of organised ostracism. He had already experienced fresh difficulties with the tenantry round Lough Mask which was not surprising, as his residence lay in the heart of the Land League country. In August 1880, his own labourers, emboldened by the League's activities and the encouragement of the local priest, John O'Malley, had gone on strike for a wage increase. To this demand Boycott had submitted, agreeing to raise the minimum pay to 9 shillings a week and the maximum to 15 shillings, instead of the previous 7–11 shillings.* By the beginning of September he was in further difficulties, this time in connection with his role as agent for Lord Erne. His lordship's rents for November 1879, or in the case of the yearly tenancies for May 1880, were due for collection. Lord Erne had instructed Boycott to allow a 10 per cent abatement for the bad harvest and conditions generally, but when he presented the rents to the tenants all but two of them demanded a 25 per cent abatement. According to Boycott 10 per cent was fair as it brought the rents below Griffith's Valuation. This had existed since 1852 in which year Sir Richard Griffith had been appointed to value property in Ireland in fact for taxation purposes, but over the years it had acquired the status of a letting valuation. In this particular instance, the tenants denied that the 10 per cent abatement brought their rents below Griffith's Valuation and stuck to their demands for what they considered to be the just reduction of 5 shillings in the pound. Boycott said he wrote to Lord Erne informing him of the situation but that his lordship refused to grant further abatement, while the tenants said Boycott issued the demands and then, without giving them time to consider or

* For comparison, the wages of many English agricultural labourers were 9 shillings a week. At this period a bitter campaign was being fought between Joseph Arch's National Agricultural Labourers' Union and the squirarchy for better pay and conditions. Arch succeeded in raising wages by an average of 2 shillings a week but lost the overall fight, as the union was defeated, partly due to the weapon of eviction which existed in England, too. The two battles in England and Ireland remained differently based and entirely separate.

to find the money, obtained eviction notices against eleven of them.

Thus, on September 22, only three days after Parnell's Ennis speech, the local process server whose name was David Sears, accompanied by a seventeen-strong constabulary escort, set off from Ballinrobe to deliver the eviction notices to the eleven selected tenants. The first three notices were successfully served, not on the titular heads of the households concerned but on their wives. At the fourth cabin, a Mrs Fitzmorris refused to accept the eviction notice, and raised the alarm by waving the red flag which warned other cottiers that the process server was on his rounds. It was the women of the Lough Mask area who descended on David Sears and the constabulary, pelting them with mud, stones and manure, stopping them from serving the remaining notices and eventually driving them to seek shelter in Lough Mask House. Boycott himself was out for the day but when he returned in the evening he found Sears and the constables still sheltering in the house, and heard the story of the howling ladies and their successful resistance.

The next day a further attempt to serve the processes was made, as the legal time limit to meet the next Ballinrobe Quarter Sessions was fast approaching. One observer said that David Sears, surrounded by a hostile crowd, refused to make a second attempt; but the *Connaught Telegraph* reported that it was while Sears was waiting for a stronger constabulary escort to arrive that 'a curious scene was enacted. As if by one sudden impulse every man in that vast throng rushed towards Lough Mask House, the residence of a very unpopular land agent'. At that precise moment it undoubtedly was a mass impulse, a sudden spontaneous combustion that drove the crowd along the road from Ballinrobe to Lough Mask House, but behind it lay the figure of Father John O'Malley and to a lesser extent that of the American journalist, James Redpath.

John O'Malley was not the parish priest of Ballinrobe but of The Neale, an undistinguished hamlet lying on the road from

Ballinrobe to Cong. He possessed the immense authority vested in any parish priest in Catholic Ireland but in his own right he was a forceful character. He was also loved by his parishioners, probably as much for his weakness for the bottle as for his humour and conviviality – journalists later wrote of 'the ingenious excuses of inclement weather and long journies that he made in order to induce his guests to taste whiskey so early in the day'. In most respects, like most Irish parish priests, he was a conservative character but he had from the inception of the Land League – considerably earlier than the majority of his brother priests and superiors in the hierarchy, who had only recently aligned themselves behind Parnell – recognised that this particular movement would attract the mass of the peasants and could gain for them a settlement of the question that bedevilled their lives. After the first day's successful resistance to the process server, O'Malley addressed the jubilant crowds, advising them not to offer violence should David Sears return with the eviction notices but instead suggesting they strike against the landlords. It was thus O'Malley who pointed the finger in the direction of landlord ostracism and withdrawal of labour.

James Redpath also played a part in creating the atmosphere that led to the inauguration of 'boycotting'. He was a distinguished American journalist, widely known for his ardent support of John Brown's anti-slavery campaigns in the United States. He came to Ireland early in 1880 as the special correspondent of the *New York Herald* and *Inter-Ocean*. Later he stated that he arrived in the country with an open mind, not knowing who was in the right or wrong in respect of the land question. If his mind was as open as he claimed on arrival, it quickly underwent the most dramatic conversion, and Redpath brought all the enthusiastic one-sidedness of the convert to the tenants' version of Irish land ills, propagating views that were as extremist on the one side as William Bence Jones's were on the other. He wrote of a Land League meeting in Straide, Davitt's birthplace – 'That ruined cabin where Michael Davitt threw out the flag of the Irish land war', prophesying (not very accurately) that in time to come it would be pointed out 'as the Runnymede of the Irish people'; he wrote of the English Parliament as the lackeys and executioners of the Irish landlords; he urged the peasants to dispel the Egyptian darkness of the ancient despotism by means of the Land League; and he addressed meetings on the same lines, notably the one in Claremorris where he advocated the same sort of moral ostracism as Parnell had at Ennis, although in much more turgid and verbose language. Undoubtedly the speeches and writings of this American journalist who claimed to be a dispassionate, objective observer, encouraged the Irish tenant farmers to take stronger action, particularly in Mayo where he focused his attention, specifically in the Lough Mask area where he forged a friendship with the convivial Father O'Malley.

Thus Michael Davitt had laid the foundations for a policy of social ostracism, Charles Stewart Parnell had presented the bricks with which to build it in his Ennis speech, Father John O'Malley and James Redpath created the local enthusiasm for building to which Charles Cunningham Boycott further contributed by his own unpopularity, but it was the inhabitants of the Ballinrobe area who, with the 'one sudden impulse' driving them along the road to Lough Mask House, started to construct the edifice. For when the people reached their destination they proceeded to roam about the grounds, invade the actual house, and advise (the choice of verb is James Redpath's) Boycott's servants – his farm labourers, his herdsmen, his coachman, his stableman, his servant girls – to leave his employment immediately and never to work for him again. Boycott himself said that several of his employees were intimidated by the crowd and forced to leave 'under threat of ulterior consequences'. Some measure of coercion is borne out by the statement of one Martin Branigan, who in November, took Boycott to court for non-payment of three days wages. Branigan, who had worked for Boycott for seven years, said he was paid by the day and that he only left without notice at midday on September 23 because he was afraid of the fifty or sixty people who came into the field where he was working, therefore he was entitled to his wages for the three previous days. (The Ballinrobe Petty Sessions adjudged in his favour, and Branigan obtained his 7/6d.) Whether or not Boycott's indoor and outdoor employees went willingly or under threat of dire consequences if they failed to obey the will of the crowd, they all left, and by the evening of September 23, Captain and Mrs Boycott, their young niece, their young nephew, Arthur St John Boycott, and Ashton Weekes, all of whom were staying at Lough Mask House, were left to themselves. Ashton Weekes was Boycott's young friend, late a Captain in the 13th Hussars, who appeared to live at Lough Mask House, and when matters came to a head shortly afterwards he was noted by the newspaper correspondents as being a friend of Boycott's – his only one according to nationalist sources.

Once started, the process of isolating Boycott did not stop at denuding him of his servants and labourers, thus forcing him to run his estate and harvest his crops without help. Within a few days the blacksmith and laundress had refused to shoe his horses or do the washing, under threat of murder according to Boycott, but they may have acceded to local pressure more willingly than this implies. The next person to cease giving service to Lough Mask House was the twelve-year-old boy who had acted as postman, carrying letters to and from Ballinrobe. When their young nephew, Arthur, volunteered to undertake this task he was intercepted *en route* from Lough Mask to Ballinrobe and told he must stop, otherwise he would be in danger. The shopkeepers in Ballinrobe were also persuaded, or agreed, not to serve the Boycotts, so that they had to obtain their food and household necessities from Cong, by boat up Lough Mask as the roads were patrolled by Land League supporters. Boycott said his farm became public property, people wandered across it as they chose, leaving gates open, breaking down fences, trampling on his crops, letting his cattle wander into the road, though James Redpath and nationalist sources denied this latter form of harassment.

Whether the situation extended to treating Lough Mask House as an open house or not, by the early weeks of October the Boycotts were in an unenviable position. Immediately after the invasion of the house and grounds and the withdrawal of the employees on September 23, Boycott had applied for constabulary protection. This had been as immediately supplied – the first letter on the subject of Mr Boycott was written by the local Resident Magistrate, Mr McSheehy, to the Chief Secretary's office at Dublin Castle on September 24. At this point in time, the fact that a Mr Boycott of Lough Mask House, Ballinrobe, County Mayo, had applied for and been granted police protection was of no great import. Many gentlemen in various parts of Ireland, but particularly in the west, were applying for and being granted police protection, and all that this case seemingly did was add to the statistics, underlining the mounting power of the Land League and the lessening power of English law. On September 28, the Chief Secretary's office was asked to authorise the despatch of a hut to Lough Mask to provide shelter for those policemen the house itself could not hold, but despite the presence of a largish number of constables which offset the anticipated violence, the Boycotts' situation remained extremely unpleasant.

They were isolated in their previously comfortable house, Mrs Boycott having to wash and cook and clean herself – a startling position for a well-born lady – Boycott himself having to rise at 4 a.m., feed the cattle, muck-out the stables, milk the cows, attend to the hundred and one tasks on his estate, with only Ashton Weekes and his young nephew to help him. Supplies had now to be organised from Cong, and if any member of the household set foot outside the grounds, they were hooted and hissed at and generally derided. Apart from the strain of the material situation, allied to the tension of living under protection and having policemen permanently around the house and grounds, there was the larger issue. Lough Mask House was the Boycotts' home, and the estate their means and way of life. They were aware that it was the object of the Land League to intimidate them as members of the landlord class, if not actual landlords, and perhaps force them to leave Ireland. Should they submit tamely to this intimidation, pack up and return to England? How could they? Most of their capital was tied up in the estate. And why should they? They were the legal leaseholders of Lough Mask House, Boycott himself was Lord Erne's legally appointed agent, and in their own eyes they had done nothing wrong. As the days passed and the isolation deepened, the Boycotts must have deliberated upon these questions and also upon the measures they could or should take to counteract what seemed to them the insane, unwarranted, lawless treatment to which they were being subjected.

CHAPTER II

'A Sight Unparalleled in Any Civilised Country'

At the end of September and beginning of October 1880, the Boycotts' plight was well known within the Lough Mask area, and it was discussed in Ballinrobe and Cong and further afield in Claremorris. The treatment was proving highly effective, the family was isolated, a minor landlord and disliked land agent was increasingly less able to function in either capacity. At this moment the aim of the enterprise was limited to utilising the new-found unified strength either to force Boycott to leave Lough Mask, or to force Lord Erne to replace him with another land agent. No attempt was made to use the weapon of concerted ostracism against other landlords or land agents, no publicity was given to the Boycott affair even in the local papers, consequently, to the world at large, the family's situation remained unknown. It was partly due to Boycott himself but more largely due to the journalistic instinct of a London reporter that the affair reached the headlines, but it was not initially as a result of the Land League's publicity that 'boycotting' became news, although they made the maximum use of it once the story had broken.

However, the Lough Mask area itself was headline news in Irish, English and American newspapers at the end of the month because, on September 25, the body of Lord Montmorres was found riddled with bullets near Clonbur, on the narrow neck of land lying between the southern shores of Lough Mask and the northern shores of Lough Corrib. Montmorres was only a small landlord – according to local sources he had nine tenant farmers although other sources stated fifteen, and nobody said he was a particularly bad one. Indeed in local quarters his position as a landlord was played down, and emphasis was laid upon his corruptness as a magistrate – the *Connaught Telegraph* said: 'in some of his more intoxicated moods, the decisions arrived at in some cases astonished even his brother disciples of justice'. Despite the efforts of the Land League supporters to imply that Montmorres had been murdered by one of the distraught victims of his corrupt magisterial verdicts, the connection was inevitably made with the activities of the League, for by this time nobody on any side regarded the League as a passing shadow; its mounting force and power was everywhere recognised. And was not Clonbur on the borders of Mayo, the home of the Land League, the area where it possessed the greatest power and authority? At the funeral service it was asserted that the deed 'was not so much an act of revenge against Lord Montmorres as an act of intimidation to the class to which he belonged', while the Dublin *Evening Mail* stressed the point more firmly when it wrote of the murder as 'the coping stone of a huge edifice of lawless outrage which has ruled the West of Ireland under a reign of terror as powerful and as absolute as that of the French Revolution'.

The involvement of the Land League in the Montmorres murder was never proven. Certainly Michael Davitt deplored such violence, but there was a not entirely unjustified suspicion that other members of the League held the sanctity of human life in less esteem and considered the despatch of the odd landlord a matter of no great import if it helped achieve the right end. The ambience of the League, the wildness of many of the speeches, and the constant use of the threat of violence undoubtedly affected people in an area, indeed in a country, where for many and varied reasons the sanctity of human life was not esteemed in a manner which Englishmen considered appropriate. To a degree the Montmorres murder helped pave the way for the reaction to Boycott's desperate situation once the latter became widely known. The loyalist papers in Dublin and Belfast had been thundering for months about the scandalous condition of much of rural

Ireland gripped in the vice of the Land League, about the primary duty of any government to protect life and property and to employ public forces to keep public law. In recent weeks they had been concentrating their attention on the Liberal administration's failure to tackle the problem, and the consequent need for loyal citizens to take action themselves. The Montmorres murder obviously increased their alarm, the feeling that they themselves would have to act concomittantly increased, and at the beginning of October they were casting around for a specific issue on which they could take action.

The actual term 'boycott' came into being before anybody in the outside world had heard of the man himself. James Redpath later related that on September 23, only a few days after the initial excitement at Lough Mask House, he was dining with Father O'Malley at the presbytery of The Neale and they discussed the recent events. Redpath's record of the conversation went as follows:

'I said, "I'm bothered about a word."

' "What is it?" asked Father John.

' "Well," I said, "When the people ostracise a land-grabber we call it social excommunication, but we ought to have an entirely different word to signify ostracism applied to a landlord or a land-agent like Boycott. Ostracism won't do – the peasantry would not know the meaning of the word – and I can't think of any other."

' "No," said Father John, "ostracism wouldn't do."

'He looked down, tapped his big forehead, and said: "How would it do to call it to Boycott him?" '

The delighted Redpath agreed to propagate the word 'boycott' in his speeches and writings, and thus Father O'Malley became 'the neologist of an immortal term'. It was indeed Redpath who first used the term in print, in an article describing the events that had occurred around Lough Mask House which was published in *Inter-Ocean* on October 12, again, before anybody in the outside world had heard of Boycott.

In the meantime, in furtherance of the immediate objective of getting Boycott removed from his job as land agent, a series of letters passed between the Lough Mask tenantry and Lord Erne. The first one was written on September 25, and listed the tenants' grievances which we mentioned in an earlier chapter, such as Boycott's refusal to allow wood to be collected from the estate 'although he has been using the timber freely for his own use', his imposition of petty fines and his general tyranny. It went into the ramifications of how much abatement other landlords in the area had granted, and said how willing the humble and grateful tenants were to pay a *just* rent. It also said they were convinced that they could not hope for justice as long as Boycott continued to poison Lord Erne's mind against his humble tenants, and were therefore unanimously and irrevocably resolved not to have any further dealings with Boycott, and prayed that Lord Erne would now see the true light and at last look after them properly. The postscript added: 'An early reply sent to Mr David Connor (but not to Boycott) is respectfully requested.' Lord Erne's reply came on October 1 from Crom Castle. It was about a quarter the length of the tenants' humble petition, said that most of the complaints seemed to be of a frivolous nature and that he must therefore decline to examine them, that his rents were fair and he could only believe that the present conduct of his tenantry was due to their having been misled by bad advice. On October 7, the tenants riposted with another lengthy epistle which went into details of how unpopular Boycott had been on Achill Island, and when acting as agent for other landlords. (Boycott had held other agencies, which he claimed he relinquished of his own free will, but which the tenants said were taken from him when the land-lords realised what a wretch he was.) There was much about the justice of a rent reduction and how Boycott had swindled the tenants out of their Parish Relief by promising them seed and potatoes which he did not deliver, or when he did, grossly over-charging for them – the point of this detail being to prove the obnoxious character of Lord Erne's chosen agent. On October 13 his lordship replied to this onslaught in even briefer terms. He was sorry that his tenants had reiterated their charges against Captain Boycott which he judged to be entirely without justification, and he referred them to his previous letter as he had nothing further to say.

By this date Boycott's position had worsened, partly as a result of the tenants realising they were not going to obtain his removal by appeals to Lord Erne. On October 11 he felt it necessary to apply for extra police protection because of further ill-will and harassment and, as the postmistress in Ballinrobe had refused to send up an urgent telegram to Lough Mask House, he had also applied for permission for the RIC to carry his mail. If the tenants had realised that Lord Erne was unlikely to uphold their claims, Boycott had by now appreciated that the only support he would obtain from that quarter was moral, positive only to the extent that his lordship would not submit to the tenants' demands and sack him. It was therefore up to him to take action, and accordingly, in an attempt to publicise his parlous situation and thereby hopefully have it remedied, he wrote a letter to *The Times* on October 14. As letters to *The Times* went, it was short and to the point – one thing of which Boycott could not be accused was verbal excess. It said that the following details might be of interest to readers as an example of the power of the Land League, and proceeded to enumerate the events which had occurred, the flight of the process server to his house, the descent of the howling mob the next day, the coerced withdrawal of his employees, the refusal of the blacksmith and laundress to serve his family, like-wise the local shopkeepers, the intimidation of the post-boy and his young nephew, and the use of his farm as public property. He finished by saying he could get no workmen to do anything for him and his ruination was the openly avowed intention of the Land League.

The Times printed his letter on October 18, and in editorial made the following comment: 'A more frightful picture of tri-umphant anarchy had never been presented in any community pretending to be civilised and subject to law. The persecution of the writer, Mr Boycott, for some offence against the Land League's code, is an insult to the government and to public justice. If such monstrous oppression and spoliation cannot be put down by "the constitutional powers" about to be set in motion against the leaders of the League, Mr Forster must, however reluctantly, proceed to the alternative he has already recognised.' The reference to 'the constitutional powers' Mr Forster was about to set in motion was the prosecution of Parnell and other Land League leaders on charges of conspiracy to prevent the payment of rent, a measure over which Forster had been agonising since the beginning of October. The hint about the alternative Mr Forster had already recognised was the urgent need, as *The Times* and many politicians and private persons saw it, to introduce a new Coercion Bill for Ireland. It was on the necessity of breaking the mounting power of the Land League and re-enforcing law and order, that *The Times* was concentrating its attention. Although it printed Boycott's letter and used the contents to illustrate the frightfulness of the situation in rural Ireland, it was in a glancing manner, as one aspect of the general pattern. In its view what really mattered was the overall lawlessness and how Forster and the Liberal administration intended to control it. *The Times* did not mount a journalistic crusade on Boycott's behalf but it had printed his letter and many people heard of it or read it. Although the letter, in itself, did not prove to be the catalyst, once the ball had started rolling the publication was of assistance as interested parties were able to refer to Boycott's precise summary in the correspondence columns of England's most august newspaper.

The man who actually rolled the ball to the top of the hill and poised it in a position that enabled eager hands to send it hurtling down was Bernard Becker. He was the special correspondent of the London *Daily News* (or special commissioner as he was then entitled) who was sent to the west of Ireland by his newspaper to do a series of articles on the true conditions in this disturbed part of the United Kingdom. Before he left Dublin, Becker was given a graphic description of the conditions he would discover in Connaught – mainly by people who had not been there. He was told of the population going in fear of their lives, with attacks on people and property a daily occurrence. He made for Westport as the largest town in the Land League's home county of Mayo, and as he travelled round the triangle marked by Westport, Castlebar and Claremorris he was depressed by the general atmosphere, the poverty and the attitude of many people, but he was also struck by the apparent normality of everyday life and the comparative calm of the area. It was only when he was in Claremorris and made enquiries about Boycott – whose letter to *The Times* he had read – that he began to sense the tensions beneath the surface, what he called 'the *spectre vert*' that was the threat of revolution he had heard so much about before leaving Dublin. For, as soon as he mentioned Boycott's name, conversation stopped abruptly and nobody knew anything about the gentleman, what he was doing or was being done to him. This conspiracy of silence was more than sufficient to rouse Becker's journalistic interest and he promptly travelled to Ballinrobe to try and discover exactly what was happening at Lough Mask House. In Ballinrobe he came up against another wall of silence and could find nobody to drive him out to Lough Mask, but eventually he managed to borrow a carriage. When he reached the tall iron entrance gates he found them guarded by armed constables who refused to conduct him to the house or to allow him to enter the grounds. Undaunted, he decided to wander round the outside of the estate and as he walked down the road and turned a corner luck was with him and fate, one could say, was with Boycott.

Becker described the sight that greeted his eyes as he rounded the bend thus: 'Beyond a turn in the road was a flock of sheep, in front of which stood a shepherdess herding them back, while a shepherd, clad in a leather shooting-jacket and aided by a bull terrier, was driving them through a gate into an adjacent field. . . .

Both were obviously amateurs at sheep-driving, and the smart, intelligent bull terrier was as much an amateur as either of them ... Behind the shepherd were two tall members of the RIC in full uniform with carbines loaded.' The shepherd and shepherdess were, of course, Captain and Mrs Boycott and the enterprising Becker obtained from the former about the longest interview he granted to any journalist. Doubtless, at this moment of isolation and desperation, the normally taciturn and reserved Boycott was only too delighted to have an interested ear into which he could pour out his woes. After the meeting Becker returned forthwith to his hotel and proceeded to write a lengthy despatch with the dateline Westport, October 24, 1880. He was an excellent journalist with a clear readable style, a retentive ear for the descriptive phrase, a sharp eye for the revealing incident and he was sufficiently unbiased to avoid distortion. He reported what he had seen and heard at Lough Mask in vivid, but not too brightly-hued, prose and what he had seen and heard was quite extraordinary. The despatch started with some general comments on the Connaught atmosphere in which no horror at crime was displayed, nor disgust with a state of affairs where murder could pass unnoticed and humour found in the vilest situation. Becker also commented – as did nearly every outsider – on the miserable hovels crowded with men, women, children and animals – 'the like of which, on any English estate would bring down a torrent of indignation on the landlord'. He then came to the crux of the article, which was the situation confronting Captain and Mrs Boycott. He provided good biographical details – Norfolk man, commissioned in the 39th Foot, farmed in Ireland for twenty-five years – which helped underline the social position of the ostracised family. His descriptions of the events that had overtaken the Boycotts, and their living in a state of siege, were excellent. He also pointed out that Boycott had £500 worth of root crops that would rot in the ground unless help could be obtained to harvest them. It was the publication in the *Daily News* of this lengthy despatch entitled 'The Isolation of Captain Boycott' that alerted the outside world to Boycott's position and to the new weapon forged by the Land Leaguers of Lough Mask.

The article was reprinted in the *Belfast News-Letter* and the Dublin *Daily Express*, both staunch upholders of the Union and fiercely anti-Parnell and the Land League, and thereby focused attention on Boycott's situation. Both newspapers had in fact reprinted his letter to *The Times* but this had occasioned no particular interest, being submerged in the general run of anti-Land League correspondence, but the Becker article with its readability and personal detail was a different matter, it attracted widespread and, in loyalist circles, horrified attention. On October 29, the Dublin *Daily Express* published the letter which gave the ball its next heavy kick. This letter was signed 'Combination' and said it seemed to the writer it would be the most cowardly thing to leave Mr and Mrs Boycott to be starved out, with their crops rotting in the ground, and proposed that a fund be set up with a target of £500 to finance a body of men who would go to County Mayo, under the leadership of the writer, to save Boycott's crops. There was a P.S. which stated that the writer had 'never seen or heard of Captain Boycott until his name appeared in the papers'. In an accompanying article the *Express* heartily endorsed 'Combination's' proposal, saying it would be to the lasting discredit of loyal property-owning Irishmen if they abandoned one of their own class in his hour of need, and the scheme would have the additional advantage of proving to the agitators that their intended victims would not be forsaken but could rely upon the support of loyal Irishmen. The identity of 'Combination' was soon revealed as a Mr Manning, a land agent, who currently lived in Dublin but who for many years previously had lived in Monaghan, where he had been the deputy agent for the Castle Shane estate.

If it was Mr Manning in Dublin who proposed the idea of salvaging Boycott's crops, it was in Ulster that the notion was enthusiastically adopted and developed. On November 3 two letters appeared in the *Belfast News-Letter*, one from the Reverend

William Stewart Ross, the other from 'A Lover of Law and Order'. The latter was six times the length of the former and basically reiterated what Mr Manning had already suggested in the *Express*, namely that practical sympathy be shown for Boycott by means of a relief fund which would furnish men to save his crops. In addition to signing himself as 'A Lover of Law and Order', the author elaborated upon this theme, laying stress upon the American money flowing into Ireland, most of which was finding its way into the pockets of the very people who were now resisting law and order. He went on to say that a fund to save Boycott's crops and indemnify him against the losses he must otherwise sustain would be a blow struck for law and order. He also predicted, accurately, that such methods as were being used against Boycott would be used again by the Land Leaguers, but forecast, less accurately, that if all lovers of law and order rallied to Boycott's side and defeated the League by saving his crops, the method would be rendered useless. The Reverend Stewart Ross's letter endorsed everything 'A Lover of Law and Order' had written – he had had a preview of its contents – and repeated that immediate aid should be sent 'to our suffering fellow-Protestant, Mr Boycott', and affirmed that he as an Orangeman and Protestant would be only too happy to subscribe to a relief fund. The sectarian element as expressed by the Reverend Stewart Ross – sound loyal Ulster Protestants versus unstable revolutionary Connaught Catholics – was made an issue from the start, although at various subsequent moments attempts were made to blur the edges into a contest between the upholders of law and order, of whatever religious persuasion, versus revolutionary malcontents; Parnell, after all, was a Protestant.

It was these two letters which sent the ball Bernard Becker had put into position hurtling along, with a velocity that took everybody by surprise. The next day the *Belfast News-Letter* had a column headed 'The Boycott Relief Fund' with a list of subscriptions already received and a further column containing letters on the subject of 'The Boycott Relief Expedition'. Included among

these was one from a Protestant vicar in Antrim and one from a
'Repentant Whig' both of whom approved heartily of the idea of
a relief expedition, one from a lady who could only afford to send
10 shillings but wished the enterprise every success, one from a
medical student who would gladly march to the relief of a fellow
Protestant and one from an ex-sergeant pensioner who was a
total abstainer and who freely offered his services. The next day
there were further letters and subscriptions from 'A Lover of my
Country', 'On to Mayo, boys', 'A Lurgan Orangeman', 'A
Derryman' and others. What had happened was that the anti-
Parnellites, the anti-Land Leaguers, the upholders of the *status
quo* and the benefices of the Act of Union – all those who were
alarmed by the Land League's activities, who feared lawlessness
and felt helpless in the face of its rapid spread, who believed
something must be done to stem the tide of revolutionary feeling
– had found their cause. Bernard Becker had depicted the plight
of a single individual – always much easier to comprehend and
identify with than the plight of thousands or millions – and the
situation of Captain Boycott was such that the Land League
opposition not only could act now, but must act now, if his
crops were to be saved. In Belfast the plans for the Relief Expedition gathered momentum, an organising committee was set up
headed by prominent Ulster loyalists, the Reverend William
Stewart Ross placed the Christ Church mission room at the
committee's disposal, subscriptions continued to pour in, Ulster
labourers flocked to enrol as members of the expedition. Negotiations were entered into with the directors of the Midland Great
Western Railway to provide special trains to convey the contingents from Ulster to Mayo and, ominously, there was talk of the
relief expedition being armed, since they felt it was unsafe for
them to go into such an area as Mayo without means of self-
defence.

In their enthusiasm for the project the Ulster organisers
genuinely do not seem to have considered the implications of
sending a large body of armed Ulstermen – albeit armed only for

self-defence – into Mayo. Nor do they seem to have consulted Boycott himself, to have asked him whether he wanted hundreds of Ulstermen to come to his aid. They had their eyes firmly fixed on their cause, they were going to assist a decent, respectable gentleman menaced by the forces of lawlessness, they were finally and justifiably going to cry halt to the Land League's communistic, revolutionary, anarchic, destructive activities.

Within a few days, however, there was strong reaction in nationalist circles. On November 5 the *Freeman's Journal* entered the lists. Hitherto, the paper had been preoccupied with setting up its own Defence Fund for Parnell because he and other nationalist leaders, including Joseph Biggar, John Dillon, T. D. Sullivan, Thomas Sexton, Land League treasurer Patrick Egan (but not Michael Davitt) had been served with subpoenas informing them that they were to be prosecuted for a conspiracy to prevent the payment of rent. The *Freeman's Journal* had been devoting most of its space to the injustices of trying Parnell and the other Irish leaders – why, it demanded, were they to be prosecuted for combining against the landlords when trade unions in England could legally combine against their employers? Probably up to this point the *Freeman's Journal* – and other nationalist sectors – had not taken seriously the proposal to send an armed expedition to harvest the root crops of some unknown English gentleman in remotest Mayo, but, by November 5, the paper was sufficiently alarmed by the frenetic activity in Belfast to find space to denounce the promoters of 'warlike expeditions'. It further asked whether any newspaper favouring the Land League had gone so far as to advocate the relief of suffering tenants by armed force. To the accusation that the Boycott relief expedition aimed to relieve a suffering land agent by force, the *Belfast News-Letter* responded immediately, but its reply continued to avoid the implications of their crusade. The *News-Letter* said the object of the expedition was not to promote discord in Mayo but was merely one of kindness and mercy towards the besieged family at Lough Mask House and the expedition organisers asked nothing in the way of weapons except that the Northern labourers be armed in self-defence. However, the organisers were already asking considerably more for they had suggested that the government should ensure the expedition's safe passage to Mayo and protect it while Boycott's crops were harvested, and the only way the government could do that was by the use of troops.

CHAPTER 12

'A Narrow Escape from an Orange Invasion'

In the meantime the besieged Boycott had managed to escape from the confines of Lough Mask on one or two occasions. On October 22, before his story burst on the astonished world, he was in Galway where he gave evidence to the Bessborough Commission. In the course of this evidence he detailed the inconvenience, malice and harassment to which he had been and currently was being subjected. He stated his firm belief that his persecutors aimed to drive him from his farm because he had, in the course of his duty as Lord Erne's agent, served eviction notices. He gave his opinion that an amendment to the land laws would doubtfully affect the general situation in rural Ireland; that it would certainly not affect his position because Lord Erne was already offering an abatement* which brought the rents below Griffith's Valuation, and that therefore the only solution which would apparently satisfy the Lough Mask tenantry would be to let the land free of charge, not in his opinion a sane proposition. After Boycott became news it was also stated in nationalist circles that he continued to race his horses at the Curragh and had been able to visit Dublin 'while the honest Orangemen were picturing him to themselves holding a sort of Ekowe on half rations, against a host of Connaught Zulus thirsting for his blood'. (Analogies between what was happening at Lough Mask

---

* In his evidence to the Bessborough Commission Boycott in fact said Lord Erne had granted a 20 per cent abatement but elsewhere he said it was only 10 per cent, the figure quoted by all other observers and interested parties.

and the recent Zulu campaigns became popular in all newspapers and remained so for the duration of the Boycott affair.) In connection with the racing allegations, the magazine *Vanity Fair* also ran a story about Boycott the horseman. It said, 'At the beginning of his unpopularity, he heard just before a steeple-chase, that the "boys" intended to knock him over during the race; a determination he frustrated by giving their champion and leader Mr Nally . . . a mount on his second best horse, and riding boot to boot with him from start to finish'. The magazine did not elaborate on this thrilling encounter or say where it occurred but legend in the Lough Mask area affirms that it was at Ballinrobe Races and, inevitably and symbolically, the Captain lost the race. Boycott himself never mentioned the incident, neither did other newspapers or magazines but it suggests that up to the last minute there was ambivalence in local attitudes towards him. Incidentally, the Mr Nally who was loaned the second best horse and rode boot to boot with Boycott, had been prominent in the foundation of the original Mayo Land League, was among those indicted with Parnell on the charge of conspiracy to prevent the payment of rent, and was on the scene in Claremorris, Ballinrobe and notably at Lough Mask itself during the whole period of the Relief Expedition.

By the first week in November the nationalist papers had committed themselves to the fray, and to counteract the impression built up by the loyalist newspapers of the decent, respectable, law-abiding English gentleman who had farmed peaceably in Ireland for twenty-five years and was now beset by the unwarranted intimidation of the Land League, they started to propagate the tenants' version of the events that had led to Boycott's isolation and to lay emphasis on the unpleasantness of his character. One or two of the examples they chose to illustrate his personal traits were a trifle odd. For example, the *Freeman's Journal* asserted that he was glorying in his sudden fame and was actually enjoying the menial occupations he had been forced to undertake by his workers' withdrawal of their labour. It embarked upon a long story to illustrate this latter claim which went thus: an archeological association was currently working on one of the many islands lying in the waters of Lough Mask, and the foreman of the enterprise had rented a cottage from Boycott and wanted to fix a gate. A mason in Ballinrobe agreed to perform the task as it could not be counted as a service to Boycott himself, but on arrival at the cottage found that a mason's labourer had not been engaged. The man refused to act as his own labourer and was about to return to Ballinrobe when Boycott appeared on the scene, was told about the problem and proceeded to offer his services, personally breaking the stone wall. One could say this particular incident showed Boycott in a friendly, helpful light rather than demonstrating a peculiar love of manual labour, as the *Freeman's Journal* contended.

However much the nationalist papers might play down the more lawless aspects of the situation and play up the nastiness of Boycott's character and the justification for his ostracism, the position in which he found himself was deteriorating. On November 1, he had to attend the Petty Sessions in Ballinrobe in connection with the action of Martin Branigan for the payment of his three days' wages. As he left the court Boycott was surrounded by a mob of some five hundred people which hooted and hissed and hustled him, and he was forced to seek shelter in the infantry barracks. The RIC were then called and arrived at the barracks under the auspices of Mr McArdle, the Sub-Inspector, and Mr McSheehy, the local Resident Magistrate, and it was with a constabulary escort that Boycott was finally conducted back to Lough Mask House but not before Mr McSheehy had read the Riot Act. The *Ballinrobe Chronicle* admitted that the streets of the town had presented 'an untoward appearance' and that the situation had been somewhat disagreeable, but insisted the incident had not measured up to the exaggerated reports in newspapers not on the scene. One paper which obviously utilised the incident was the *Belfast News-Letter*. It quoted Boycott himself as saying that it demonstrated that 'the spirit of terrorism towards me is decidedly on the increase, and the determination to hunt me out of the country more openly expressed'. It further stated that such behaviour only emphasised the urgent need to assist the Captain, and said that if the government would not move to save a peaceable citizen from ruin and intimidation, then the loyal men of Ulster would.

By the end of this first week in November the plan to send the relief expedition was established; it was assumed the organisers were well ahead with their preparations but there remained official vagueness about the date of departure and, most vitally, about the precise number of Ulster labourers it was intended to convey, by special trains, to Mayo. The vagueness about numbers allowed rumour to proliferate – between three and five hundred men was the figure widely mooted – and nationalists were not alone in viewing the descent of such a body of armed Ulstermen upon Mayo as an act of invasion and the prelude to inevitable strife; on November 8 Mr Forster wrote to Gladstone, 'This would be civil war, we know the whole countryside would be up against them'. Up to this point, although the expedition's organisers in both Belfast and Dublin had insisted the government must provide protection for the expedition – and Dublin was active, if considerably less vocal in its activities than Belfast – the Chief Secretary's office had made no comment upon any aspect of the affair. This had laid the government open to attack in loyalist circles and increased the loyalists' justification for taking action themselves, but behind the scenes Mr Forster had been busy. His office had been in contact with Boycott for some time, indeed Mr Forster said in a letter to Gladstone as the affair reached its first peak on November 8, 'We will do what we have always promised to do and in fact urged him to enable us to do – viz. to protect his farm and away from his farm and at his farm as many men as are necessary for the *bona fide* work on his farm'. Boycott himself insisted that this was precisely what he had wanted from the government – a small body of labourers with adequate protection – but that it had failed to act. There is some truth in both

cartoon of Charles Cunningham Boycott by 'Spy' which appeared in *Vanity Fair* January 29, 1881.

A cartoon of Charles Stewart Parnell by 'Spy' which appeared in *Vanity Fair* on September 11, 1880.

A cartoon of William Ewart Gladstone, captioned 'The people's William', by 'Spy'
which appeared in *Vanity Fair* on July 1, 1879.

An engraving of W. E. Forster from the *Illustrated London News* dated July 31, 1880.

A drawing of Michael Davitt addressing '10,000 persons at Jones' Wood', USA. It is captioned 'Our object is to teach the people of Ireland, generally, that the Land of Ireland was made by God Almighty free for the people He created to live upon it.' It appeared in the *Irish World* on June 5, 1880.

The troops escorting the relief labourers from Claremorris to Ballinrobe. From *The Graphic*, November 20, 1880.

The 'careworn' Captain Boycott, a drawing which appeared in the *Penny Pictorial News* on November 20, 1880.

Captain Boycott and his friend Ashton Weekes with a constabulary escort. From *The Graphic*, November 20, 1880.

'Tasting the beer' in the camp at Lough Mask, from *The Graphic*, November 20, 1880

The constabulary and line encampment in the grounds of Lough Mask House. From *The Graphic*, November 20, 1880.

A drawing of Ballinrobe during the military occupation, from *The Graphic*, December 11, 1880.

Driving Captain Boycott's cattle from Lough Mask to Claremorris. From *The Graphic*, December 4, 1880.

The last meal at Lough Mask House, from *The Graphic*, December 4, 1880.

The convivial Father O'Malley at home. From the *Illustrated London News*, December 11, 1880.

A photograph taken on the steps of Lough Mask House. Boycott is at the back,
4th from the right, behind his wife. Next to him are his nephew and niece (blurred);
in front are Mr Ashton Weekes and Mr Robinson in their tam o'shanters.

A group photograph, including the relief labourers, taken in the flooded grounds of
Lough Mask House. Boycott is in the centre, holding a staff.

A photograph of members of the Royal Irish Constabulary parading for duty in the grounds of Lough Mask House.

. photograph of the Royal Irish Constabulary on eviction duty near Lough Mask
ouse shortly after Boycott's departure for England. (Note the battering ram on the
rt.)

The departure of the Boycott relief volunteers from Lough Mask House. From the *Illustrated London News*, December 11, 1880.

versions of what did *not* happen; Boycott did ask for labourers and protection, but while the Chief Secretary's office was slowly considering his request – one among many from outraged victims of the Land League's activities – events overtook and overwhelmed it in the shape of Bernard Becker's despatch, the loyalist reaction and the rapid formulation of the plans for a civilian relief expedition. Unfortunately, although Boycott himself appreciated that what was happening to him was something extraordinary and novel, as did the loyalist sectors once the story became news, the Chief Secretary's office (like the nationalists) initially failed to grasp the implications and when they did it was too late for discreet government aid.

However, Forster did keep pace with the rapid movement of events once the civilian front had blown the incident up to outsize proportions. On November 3, after the contretemps at the Petty Sessions in Ballinrobe, Mr McSheehy wrote to Forster requesting that the infantry force in the town be immediately augmented, and the next day orders were sent from Dublin Castle to fill both the infantry and cavalry barracks to their maximum capacity, while a further urgent memorandum was sent by Forster to the Military Secretary asking 'that the military stations at Ballinrobe may be at once instructed to patrol the roads as frequently as possible in the direction of Captain Boycott's residence' and urging the fullest co-operation between the civil and military authorities in the matter. Plans for a large transfer of extra troops into the disturbed area were also urgently made, but finding accommodation for them proved difficult from the start. On November 4, the local government board in Claremorris, which was the nearest railway station to Ballinrobe and Lough Mask House and therefore of the utmost importance, received a telegram stating that the government wished to place a company of infantry in the workhouse and requesting the immediate compliance of the Board of Guardians. The board was not co-operative, initially it was unable to obtain a quorum, and when it did, the members refused to accommodate the troops on the grounds that their presence would occasion hardship and suffering to the regular inmates. (Mr Forster queried whether the Guardians had the right to refuse accommodation to Her Majesty's troops and was informed they had, as full control of the management of the workhouse was vested in them.) Further on November 7, instructions were sent for the telegraph lines between Dublin–Claremorris and Dublin–Ballinrobe to be kept permanently open, while on November 8 orders were transmitted to resident magistrates in other areas to proceed to Ballinrobe to be prepared to assist Mr McSheehy in the execution of his duties, which might include an Orange invasion. Incidentally, although in the initial correspondence between Mr McSheehy and Dublin Castle and in his own published statements, Boycott had been referred to or had referred to himself without his military title, by early November he was everywhere designated *Captain* Boycott. It would seem that Bernard Becker's despatch with its biographical account of his having served in the 39th Foot had much to do with the resurrection of the military rank, apart from the desire of the loyalists to emphasise Boycott's stature and that of the nationalists to demonstrate that anybody who misbehaved in Ireland was now liable to be chastised irrespective of rank.

By November 8, Mr Forster had decided he must take firm action which he did in a most unusual, indeed almost unprecedented manner, for on that date he called a press conference at Dublin Castle. At this exceptional conference – 'It is not usual for the Government to communicate matters of news to the Press, it is not their business to do so' – Forster started by explaining why, on this occasion, he had deemed it fitting to take the press into his confidence. His reason was a tribute to the power of the printed word – for the whole Boycott affair had been inflated through the medium of the press. He admitted that there had been such widespread news coverage of the relief expedition and so many wild statements had been made in the previous week that he felt he must set the record straight as far as the government was concerned. He informed the assembled journalists that from the start of 'this unfortunate event of Captain Boycott' the government had been most anxious to give him every possible assistance, and had told both Boycott himself and Lord Erne that if arrangements were made for a small number of men to harvest the crops, the government would afford them protection to, from and at, Lough Mask House. This information was for the benefit of the loyalist papers, particularly the *Belfast News-Letter*, which had been loudly proclaiming that the government had been neglecting its duty in the preservation of law and order, and had taken absolutely no steps to succour an honest citizen menaced by the forces of violence.

However, Mr Forster continued, permitting a large body of armed men to descend on Boycott's farm was not necessary to save his crops and would inevitably precipitate what he called 'a very strong collision' in Mayo. Consequently, he had informed Mr Robinson, the proprietor of the newspaper which had first suggested the relief expedition, the Dublin *Daily Express*, that no such body such as had been suggested could be allowed to travel to Mayo, that fifty unarmed labourers would be more than sufficient to harvest the crops, but that the government would be willing – indeed would consider it their duty – to provide this small group with protection. He also stated that the government had already ordered the despatch of a large number of extra troops to the disturbed area, which information was again for the benefit of the loyalist sectors as an answer to their accusations of governmental neglect. Prior to the press conference, Forster had told the directors of the Midland Great Western Railway that the government would not guarantee the safe passage of the special trains ordered by the Ulster organisers of the relief expedition and in consequence the railway had cancelled the trains. By these actions Mr Forster curbed the ardour of those who were in danger of precipitating violence in the name of law and order, and halted a drastic 'invasion of Mayo', as the expedition was already being designated in nationalist quarters. If the organisers had had their wings clipped they had none the less achieved something – official government recognition of, and intervention in, the Boycott affair, and Mr Forster's public promise of protection for the smaller relief expedition. The organisers, in fact, protested they did not want government intervention, they only wanted government protection in the shape of troops, but, as with the setting up of the relief expedition, they overlooked the implications of government involvement.

Both the Dublin *Daily Express* and the *Belfast News-Letter* expressed righteous indignation at the statements made by Mr Forster at his press conference. The *Express* brushed aside his explanation about the earlier help offered to Boycott and the large troop movements westward, and reiterated its belief that the government had done nothing previously to assist the Captain in his cruel isolation or 'to put down the malignant power which had been set up to supersede the Queen's authority' (i.e. the Land League). On the contrary, it said, it was only when a body of loyal men proposed to aid the victim of this malignant power that the government showed interest and further displayed 'an unexpected resolution to thwart their benevolent purpose'. In the matter of the government's pressure on the directors of the Midland Great Western Railway, causing the withdrawal of the special trains, the *Express* was equally indignant. No difficulty had been experienced by the leaders of the Land League in chartering special trains when the known object of these leaders was to promote agitation and defy the law (it was true that Parnell was addicted to hiring special trains, always preferring not to waste time). Why, therefore, should similar facilities be withheld from those whose only aim was to rescue one of the Land League's victims and to prove that the reign of anarchy and assassination was not supreme in Ireland? The *Express* felt sure that the general public would find it hard to understand the reasons for such partiality and would be forced to draw its own conclusions, namely (although it did not state this explicitly) that Gladstone's Liberal administration was feeble and incapable of dealing with the menace of the Land League. The sentiments of the *Belfast News Letter* were on much the same lines, and its indignation at Mr Forster's intervention was even more vociferously stated.

However, the Dublin and Ulster upholders of law and order were not altogether in accord, and the inbred, historic antagonism between Protestant North and Catholic South reappeared at the time of Forster's press conference. On November 8 the *Belfast News-Letter* asked: 'What are our friends in Dublin about? There is a large sum of money available in that city; and why do they not communicate with Belfast, where the men are? It is to be hoped that the matter may not be delayed any longer'. The next day the Dublin *Daily Express* replied at length to these queries, casting itself and its southern Irish compatriots in the role of 'Reasoned Restraint' and the *Belfast News-Letter* and Ulster in that of 'Wild Zealot'. The *Express* began its reply by saying that the time had come when its readers must be put fully in the picture, and mentioning in an offhand manner that the idea for the relief expedition to save Boycott's crops had originated in its columns with the strong approval of its proprietor. Having proposed this praiseworthy scheme, the *Express* (and all reasonable southern Irishmen) had deemed it advisable to show restraint while reaction was tested and, when this proved favourable, while arrangements went ahead; as the *Express* pointed out severely, 'such arrangements could not be made in a day'. Moreover it had felt that any premature publicity might tend to mar the purpose of the expedition which was to show practical sympathy to Captain Boycott and, at the same time, to teach his persecutors a lesson. Unfortunately, once the project had been suggested in Dublin and plans to implement it were going ahead, the zeal of the Ulster sympathisers had reached such proportions that supporters of the Land League had been able to raise the alarm and declare that an armed invasion of County Mayo was in preparation. The *Express* felt sure that the League supporters had no real justification for these wild accusations, it was certain that the Ulstermen had no such warlike intentions but had been prompted by over-enthusiasm. However, it had to be admitted that the schemes and proposals emanating from Belfast had produced an effect deleterious to the relief expedition. They had provided ammunition for the Land Leaguers and had made reasonable people suspect that their aim was not merely to succour Captain Boycott and teach his tormentors a lesson, but that the promoters of the expedition intended openly to challenge 'the assassins and their friends' which would undoubtedly result in a serious breach of the peace. Had the Ulstermen been content to follow the wise lead of 'Combination' (Mr Manning) and to leave all arrangements in the hands of loyal southern Irishmen, the uproar which had ensued would have been avoided and a nice, orderly expedition could have embarked without trouble or government intervention. At least, this was what the *Express* strongly inferred. On the subject of government intervention, however, the *Express* was at one with its Ulster brethren, even if it did suggest that the blame for this lay at Ulster's door.

While the newspaper organs of Protestant North and Catholic South were snapping their sectarian and racial teeth at each other, the actual organisers of the relief expedition, their initial plans having been thwarted, were hastily reorganising the curtailed foray into Mayo. First they had to whittle down the numbers, turning away innumerable, eager volunteers; they finally settled for a contingent from Monaghan and another from Cavan.* As the special trains had been vetoed, they worked fast, and by November 10 the Boycott relief expedition was ready to leave.

In the meantime, the extra troop reinforcements promised by Mr Forster had been sent to Mayo. In the early hours of Tuesday morning, November 9, four troops of the 19th Hussars – one under the command of Brevet Lieutenant Colonel Twentyman,

* Ironically, when the Irish Free State came into being and accepted, if reluctantly, the proposals of the Boundary Commission on Northern Ireland, both Cavan and Monaghan were among the Ulster counties which formed part of the Free State (Donegal being the other). However, in the 1880s both Monaghan and Cavan were very much part of the loyal Protestant province of Ulster.

the other under Captain Webster with Major Coghill in overall command – were ordered to Broadstone Terminus in Dublin from the Island-bridge barracks. They arrived at about 2 a.m. and the activity – engines being shunted, wagons hitched, horses loaded into travelling boxes – caused the *Irish Times* to comment, 'Probably since the period of the Fenian uprising no such scene as that which took place at Broadstone terminus between 3 and 4 o'clock this morning has occurred in Ireland'. The Hussars were shortly joined at the station by a detachment of the Army Service Corps from Portobello Barracks, including ambulances – the Hospital Corps being under the command of Surgeon Major Reynolds V.C., the hero of Rorke's Drift. As dawn began to break, the special trains bearing the Hussars, the Army Service Corps, the Hospital Corps, the horses, the ambulances and the supplies steamed out of Broadstone terminus on their journey westward. A few hours later there was similar activity at the Curragh, four hundred men plus officers of the 84th Regiment, and a large quantity of tents, were despatched via Portarlington to Athlone where they were able to join the Midland Great Western Railway and proceed to Claremorris.

When the special trains from Dublin and Athlone arrived in Claremorris the weather was foul and, according to the *Connaught Telegraph*, 'the poor soldiers had to stand in slough and rain, with empty stomachs, for long hours awaiting orders to march to Ballinrobe' – a distance of thirteen miles. It was not until the early hours of Wednesday morning that they arrived in the town and, again according to the *Telegraph*, 'the whole army of invasion had to take refuge in nooks corners and corridors – no shelter, no food, nor order or discipline – all one conglomeration of red-coats, horses, baggage, etc. . . . The Army Service Corps and the commissariat, true to their names and traditions, broke down in transit, forgetting their picks, tent-pegs, and camp kettles, three species of utensils indispensably necessary to carrying out operations'. Although the *Telegraph* enjoyed itself hugely in this article, entitled 'Our Invaders', other newspapers agreed about the disorganisation and said that when camp was finally pitched on the green between the infantry and cavalry barracks, it was a sodden and miserable spectacle. The reporter from the *Freeman's Journal* commented upon the disorganised arrival thus: 'There is a story of the Colonel of Hussars lying on the cold ground with his martial cloak around him, but I can hardly credit that things reached that pitch'.

It is not surprising that the troops, denied accommodation in Claremorris, caused chaos in Ballinrobe which consisted only of one short main street, a few ancillary streets, a handful of shops, one good hotel, the green and two barracks. By Wednesday, November 10, there were one hundred and twenty officers and men of the 19th Hussars with their horses, over four hundred officers and men of the 84th Regiment, a corps of the Royal Engineers hastily constructing water courses to drain the saturated camp, and detachments of the Army Service Corps and the Hospital Corps quartered in this small town. That was in addition to a troop of the 1st Dragoons and the men of the 76th Regiment already stationed at the barracks, and extra forces of the RIC, both mounted and foot, which had been summoned to support the local constabulary. It was estimated by nationalist and loyalist newspapers, with a remarkable degree of unanimity, that there were at least one thousand troops in Ballinrobe. Apart from the military influx there was another – that of the newspaper correspondents who had descended from Belfast, Dublin, London and the United States – for, as *The Times* reported: 'The Boycott expedition is the most exciting topic of the day. It has withdrawn attention from the prosecutions and the agitation (i.e. of Parnell and the Land League leaders), and filled the minds of the public with mingled curiosity, irritation and fear'. Ballinrobe itself, the headquarters, as the *Freeman's Journal* reported, 'of the nearest approach to any army beheld in Mayo since Humbert and his Frenchmen were at Castlebar in '93', was filled with more than curiosity and irritation, it was seething with excitement and swirling with rumours.

What precisely the army had come to do was the subject of much speculation, but the chief rumours concerned the number of Ulstermen supposed to be *en route* from the North. At the beginning of the vital week in November, there were wild stories that five hundred Orangemen had arrived in Westport and were already marching, fully armed, on Ballinrobe; other reports spoke of hundreds of armed Orangemen proceeding up Lough Corrib to Cong, whence they would march to Lough Mask House. There was a basis of truth in this rumour because the original intention of the organisers of the relief expedition had been to make for Galway and then up Lough Corrib, but Mr Forster had vetoed this plan as the idea of Orangemen marching through Galway, a notoriously disturbed and Catholic town, did not appeal to him. The wildest rumour of all was that two thousand Orangemen had detrained in Claremorris, but it later turned out to be a special train which had actually arrived in the town but which contained Irish farm labourers returning from seasonal work in England. The rumour was scotched when 'the lusty cheers of the harvest men for Parnell and the Land League established their identity'. Another rumour which caused a great deal of local indignation was that the troops themselves were going to dig up Boycott's root crops – this was sparked off when the engineers appeared with their picks and shovels to construct water courses and latrines.

In general, however, the troops were received with remarkable equanimity and no hostile demonstrations ensued, although some people considered their arrival as the most direct insult that could have been put upon Connaught. However, everybody agreed that the unnatural quiet depended upon what the Ulstermen intended to do when they arrived, or at least what the government intended to let them do. If they moved directly to Lough Mask House and proceeded to harvest Boycott's root crops then, asserted the local Land League leaders, there would be no trouble, although they equally firmly stated that the whole business of the relief expedition was ridiculous and unnecessary; but if, as many people suspected, the Ulstermen came in the role of 'armed fili-busters' then the men of Mayo would rightly and righteously resist, and there would be terrible bloodshed. Among some sections of the population feelings ran higher and the risk of bloodshed took second place to pride, as a placard that appeared in Claremorris illustrated: 'Men of the barony of Claremorris, will you allow the men of the barony of Kilmaine to be walked upon by a handful of Orangemen? Let your answer be, "No, we'll not." Onward, then, in your thousands to Lough Mask tonight. Strike for your religion, your lives, and your liberty.' Most of the assembled newspaper correspondents agreed that armed resistance was to be expected – there were stories of old Enfield rifles being sold, and the police believed that many young men in the area had revolvers. As the Ulster relief expedition was a provocative act and the West of Ireland was not noted for its lack of violence, this was a reasonable assumption. However, the correspondents were, to some degree, trapped by the atmosphere they themselves had helped create. If there was not to be strife their presence in such large numbers seemed a trifle unnecessary, particularly as some newspapers had sent their war correspondents.

Boycott himself did not appear to be revelling in his notoriety, whatever the *Freeman's Journal* might say, nor did he seem enthusiastic about the projected arrival of his Ulster saviours. He had written to the Dublin *Daily Express* to thank the editor and its readers for giving his case publicity and for their generosity and assistance, but he had also given interviews to the Press Association correspondent and to Bernard Becker who was back on the scene. To the former he stated that he had succeeded in saving his grain and only needed minimal assistance, say ten or fifteen labourers, to harvest his root crops. What he did not require was the arrival of a large number of Ulstermen, as he feared their presence would lead to sectarian war; moreover, he had no idea where the Ulstermen would obtain food, or fuel to cook it, as the tradesmen in Ballinrobe were refusing to serve the police already billeted on his estate. To Bernard Becker,

Boycott was more forthcoming, or perhaps it would be more accurate to say that Becker, as a special correspondent, composed a more colourful and human despatch than the agency reporter.

Becker, who had been reporting from Galway, hastened by steamer up Lough Corrib upon hearing the news that 'the Boycott brigade was actually going to invade Lough Mask'. He had to travel via Ballinrobe, as nobody would take him direct to Lough Mask House, and in the town he noted that 'the illuminated tents light up the foreground pleasantly, while the moon tinges the tree-tops and the river Robe with silver. All is beautiful enough were it not for the persistent rattle of the sabre and the jingle of the spur.' Having eventually managed to hire a private carriage he arrived at Lough Mask House on November 10, and immediately commented that the extraordinary situation he had depicted in his original article was in no way diminished, on the contrary, it had been exaggerated almost to distortion, and Captain and Mrs Boycott and his family were living under conditions that would have driven most people mad.

Despite the appalling conditions under which the Boycotts were living, according to Becker, they remained defiant, and he wrote of Boycott with his 'grey head and slight spare figure bowed, but by no means in submission'. He also reported on a letter that Boycott had received from the tenants, dated November 10, intimating that they wished to appoint a day to pay the disputed rents. Accordingly Boycott replied saying he would receive the rents at ten o'clock on the morning of November 11, shortly after which hour he was given a further missive from the tenants which read as follows: 'The tenants request an answer to the following before they pay the rent: 1st Don't you wish you may get it? 2nd When do you expect the Orangemen, and how are they to come? 3rd When are you going to hook it? Let us know, so that we may see you off. 4th Are you in any way comfortable? Don't be uneasy in your mind: we'll take care of you. Down with the landlords. God save Ireland.' The *Freeman's*

Journal also reported on this singular decision of the Lough Mask tenantry to accept the 10 per cent abatement and to offer to pay the rents (although it omitted to mention the second unpleasant letter received by Boycott), but its conclusion was that the action should be viewed as 'an embitterment of hostility . . . rather than a surrender'. In any case, the rents were not paid.

Becker finished his article by saying that indiscreet friends were perhaps almost as troublesome as sworn enemies, and intimated that he fully sympathised with the unfortunate Boycott who, wishing for a few labourers to harvest his crops, was now facing an Ulster invasion. Even though the government's intervention had reduced the proportions of this 'Ulsterior force' – as Becker had heard the expedition called in Galway – the arrival at Lough Mask House of fifty labourers with baggage and implements was indeed 'a hideous infliction', Boycott having neither sufficient accommodation nor food for them. As final proof of the unfortunate nature of the assistance Boycott was receiving, Becker noted that an advance squadron of the 19th Hussars and one hundred infantrymen had already arrived and installed themselves in the grounds of the estate.

Whatever Boycott might feel about the fantastic events that had enveloped him – and his interviews with the PA correspondent and Bernard Becker indicated that he was far from happy – they had progressed too far and too fast for anybody to halt them. It was a question of waiting and seeing what happened once the Ulstermen arrived, and in a state of high excitement that was what the inhabitants of Ballinrobe did, while the advance guard of their invaders – the troops and the press – attended on future events in only slightly calmer mood. At the eleventh hour a rumour, to the effect that Boycott, worn down by the suffering he had undergone and the isolation to which he had been subjected, had cut his throat, threw everybody into a panic. On November 11 most newspapers carried a telegraph item with this startling news, but it proved to be false and the atmosphere in Ballinrobe returned to its state of fearful anticipation. The outside world – alerted by the vast newspaper coverage, by Mr Forster's press conference, by the government's intervention and the military preparations – held its breath, part of it hopeful that a bloody collision would ensue and matters in Ireland be brought to a head, part of it praying that reason would prevail.

CHAPTER 13

'The Queerest Menagerie that Ever Came Into Connaught'

The first contingent of the relief expedition left Monaghan on the evening of Wednesday, November 10, under the leadership of Mr Crawford. The man who had originally intended to command the Ulster force was Colonel Lloyd, the agent for Lord Rossmore's large Monaghan estates and a prominent Ulster loyalist, but when government intervention limited the relief expedition to fifty men, Lloyd decided it was too small to warrant his personal attention and relinquished the local command to Mr Crawford. However, he did address the members of the Monaghan contingent, most of whom lived on the Rossmore estate and were, according to the *Belfast News-Letter*, 'stout and respectable young men, the sons of well-to-do farmers'. (Nationalist newspapers were to describe them differently.) Lloyd told them they were embarking upon a noble and patriotic expedition, to save the crops of a gentleman who was as brave and courageous as himself; he did not believe in hiding his own light under a bushel. He warned them they were venturing into a very rough part of the country, but as the government had promised protection, he thought they had no reason to expect interference from 'the bludgeon men of Mayo', particularly if they showed themselves for what they were, namely respectable yeoman of the north who loved order and fair play. He then turned to practical matters; as they would have a considerable amount of marching to do – Claremorris to Lough Mask House was a long haul – he advised them not to wear new or tight boots but to take worn and easy ones, and, as finding accommodation in the area might prove difficult, he also advised them to take their greatcoats in case they had to sleep in haylofts and the like. After this address the members of the contingent collected their belongings, were given 'an ample quantity of tobacco . . . to consume during their sojourn at Ballinrobe', and entrained for Clones.

In Clones they stayed overnight, and the next morning were joined by another small contingent under Mr Morris Goddard who was a solicitor. They were subjected to another speech, this time from 'Combination' himself – Mr Manning – who had arrived from Dublin. Mr Manning addressed them in much the same manner as had Colonel Lloyd, although he omitted such practical matters as boots and coats and concentrated on the noble aspect of the enterprise and the necessity for the expedition to conduct itself in a manner worthy of Protestant Ulster. Meanwhile in Cavan, the Honourable Captain Somerset Maxwell, who had unsuccessfully contested that seat against Joseph Biggar in the recent general election, was in charge of a further group of volunteers, 'a stalwart body of men, of evident respectability, and remarkable quietness of demeanour', according to the Dublin *Daily Express*, although the nationalist papers had other descriptions for them, too. On Thursday morning, November 11, the two contingents converged on Mullingar where they were put under the joint command of Mr Manning, Mr Goddard and Captain Somerset Maxwell. From Mullingar they proceeded to Athlone where they awaited the arrival of the normal scheduled train from Dublin to Claremorris. While standing on Athlone station, the volunteers, who numbered an exact fifty according to the Dublin *Express*,* were issued with revolvers, apparently with the approval of 'a high official of the Castle'. Whether it was with the approval of Mr Forster remains doubtful, as he had insisted that the volunteers should travel unarmed, but the organisers

---

* There was some confusion about the number of men in the relief expedition. However, the *Belfast News-Letter* later published a list of the names of the men involved (see Notes and Sources) which numbered fifty-seven, so we can assume this to be the correct figure.

said that the un-named high official had agreed the men could not travel to such a part of the country as Mayo without means of self-defence. However, the official had also stipulated that the revolvers must not be openly displayed, and on Athlone station their leaders instructed the men to comply with this order. When the train drew into Athlone in the late morning of Thursday, November 11, in addition to its complement of ordinary travellers it contained a small body of the RIC and the supplies necessary for the relief expedition. To satisfy its readers, all loyal Irishmen and friends and relatives of the volunteers, that the latter's need had been thoroughly attended to – by Mr Robinson the proprietor of the Dublin *Daily Express* – this newspaper presented a list of items included in the supplies, to wit: '2 sacks of oatmeal, 3 barrels and 1 sack of biscuits, 3 cwt of tinned meat in cans, 2½ cwt of bacon, 2 large hams, 1 large cheese, 25 lb butter, 25 lb tea, 1 cwt of sugar, 25 tins of Swiss condensed milk, 25 tins of concentrated coffee and milk, 6 drums of salt, 30 lb tobacco, 14 gallons of whiskey, 6 stoves, 2 cooking stoves, 1 large one (?), blankets, towels, soap, candles, tins for drinking, plates, knives and forks, with carvers, flare lanterns, dark lanterns, a gross of lucifer matches, four foghorns for signalling purposes, 100 empty sacks, and 6 carts and horses to bring down the provisions and bring back the oats which the party have to thresh for Captain Boycott'. Unfortunately, Mr Robinson's efforts to procure tents had been unsuccessful and the organisers could only hope, as they left Athlone, that suitable arrangements for sleeping could be made on arrival at Lough Mask House.

Although it was on the ordinary scheduled train that the volunteers travelled to Claremorris, it was preceded by a special pilot engine to ensure that the line was safe from interference by the Land Leaguers, and the route was also patrolled by members of the RIC, in increasing numbers as the train approached Claremorris. Various representatives of the press were in the train, including *The Times* reporter who, having travelled in the same compartment as the Cavan volunteers, could assure the public that calling the expedition 'the invasion of Mayo' was ridiculous, that the task ahead would be performed efficiently and peacefully, and that if there were any trouble the Ulster volunteers would not be its perpetrators. *The Times* man added that the Cavan labourers detested Mr Parnell and swore their undying allegiance to the Crown and Constitution. All the stations along the line had small crowds which booed and hissed as the train passed through or stopped briefly, but it was at Ballyhaunis, eleven miles from Claremorris, that the first major demonstration of Connaught hostility to the Ulster presence showed itself. A largish crowd had assembled on the platform and it groaned and hooted and hissed at the train 'with perfect impartiality', according to the Dublin *Daily Express*, for, although it knew the relief expedition was on the train it did not know in which compartments. There were shouts of 'Why don't the blackguards come out?', 'Not one of them will ever come back' and one man was particularly noisy, complaining he wanted to see the Orangemen because he hadn't slept for four nights in anticipation of their arrival.

Meanwhile in Claremorris itself the government had organised a large reception party for the expedition. Mr Forster had issued instructions for an extra escort of cavalry and infantry of 'one Field Officer, 20 men Royal Dragoons, 150 men of the 76th Regiment with proportion of officers' to proceed from Castlebar to Claremorris station, there to assist the civil powers in protecting a party of fifty labourers. In addition to this force from Castlebar, which was to escort the labourers as far as Hollymount before handing over to another detail from Ballinrobe and returning to its own barracks, two troops of the 19th Hussars under the command of Major Coghill had also been sent from Ballinrobe to Claremorris to meet the volunteers' train. Further there was a strong body of police drafted from various parts of Connaught with a good sprinkling of officials, including Colonel Bruce, the Deputy Assistant General of the Royal Irish Constabulary, and numerous resident magistrates who had also been summoned into the area from as far away as Portarlington. However, the nominal command of the operation remained in the hands of the Ballinrobe resident magistrate, Mr McSheehy, as it was officially both a local and civil affair, the military being present only to assist the civil powers in the execution of their duty. Ominously, among the troops and constabulary that marched or rode the thirteen flat, dreary miles from Ballinrobe to Claremorris that morning, there was an ambulance wagon under the command of Surgeon Major Reynolds, V.C., and that he was the hero of Rorke's Drift was mentioned by all newspapers. The suggestion that the authorities were anticipating a Mayo battle on a similar scale was further emphasised by widespread reporting that Major Coghill of the 19th Hussars was the uncle of 'the lieutenant of that name slain on the retreat from Isandula'.*

By 2 p.m. Claremorris station had been sealed off, a cordon of Hussars with drawn swords had been placed round the long passage leading from the town to the station entrance, in front of the entrance itself were more Hussars and Dragoons, while Infantrymen of the 76th Regiment were drawn up on the platform, and armed policemen of the RIC were positioned in skirmishing order in the fields and hedges surrounding the station. Only those members of the public who could show urgent reason for their presence were permitted to enter the station precincts, but press correspondents were allowed on to the platform. Among those who thus entered was James Daly of the *Connaught Telegraph*, and he enlivened the weary wait by launching into a vigorous denunciation of landlordism, which was permitted despite the military presence on the platform. He assured the assembled company that the people were bound to win because all the bayonets in the world could not prevail against right and justice.

At about ten past three the pilot engine chugged in, causing a flutter of anticipation, but then the word came that the actual train

* Isandula was where the Zulus inflicted a disastrous defeat on a British force under Lord Chelmsford in January 1879, and the successful defence of Rorke's Drift followed thereafter.

had been delayed by the hostile crowd at Ballyhaunis. Eventually, at three-thirty, a bell rang announcing its arrival, the cavalry bugles sounded the fall-in and, as the train steamed alongside the platform, the infantry were marched to the main entrance and formed into fours with bayonets fixed, although they were instructed to use them only if the Ulstermen were attacked. Mr Manning, Mr Goddard, Captain Somerset Maxwell and the other gentlemen in charge of the expedition emerged from first class compartments and met the assembled resident magistrates, then after a brief delay the labourers were ordered to get out of their third class compartments, and their appearance on the platform occasioned a hoot of derision from the few civilians who had managed to gain admittance. According to the *Freeman's Journal*, it would have been impossible to have picked out from the Belfast slums 'a sorrier or more wretched crew ... shabbily dressed, and of poor physique, and anything but prepossessing features'.

The volunteers were mustered into double line and eventually given the signal to move off, but not before James Daly had taken the opportunity of addressing them, in a manner quite dissimilar from Colonel Lloyd or Mr Manning. Seeing they looked 'as nervous as half-hanged dogs', Daly told them to cheer up, Connaughtmen would not soil their hands with them and they would return north unharmed, but perhaps with different impressions of Mayo from those with which they had arrived. One of the labourers asked, 'What kind of b—— is this Boycott?' and Daly replied, 'He is not worth all the fuss. He is a self-made martyr.' He added that Boycott was an inefficient farmer, that he had raised the alarm to obtain Orange and/or government money to extricate him from his own bad management, and that, as a result of the uproar, he would assuredly leave Ireland a richer man than when he came.

The labourers were led off the platform by Mr Manning and Captain Somerset Maxwell who, according to the *Freeman's Journal*, 'were got up in campaigning frieze, with knapsacks strapped at their backs'. Their appearance outside the station, between the lines of the 76th Regiment with its fixed bayonets, was the signal for a storm of groans, hissings, hootings and booings from the assembled crowd, an outburst of execration such as several correspondents had never heard before and hoped never to hear again. Women predominated in this hostile Claremorris crowd, exhausting their considerable vocabulary of expletives and derogation in ridiculing 'Boycott's angishores', while the 'angishores' themselves made a brave show of indifference, according to loyalist observers, or looked more like trembling prisoners inside their cordon of 76th steel, according to nationalist ones. In the face of this noisy hostility, the party did not wait long in front of the station, the bugle was quickly sounded, Major Coghill gave the order for the Hussars to move forward, and the extraordinary procession set off.

At its head rode Major Coghill and the 19th Hussars, followed by armed mounted police, with fifty more armed constables riding in carriages, then came the solid body of the 76th Regiment on foot, encasing the Orangemen, also on foot; the rear was brought up by the ambulance wagons, the wagons carrying the expedition's supplies and finally the Dragoons, together with the carriages and horses of the press correspondents. Through Claremorris wound the cavalcade, the greatest, most imposing, most fantastic its undistinguished streets had ever witnessed, the crowds increasing at every yard, the cries of indignation and execration growing in volume as the early winter darkness started to fall and the rain to lash down in blinding sheets. It was an occasion, said one correspondent, to make the blood run cold and even the most sanguine person fearful for the future of the expedition. In fact, the only mishap that occurred in Claremorris was to Major Coghill whose horse – unsettled by the noise – reared and threw him; either fracturing or breaking his leg and causing him to withdraw from the operation. However, half a mile outside the town there was trouble. Most of the correspondents arrived late on the scene, having either stopped to telegraph copy in

Claremorris or, in the darkness and rain, become entangled with the body of the procession.

The cause of the trouble was the carriages hired in Ballinrobe – not without difficulty – to carry the police. Now that Claremorris was behind them, the resident magistrates in charge, Mr McSheehy and Mr Hamilton, thought it would be an excellent idea if the labourers were transferred to the carriages and driven to Ballinrobe as quickly as possible. One or two of the Ulstermen had already climbed into the carriages when their owner, a Mr Ansbro, called a halt, because he had signed an agreement to transport only the constabulary and he was definitely not carrying any members of the relief expedition. While Messrs Hamilton and McSheehy pleaded with him, a largish crowd gathered, including prominent local Land League leaders who exhorted Mr Ansbro to stick to his guns and cheered when he did so. The magistrates argued on, the rain continued to pour down and several of the Ulstermen refused to climb out of the carriages. Mr Ansbro would not move until they did, and the sodden waiting soldiers of the 76th Regiment called out, 'Charge him' and were severely reprimanded by their officer. Eventually Mr Ansbro won the day and the cavalcade continued with the police in the cars and the Ulstermen on foot, amidst loud cheers from the Land League onlookers.

Most of the newspaper correspondents now galloped on ahead, or were conveyed by carriage, anxious to be in Ballinrobe to greet the arrival of the expedition. As they passed through Hollymount, six miles from the town, they encountered the 84th Regiment which had been detailed to take over from the 76th and escort the labourers into Ballinrobe. The men of the 84th had been waiting for hours in the slashing rain, some were lying huddled in their greatcoats by the side of the road, while others sheltered in the woods. Several called to enquire after the whereabouts of the procession, and the information that it was at least three miles behind, and proceeding at a very slow pace, 'elicited responses better understood in birdcage walk than in the wilds of Connaught.' It was not until half-past nine at night, five hours after they had left Claremorris, that the weary, wet, footsore labourers eventually reached Ballinrobe, passing through streets lined by infantrymen with fixed bayonets. Their reception was much the same as it had been in Claremorris: cat-calls, jeers, boos, groans for the Orangemen and Boycott, cheers for the Land League and Parnell. By ten o'clock they were ensconced in the infantry barracks and the Boycott relief expedition had reached the end of its first day.

Friday, November 12, dawned as grey and miserable as its predecessor – and there are few places more miserable than a small Irish town on a grey November day. It was in drizzling rain that the Ulster volunteers left the infantry barracks on the last lap of the journey – the four miles from Ballinrobe to Lough Mask House. They did not finally depart until eleven o'clock in the morning, the lateness of the hour being attributed to their need for rest after the previous day's endeavours. (Bernard Becker said they looked 'terribly knocked up', their appearance not auguring well for the labours that lay ahead, and other correspondents agreed.) The departure from the barracks was attended by the same military preparations as on the day before; in front of the cavalcade rode a corporal's guard of the 19th Hussars, followed by a sixty-strong constabulary force and another detachment of Hussars with men of the 84th Regiment forming a phalanx round the volunteers.

The entire population of Ballinrobe was at windows and doors or in the streets to watch the spectacle, and was loud in its expression of what the *Express* reporter tactfully designated 'very uncomplimentary remarks'. The limits of the town were soon left behind, and the right fork to Lough Mask was taken, and the convoy proceeded slowly along the long, flat road, past the grey stone walls, the patches of boggy turf, the acres of cultivated fields and the occasional squat farmhouse. There were few people on the roads (a fact commented on by the correspondents present), and those who turned out to witness the advent of the relief expedition and the British army were mainly women and children, who taunted the Ulstermen with cries of 'Hurry up, the turnips is boiling', 'Three cheers for the American Republic'; and by singing Land League songs.

As the cavalcade wound its way towards Lough Mask 'like a huge red serpent with black head and tail', in Bernard Becker's vivid words, the drizzle stopped and a watery sun broke through the clouds, glinting on the orange and gold of the autumnal leaves, throwing into relief the mountains of Maam Turk which lay behind the waters of Lough Mask. At the iron gates of Boycott's estate not a solitary civilian member of the Connaught population was to be seen, only the patrolling constabulary with their loaded rifles. Through the gates wheeled the cavalcade, to be greeted, in the parkland which stretches back to the house, by Boycott carrying a double-barrelled rifle, and his friend Ashton Weekes with a Winchester repeater. These weapons were not to demonstrate hostility to the relief expedition but to emphasise that the situation was such that both men were forced permanently to carry arms. However, most of the correspondents commented upon the lack of enthusiasm with which Boycott greeted Mr Manning, Mr Goddard and Captain Somerset Maxwell – 'it was the tamest and most unemotional scene imaginable', said the *Connaught Telegraph*. Nobody shook hands, Boycott's thanks to the leader of the expedition were of a perfunctory nature and he neither looked at nor spoke to any of the fifty-odd labourers who had come so far to salvage his crops. The *Connaught Telegraph* ascribed this coldness to his surly, unpleasant nature, repeating its contention that his tenants had every reason to 'boycott' him. In fairness to the man, however, it should be remembered that he was not of an emotional disposition, he had not personally initiated the expedition – indeed he had protested (if not over-loudly) that he did not require or need such a force – and it would have been unreasonable to expect a warmer welcome. Moreover, he had realised what having a small army encamped on his property entailed; the advance party of the 19th Hussars and 84th Regiment had already churned up the parkland, supplemented their army rations by purloining, slaying and cooking numerous sheep, chickens and geese, and chopped down for camp fires several of those same trees Boycott had forbidden the tenants to touch.

The inability of Mr Robinson, of the organising committee in Dublin, to provide tents for the expedition proved not to be disastrous, for the army had already provided them, five having been erected for the Ulstermen – ten to each tent – 'with their feet all pointing towards the centre pole', as the Dublin *Daily Express* studiously noted. It was already 1 p.m. by the time the cavalcade reached the estate, so the volunteers proceeded to sort themselves out and make preparations for dinner, and no work was done that day. Even had the men wanted to set to work immediately on their arrival, they would not have been able to do so, as their main baggage including implements, were still *en route* under a cavalry escort. Sleeping arrangements proved difficult, as the men from Monaghan refused to share tents with the men from Cavan and there were arguments about who should have what seemed to be the better-sited tents. Eventually, however, harmony was restored and the spectacle of Cavan fighting Monaghan in Mayo was averted, much – as Bernard Becker recorded – to the sorrow of one Mayo onlooker 'whose eyes sparkled and whose mouth watered at the delicious prospect'.

If Boycott was not over-warm in his greeting at the gate, he did entertain the leaders of the expedition to dinner that night together with the officers, including Colonel Twentyman, who was in command of the troops actually stationed at Lough Mask House, and the resident magistrates, Mr McSheehy, Mr Hamilton, Mr Beckett and Mr Harrall, who were to take it in turns to be on duty in the House during the relief operations. However, there were also reports of dissension during dinner; according to nationalist sources, Mr Manning raised the question of what exactly the Ulster labourers were required to do, and when Boycott replied that they were to dig up his root crops, thresh his corn and generally assist in running the farm, Mr Manning was supposed to have retorted that the labourers were poor, money was short and if Boycott required this extra assistance he would have to pay something towards it. This story seems suspect, it was not true that finances were low – the Dublin *Daily Express* was still printing daily lists of subscriptions to the Boycott relief fund – and it would appear to be an over-elaboration of the popular nationalist theme of Boycott's meanness and lack of gratitude.

While their leaders were being entertained up at the House, the Cavan and Monaghan labourers contented themselves with making their camp as tolerable as possible, building fires (with more wood from Boycott's pine plantations), swigging beer and singing songs before retiring for an early night. After Mr Manning, Mr Goddard and Captain Somerset Maxwell had dined, they retired to the boathouse, which Boycott had placed at their disposal. This was situated on the edge of Lough Mask about a quarter of a mile from the main encampment, and although no bedding was available, it was carpeted and the Ulster Leaders made the best of the inconveniences suffered in a noble cause, and allowed the *Daily Express* correspondent to share their quarters. Thus, again without incident, ended the expedition's first actual day on Lough Mask estate.

CHAPTER 14

'The Dug Out All his Praties and they Thrashed out All his Corn'

During that Friday night there was a torrential rainstorm accompanied by winds approaching gale force which battered the tents – only an unoccupied one was actually blown down – and turned the green lawns into a quagmire. It was said that only Mayo could produce rain in such profusion that it became an instrument of torture, and that the clerk of the weather had definitely enrolled in the Land League. Despite the inclement night the volunteers were up early on the Saturday morning, marching the quarter of a mile to the waters of Lough Mask to wash, returning for breakfast in a stable loft. Another part of the stables had been converted into a cookhouse, with one of the Monaghan contingent, who had previously been an army cook, installed as *chef de cuisine*. It was generally agreed that the commissariat, organised by Mr Robinson, performed its task efficiently and the men breakfasted on slices of compressed beef and biscuits, with mugs of coffee or cocoa. After their meal they lined up and were allotted their tasks; to the Monaghan contingent was given the job of lifting the mangolds, while the Cavan men embarked upon the potatoes; the number of crops the relief force was required to harvest consisted of two acres of potatoes in drills, eight acres of turnips, seven acres of mangolds, and twenty acres of corn that had been cut, but needed threshing. A few men from each contingent stayed behind to attend to the cooking and to start the threshing with Boycott's small hand-thresher. The workers marched to the potato and mangold fields accompanied by Mr Manning, Mr Goddard and

Captain Somerset Maxwell, a police escort and a patrol of the 19th Hussars. All were armed.

That night the Monaghan workers, soaking wet from their day's labour in the fields, decided they had had enough of tent life and moved into the hay-loft, temporarily accompanied by Mr Manning, because the leaders of the expedition had come to the conclusion they should share some of the rigours with their men. Since the Cavan contingent stuck to their tents, Captain Somerset Maxwell was forced to sleep under the dripping canvas. A rumour had reached the camp that a night attack was to be expected, so a password was chosen and the sentries were doubled, but nothing happened. However, rumours of an attack persisted and an extra force of the 84th Regiment was drafted to Lough Mask, thus further burdening Captain Boycott's resources. Although the Ulster volunteers were anxious to continue their labours it was deemed inadvisable to allow them to work on the Sabbath and they spent the miserably wet day amusing themselves as best they could, with divine service in the hayloft providing a diversion in the afternoon.

By Sunday night nothing untoward had happened. The Ulster volunteers had arrived with their revolvers, over one thousand armed troops and the constabulary were encamped in the area, the labourers had set to work on their appointed tasks, while the troops were guarding their every activity. The population of Mayo was apparently showing an extraordinary indifference to the whole affair. The nationalist side attributed this phenomenon to the brilliant organisation and restraining influence of the local Land League leaders, who realised that they were probably in possession of a valuable new weapon and the way to utilise it was, in today's parlance, to play it cool. Playing anything cool does not come easily to the Irish temperament and it is to the credit of the local leaders, such as Father O'Malley, James Daly and Mr Nally, that they kept a firm hand on their excitable followers, restraining the young men with their revolvers and Enfield rifles, dampening down Connaught pride, urging the population to remain calm. The *Connaught Telegraph* had a strong article to this effect: 'Be calm, be cool and, at the same time, resolute and determined ... Treat those mailed and buckshot warriors with silence and contempt ... Show the world over by your calm, but resolute demeanour, that you are worthy of your name and traditions.' It is also to the credit of the absent Michael Davitt that he had succeeded in instilling into some of those who had joined the Land League his belief in the power of non-violence, a more remarkable achievement when considered in the context of Ireland's bloody agrarian history. However, the loyalist side insisted that it was 'due not to the gentle persuasion of the Land League' that thus far peace had been preserved in Mayo, but to the firm (if belated) action of the government which showed that it intended to maintain law and order at whatever cost. At this early juncture, the loyalist sectors on the whole – particularly those who were not actually in Mayo witnessing the extraordinary spectacle – considered the right action had been taken, the threat of the Land League squarely faced, and that the latter would now back down before the government's determination to maintain law and order.

The large number of press correspondents, both nationalist and loyalist, who were actually at Lough Mask, were more equivocal in their assessments of the military endeavour and the effect it was likely to produce. They were all agreed that the situation was still potentially explosive, and would remain so as long as the Ulstermen and the army stayed in the area. Those correspondents who wrote gloomily of waiting on events were not entirely prompted by the need to hold their readers' interest; no one knew what might happen in such a tense atmosphere. The *Connaught Telegraph* had not exaggerated; certainly the eyes and ears of the Western world were upon Lough Mask House and the drama being unfolded there. The American newspapers were avidly following the progress of the relief expedition and if there was not quite the same high degree of enthusiasm on the Continent, there was considerable interest. *Le Figaro*, for example, devoted its weekly 'Correspondance Anglaise' column to 'Incident Boycott', explaining that in Ballinrobe, a small town in county Mayo, Ireland, there were currently seven thousand men – infantry, cavalry and regular police – whose sole mission was to protect Captain Boycott who for some time past had been courageously defying the Land League. It also mentioned the general fear (or hope) of a head-on collision between the Ulstermen and the men of Mayo. It was a justified fear for with such world attention focused on the area, any crank or hero who courted the limelight, or sought to strike a blow for Ireland, had only to perform one wild action and the fuse would be lit.

While waiting for the anticipated explosion, the small army of press correspondents was forced to tread tangential avenues in order to fill the vast amount of space allotted to the story. They complained about the telegraphic facilities – 'The wretched single telegraph wire to Ballinrobe has so utterly failed to do the tremendous duty imposed upon it, and the Telegraphic Department have so utterly failed to do theirs,' said the *Freeman's Journal*, while the Dublin *Daily Express* remarked, 'There is unfortunately only one wire from Ballinrobe to Dublin, and telegraphic communication is therefore carried on under great difficulty. It is a race between the various correspondents as to who will get possession of the wire first.' At least the wire was, on Mr Forster's orders, being kept permanently open whereas normally it was closed half the time. The correspondents expanded a good deal of space on the matter of the geese and sheep that were finding their way into the cooking pots – 'in the absence of more startling events', as the *Express* admitted – although it was generally agreed that the soldiers, not the volunteers, were the culprits. The nationalist papers, in particular, greatly enjoyed themselves elaborating on Bernard Becker's theme that Boycott was being fleeced alike by friend and foe, describing merry scenes round the camp fires as the troops roasted and consumed the purloined stock. The wood to supply the fires also came in for amused comment, and the parallel with the Prime Minister's penchant for tree-felling was made: 'Occasionally a man is to be seen, hatchet in hand doing Gladstone, felling a tree, while numbers surround him ... and as a tree falls loudly cheer the operator as a son of Hawarden Castle.' Nationalist sources also said that the soldiers gave hints to the RIC on how to make camp life tolerable. It should be remembered that some of the constables had been at Lough Mask since the onset of boycotting, as isolated as the Captain himself, in the usual ambivalent position of the police in times of civil disorder, known to the local population, in some cases even liked by them, needed when the population itself was robbed or attacked, but otherwise hated – particularly in an area such as Mayo – as the living symbols of authority. They were housed in two iron huts, whose erection Dublin Castle had sanctioned in the early days of the affair, and they had set up a cookhouse in the cellar of the ruined castle which stands near Lough Mask House. There had been complaints about the inefficient supply of food, and it was said that when Boycott finally gave permission for them to dig up some of his potatoes he himself weighed the amounts and charged ninepence a stone. This report of Boycott's meanness came not from a nationalist paper but from the *Belfast News-Letter*.

Apart from such fascinating topics as stolen geese and axed trees, rumour filled a fair amount of space in the papers; the rumour that a large armed Land League force from Tipperary was *en route* to attack the camp was mentioned, but without much conviction – as the *Express* reporter wrote,' This statement will probably prove as baseless as the others.' There were dissertations upon whether the Ulster contingents were composed entirely of Orangemen, as the nationalist papers and Mayo inhabitants claimed and the conclusion was reached that the men had come not as Orangemen, not as Protestants but as loyalists, true upholders of the Crown and Constitution, and the substantial number of Orangemen in the ranks was accounted for by the fact that they were always to the fore in any loyal enterprise. The most bored pressmen, including the special war correspondents 'full of anecdotes of Plevna, Zululand and the Franco-German war', suggested that if nobody else would attack Lough Mask camp they had better do it themselves. Apart from boredom, the wretched telegraph facilities and the difficulty of getting transport from Ballinrobe to Lough Mask – the *Express* correspondent said his driver refused to make further journeys and he and *The Times* man would be forced to walk – the reporters were also beset by the problem of accommodation. Bernard Becker said there was not a room to be had in Ballinrobe or Claremorris, and that the only decent hotel in the former, the Valkenburgh, 'was crammed to the roof with a closely laid strata of guests, from the American reporter under the roof to the cavalry officer in the front parlour'. The cramped conditions did not improve press tempers, even if they paled into insignificance beside the conditions being endured by the volunteers and troops, both at Lough Mask and in Ballinrobe itself, for a large force remained on the alert in the town, still quartered on the green, which was half under water.

The correspondent from the *Belfast News-Letter*, having spent most of Sunday at Lough Mask House talking to the soldiers and volunteers, commented upon their cheerfulness in the appalling conditions, and pointed out that the toops were, in a way, worse off than the labourers. The latter had a clear objective, they had come to harvest Captain Boycott's crops, there was a job to keep them occupied – whereas the troops, in the absence of any hostile local activity, had little to fill their days. He also commented upon the condition of the officers and troops' uniforms after four days encampment in howling gales and blinding rain, saying a cavalry officer had informed him it would cost at least £12 to replace his spoiled uniform. Finally he admitted, having now been four days in Mayo, that the military endeavour surrounding the enterprise seemed less than necessary, but in case this assertion should appear disloyal he ended with his customary gloomy, though not unwarranted statement, that none dared predict what might happen next.

Late on Sunday night the reporters had some hard news at last.

They learned that Father O'Malley was organising a fund to send fifty men from Mayo on an expedition to Fermanagh, headed by himself, with the object of seeing Lord Erne personally at Crom Castle and demanding the dismissal of Captain Boycott. The next morning, November 15, all the reporters – including the war correspondents, 'thirsting for blood' – were engaged in unearthing more information about this new enterprise which could well lead to real trouble. They had no difficulty in discovering what Father O'Malley was planning, as he had placarded the town with posters and, as Monday was market day, was personally in Ballinrobe explaining his scheme to the market crowds. The posters were addressed to 'The Irish People – Brother Irishmen' thus:

A few minions of the landlords, abusing the name of Ulstermen, have come to Mayo to thwart us in our peaceful struggles against intolerable tyranny; and the forces of the Empire have also been thrown into the scale against us, though maintaining our rights and the rights of the Irish tenant. We have violated no law. These men have been allowed to pass through Mayo without molestation, in order that no bigot might be able to say that they were insulted on account of their creed or of the province they came from. Having offered this pledge of brotherhood to our fellow-countrymen in the North, we now appeal to our sturdy brother farmers of Ulster, be they Orange or Green, Protestant or Catholic, to say whether they will allow our struggle, which is their struggle, to be defeated, or are we to be trampled by the retainers of a few Northern landlords, backed by an illegal use of national force. We are threatened, every man of us, with eviction – which the Prime Minister has called a sentence of death – not because we are unwilling to pay our rents, but because we will not pay them to a man who had made it the business of his life to torment us with the worst forms of feudalism. ...

It was a very long poster, and the remainder had more to say about Boycott's tyranny, outlined the plan to visit Lord Erne, appealed to Irishmen of every creed to send sufficient money to enable the expedition to set forth, and ended with an appeal for the support of their Northern brothers who were suffering under the same evil laws as operated in Mayo. A postscript asked that subscriptions be sent to John O'Malley, P.P. at The Neale, Ballinrobe. Incidentally, the appeal to the Ulstermen who were also suffering from the evil English land laws, followed the lines of the Land League's recent strategy. Parnell had attended meetings in Ulster, increasing emphasis was being laid on the land war as a matter above sectarian or political issues, and there was evidence that it was meeting with success in parts of Ulster.

In the streets of Ballinrobe, Father O'Malley elaborated on his scheme, explaining that it was intended that fifty Mayo men under his leadership should leave on Thursday morning, November 18, accompanied by the brass band as far as Claremorris, where they would catch the train to Cavan, stay overnight in that town and proceed to Crom Castle the next morning, returning home on the Saturday. Newspaper reports also intimated that the expedition would go armed with revolvers, although this seems to have been an assumption of the correspondents rather than the intention of Father O'Malley. The reporters were able to speculate on whether Mr Forster would allow it to proceed to Fermanagh, what would happen if he did, whether it would be met with resistance, and, if it were resisted, what would be the Mayo reaction to the Ulstermen already in their midst.

In the event, Mr Forster was not called upon to hold another exceptional press conference, for the National Land League intervened. They held weekly meetings at their office in Middle Abbey Street, Dublin, and, on November 16, the proposed Fermanagh expedition was discussed at length. The previous day Father O'Malley had telegraphed Thomas Brennan, one of the League's founder members, asking for its approval of the scheme and requesting that sufficient money be advanced to cover the expenses until such time as an adequate public subscription could be collected. Brennan had consulted those committee members he could contact at short notice, and wired back expressing disapproval of the proposed expedition. At the Tuesday meeting,

Father O'Malley's second telegram, in reply, was read out: 'We are deeply disappointed by Mr Brennan's telegram. People here would be disappointed if something effective were not done to counteract the effect of the Orange expedition. Opposition being out of the question, the plan we have hit upon seems to us the only one which combines safety with action, and it would have a great and inspiriting effect upon the agitation. This is not a question of rents but a question of whether Captain Boycott or the people shall win. If we succeed in displacing him, victory is complete. If Lord Erne remains obdurate, we will have the credit of having, unarmed, done in the North of Ireland what the Orangemen in Mayo have done under the protection of the army . . .' It was a very long telegram, brevity not being o e of O'Malley's virtues, and continued by saying that the Land League itself need not be involved or compromised, but would the Land League please advance the expenses; if they could not do that would they at least not discourage the Mayo initiative, and a prompt decision would be appreciated.

In the ensuing discussion none of the Land League leaders thus appealed to showed enthusiasm for the project. Their reasons for rejecting it were varied; T. D. Sullivan, the nationalist poet and MP, did not care for it, chiefly because the idea of the tenants trailing up to see Lord Erne and offering to pay their rents if only Boycott were removed, indicated a lack of spirit, with which view Thomas Brennan concurred. T. P. O'Connor, the noted journalist and MP, considered the project wild but supposed its poetic justice appealed to the men of Mayo, however he could not see that it would achieve anything, other than perhaps proving that the Land League members could go into the North unarmed, as had recently such leaders as Mr Parnell and Mr Dillon. It was also pointed out that Lord Erne was not in residence at Crom Castle but currently on his way to London, a circumstance overlooked by Father O'Malley. Interestingly, the point was not raised that what was occurring at Lough Mask was to the absolute advantage of the Land League, and that to spoil it by an unnecessary, rather childish piece of retaliation would be ridiculous. The meeting then wandered into other avenues, including a discussion of the steps that could or should be taken against 'those two landlord organs of slander and calumny', the Dublin *Daily Express* and the Dublin *Evening Mail*, and a resolution was passed requesting Mr James Redpath to continue in his splendid service to the Land League by propagating its cause on his return to the United States. However, a brief telegram was despatched to Father O'Malley, condensing the views of Brennan and T. D. Sullivan thus: 'League meeting fully discussed question, and considered the dignified course for the tenants to adopt is to stay at home, and let the landlord come and look for his rent.'

O'Malley accepted the decision and abandoned the project, if somewhat reluctantly, as a letter he sent to the *Freeman's Journal* indicated. In this he said his opinion on the matter remained strong and unchanged, he considered that a visit to Fermanagh would have revealed the true feelings of the Ulster tenant farmers (as opposed to the image given by the relief expedition), and that it would have achieved the desired effect of convincing Lord Erne that the Lough Mask tenantry had nothing against him personally, had no wish to withhold their rents, but that Boycott was the root of the trouble. However, he said, he yielded his judgement to that of wiser counsels, and could only thank those Irishmen in England and elsewhere who had already sent subscriptions which would be speedily returned. This piece of hard and possibly interesting news had lasted no more than twenty-four hours.

The great sensation of Tuesday, November 16, was, as the *Freeman's Journal* enthusiastically noted, 'the expedition of Captain Boycott and a troop of Hussars in search of a missing herd of cattle'. In addition to his lease of Lough Mask farm and the ownership of the Kildarra estate (which was never mentioned), Boycott also leased a farm near Kilmaine, a village five miles to the south-east of Ballinrobe. The herdsmen in charge of the Kilmaine cattle, having received threatening letters, had walked out on the Monday and during the night the cattle either strayed or were deliberately let loose. On the Tuesday morning Boycott was given the news that his herd was wandering round Mayo, and duly departed from Lough Mask accompanied by the Hussars to try and round them up. In scenes that were, according to the *Freeman's Journal*, reminiscent of the famous chase in Don Quixote when 'the warriors bold searched for the wandering beeves', all but a few of the animals were traced and led to Lough Mask farm under cavalry escort and, as the *Daily Express* reported, 'half a troop of Hussars guarding a herd of cattle along the road was certainly a most unusual sight'.

On Wednesday, November 17, the weather again changed, bitter winter arrived, with the mountains of Maam Turk wrapped in leaden grey clouds, while alternate showers of sleet and snow swept the encampment. The press corps was able to report that the mangolds and potatoes had all been harvested before the sudden shift in temperature; only a few turnips remained to be dug out. On Wednesday they also had two incidents of more riveting interest to transmit to the waiting world. The first concerned what the *Express* termed 'a day attack upon the camp' and the *Freeman's Journal* 'the irruption of Mr J. W. Nally, of Balla, the well known popular leader, into the very centre of the camp'. Accompanied by a Land League friend called Mr Joyce, Nally had been out shooting in the vicinity of Boycott's estate, after which defiant enterprise – they were men of Mayo and had the right to go shooting in Mayo – they decided to visit the famous camp itself. Despite the rigorous security precautions, the armed police on guard at the gate and the troops patrolling the grounds, the two men managed to penetrate to the heart of the camp. There they chatted to the soldiers – the volunteers were mostly out digging up the turnips – and were introduced to Mr Goddard. Nally represented his friend Joyce as a clergyman who he said was anxious to preach the true gospel to the Ulstermen. Mr Goddard accepted the proposition, '*au grand serieux*' according to the *Freeman's Journal*, asked to which denomination the clergyman belonged, and was told the Church of Ireland. However the

success of the joke went to Nally and Joyce's head and they proceeded to indulge in behaviour inconsistent with that of serious-
minded reverend gentlemen, Mr Goddard's suspicions were finally
aroused, and when he was told the gospel the visitors wished to
preach was that of the land for the people, he called the guards
and 'after a lively interchange of compliments' Nally and Joyce
were led back to the gate under heavy escort.

There was a second incident that day which united the press,
nationalist and loyalist. In the afternoon, when the press corps
arrived for its daily visit to the camp, it was refused admittance
by Colonel Twentyman of the Hussars who was in command of
the troops at Lough Mask House. The reason attributed to
Twentyman for the ban, mainly by the loyalist papers, – the
nationalist ones were simply outraged – was that a report had
appeared stating that forty-seven sheep belonging to Boycott
had been slain by the 19th Hussars. It seems an odd reason, as all
newspapers had been mentioning the disappearance of Boycott's
stock for days, but Colonel Twentyman was obviously dis-
pleased with the report and took the revenge within his power. It
was short-lived; as one body, the pressmen returned to Ballinrobe,
uttering loud words about the secrecy and irresponsibility of
martial law and the ill-advisedness of denying admission to the
one group of people upon which depended reliable reporting of a
situation of vital interest. Once back in Ballinrobe, the reporters
descended on the headquarters of Colonel and Brevet-Brigadier
General Bedingfield, R.A., who was in command of the entire
military force in the area. Bedingfield listened to the story of the
action taken by his subordinate and promptly rescinded the ban.

The main news on Wednesday, however, was that Boycott had
decided to leave Lough Mask House and return to England.
Rumours to this effect had been circulating for some time, but
had hitherto remained unconfirmed. It transpired that, on November 15, Boycott had written to a gentleman in Dublin, informing
him that he and his wife intended to leave with the expeditionary
force and spend some time with friends in England, as he was,

and would be for some time to come, 'both mentally and physically unable to undertake any active duties'. He further added – and the letter was intended for publication – that it was not only the present situation that was responsible for his condition, but also his future prospects, or lack of them: 'It is impossible for me to farm when I can neither buy nor sell; and the one word – ruin – expresses my state.'

To corroborate the news contained in this letter, Boycott gave interviews to several correspondents, notably the *Express* man, in which he stressed the toll the affair had taken on his health and the apparent hopelessness of his situation. (Incidentally, Annie Boycott's confinement to her room for several days as a result of the pressures of the last two months was reported in a nationalist paper; it was one of the few references made to the unfortunate woman.) To emphasise how unpleasant his situation was, Boycott showed the *Express* reporter some of the threatening letters he had received – his escritoire was apparently filled with them – the most lurid of which read as follows:

HEBURN, (*sic*) NOV. 14

Sir,
You have caused a great deal of disturbance in the County Mayo these last five months about your crops. You need not give yourself any trouble about the affairs of this world, for if you had all the police and soldiers in Her Majesty's Government you shall fail. You will not have protection at hand at all times to call on. You need not leave Ireland to go to London, there is too many of your countrymen there. The best thing you can do is to pray for your soul, for there is no mercy on this side of the grave, for I main (*sic*) to lay you. There is one of the Leitrim heroes on the banks of the Tyne, and I hope in providence that he will have the happiness of seeing you some time, and will put a crop in the ground that will yield fruit. None of us belong to the weast (*sic*) of Ireland; we belong to the North of Ireland, but we do not like tirney (*sic*). So no more at present.
RORY OF THE HILLS

This not over-literate epistle was accompanied by a drawing of a coffin on which was written, 'Here lies the body of the tirant (*sic*) Capt. Boycott'. According to the *Express* man, Boycott treated such letters with the contempt they deserved, and it was certainly not on their account that he was planning to leave Ireland for the time being. Indeed, had Boycott been the type of man liable to have been intimidated by anonymous letters, he would have left Lough Mask considerably earlier and the whole Boycott affair would not have happened.

On Thursday, November 18, the correspondents had little to report other than that the weather was still bitterly cold, and the relations between the press and Colonel Twentyman – 'a gallant, good-hearted, but somewhat choleric officer' – had been happily restored to their previous good footing, with the latter apologising for the language he had used during the previous day's contretemps. The *Express* was also able to report that a £30 subscription had been received for the Boycott relief fund from the Countess of Erne. (Her husband's failure to take action to succour his beleaguered land-agent had been unfavourably commented upon in several quarters, although Lord Erne had sent £5 subscription to the fund in its early days. It should be remembered that he was seventy-eight years old and, reputedly, partially senile.) On Friday, November 19, there was 'no news of the smallest interest' according to the *Freeman's Journal*, while the *Express* concentrated its attention on the £100 subscription to the Boycott fund received from the London *Daily Telegraph*.

The first week of the relief expedition's endeavours were over; the arrival of the fifty-odd Ulstermen in Mayo had passed without incident; the anticipated civil strife and bloodshed had not erupted, the only casualties being Major Coghill with his broken leg, several members of the constabulary and soldiery who were suffering from rheumatism or chest complaints brought on by the adverse weather, and the cavalry horses which were in a bad state after being quartered in the open in November, in the quagmire of Lough Mask camp. What the expedition had achieved in its first week was to focus world-wide attention on the affair and thereby on the Land League and the whole Irish situation. It had also established the use of the word 'boycott'. Newspapers were already writing of the policy that had added this ugly word to the English language and of the Captain having immortalised his surname. And it was not only in the United Kingdom, or in other countries where English was spoken, that the word was being absorbed into the language. *Le Figaro*, for example, was writing, '*Les gais irlandais ont inventé un nouveau mot, ils disent à présent 'boycotter' quelqu'un, cela signifie le mettre en interdit'.*

* The bright Irish have invented a new word, they are currently saying to *boycott* somebody, meaning to ostracise him.

'And Nothing Interrupted their Enterprising Work but the Pouring Rain from Heaven and the Wind from Maam Turk'

At the end of the first week the nationalist papers ceased to give space to 'the invasion of Mayo'. Weather reports, and how many mangolds and turnips and potatoes had been dug from Boycott's farm, had become too boring for further words. They refocused their attention on Parnell, his defence fund for the trial, and the activities of the Land League and debated what manner of land Bill Gladstone would introduce into the next session of Parliament. They also had the news of Michael Davitt's return to his native shores, in time as he himself said, 'to enjoy the discomfiture of Mayo landlordism in the costly failure of the Lough Mask expedition'.

Davitt's tour had taken him the length and breadth of the United States and in Chicago he had encountered Major Henri le Caron, the most famous English spy of the period, who had successfully penetrated Fenian circles in the States. Davitt, who had then obviously no idea of le Caron's true role, said he seemed 'a rather commonplace and by no means interesting personality' and that he kindly supplied a remedy for the insomnia from which Davitt had suffered since his years on Dartmoor. In Virginia City he met another extraordinary personality, J. W. Mackay, 'the Silver King', who put the following proposition to him – 'Why not leave the whole island to England, bring your people all over here, settled them down in Nebraska or Colorado, and call the state New Ireland or Home Rule, or whatever you like, and end the whole trouble?' Having made this simplistic suggestion, Mackay, a multi-millionaire, then refrained from contributing to the Land League funds, although Davitt admitted that as a fund-raiser he had the prime failing of not asking people outright for contributions. If he was bad at raising money he was excellent at organisation, throughout his travels he impressed people with his sincerity and integrity, succeeded in setting up branches of the Land League in the towns and cities he visited, and in generally breathing life into the American movement so that the money to enable the Irish league to continue its struggle was forthcoming.

Davitt docked in Cork on November 20, and gave a press conference which was well covered by the nationalist and loyalist papers. He announced that he was the bearer of presents from Mr Parnell's American friends, including an illuminated address granting Parnell the freedom of Chicago, and that he had a message from Mrs Parnell to her son. This told him to be of good cheer and, with typical Parnell sang-froid, said that if the forthcoming prosecution went against him a few months in jail would do him no harm. Davitt emphasised that his American tour had prospered, said that the Irish land question was now of comsuming interest to the Americans and that the majority of them favoured the Land League's policy of agitation and proposals for a settlement. He was not exaggerating, the League had succeeded in capturing American attention, a circumstance that had been greatly assisted by the Boycott relief expedition.

Nationalist sources were already writing off the expedition as a costly failure in moral as well as financial terms, but it was not yet over, and something might yet happen to upset the calm, although even the most gloomy (or optimistic) of correspondents now thought it unlikely. Several of the loyalist papers and the news agencies continued valiantly to cover the news from Lough Mask, notably the Dublin *Daily Express*, which, of course, had been responsible for proposing the idea originally. On Saturday, November 20, the weather remained fine but a sharp frost descended, freezing the water in the tents and turning the roads into skating rinks. Several of the horses were sent to Ballinrobe under escort to have their shoes roughed by the barrack farrier so that they might better cope with the icy roads on the following Monday when it was intended to bring in the hay from Boycott's Kilmaine farm. Mr Goddard proposed that sports be organised for the troops in the camp, an idea that was enthusiastically welcomed but subsequently abandoned. Two troops of the 19th Hussars were withdrawn from Lough Mask House and entrained at Claremorris for their home barracks in Dublin, a departure which underlined the government's belief that nothing further would happen, and which passed without attention from the local population. A consignment of Boycott's cattle went under constabulary escort to Claremorris, to await a cattle truck for Dublin where they were to be sold, a movement which did not, however, pass unnoticed. As soon as it became known they were Boycott's cattle, people turned out in their hundreds, hissing and booing and hooting, and everybody agreed that feeling against the Captain personally remained as high as ever. When the animals reached Dublin, the drovers threatened not to handle them but eventually, although they attracted a great deal of attention as they stood patiently in their pens at the New Cattle Market, they were sold at a reasonable profit and Boycott received the cheque before he left Lough Mask House.

On Sunday, November 21, the severe frost lessened, but a biting wind blew down from the mountains of Maam Turk and across the waters of Lough Mask, chilling the marrow of the soldiers, volunteers and constables alike, and the next day the weather again changed for the worse, the high winds bringing with them icy rain and sleet which reduced the camp to a pool of freezing slush. All the remaining correspondents started their day's news with a weather report, for the elements were of vital interest to everybody on the spot, if not to an outside world that had expected riot and bloodshed. Brevet Brigadier General Bedingfield, the officer commanding the whole area had become most anxious about the state of the cavalry horses, and the rumours that he wished to withdraw the remaining two troops of the 19th Hussars from Lough Mask were not well received by the Ulster volunteers. It was felt by them, and their leaders, that the withdrawal of the particular protection offered by the Hussars might, even at this late stage, cause trouble, encouraging the more ardent Land Leaguers in the area to attack the camp. One of the leaders, Captain Somerset Maxwell, had escaped from the miserable conditions at Lough Mask by spending several days at near-by Ashford as the guest of Lord and Lady Ardilaun. Incidentally, by other than the most ardent loyalists, the leader of the Cavan contingent was not kindly dealt with; the notion that his presence was 'an electioneering manoeuvre calculated to bring to the fore Mr Somerset Maxwell at the next contest for the county of Cavan' had a wide circulation. Otherwise, despite the inclement weather, the farming tasks continued briskly, the operation to bring Boycott's hay from his Kilmaine farm was successfully accomplished and seven loaded carts returned under a large infantry and constabulary escort, personally supervised by Mr Goddard. Threshing and winnowing continued with equal briskness and one of the lofts was already stocked with as fine white oats as the *Express* reporter had ever seen, and it was felt that the inhabitants of Mayo would learn a valuable lesson from the industry of the Ulstermen.

The big news of the day was that, at the Ballinrobe Petty Sessions, fifteen local inhabitants were charged 'with having on 1st November, 1880, at Ballinrobe, unlawfully assembled for the purpose of obstructing and intimidating Captain Boycott of Lough Mask House, and for having obstructed him in his passage through the said town upon his lawful business, to the disturbance and terror of Her Majesty's liege subjects, and against the peace and dignity of our Lady the Queen, her Crown and dignity'. This referred to the occasion when Boycott had been molested after attending the Petty Sessions to hear the complaint of Branigan for his outstanding wages. The Crown had at last felt able to assert its authority and take legal action. However the actual hearing was adjourned.

On the morning of Tuesday, November 23, the weather improved sufficiently to allow army wagons to transport the newly-thrashed corn to Cong *en route* for sale in Dublin, and, by kind permission of Colonel Twentyman, the *Express* correspondent was allowed to accompany the convoy. In a rather weary memorandum, Mr Forster had earlier sanctioned the use of the army wagons thus: 'If it be the case that without the use of the Army Service Corps wagons the military will be obliged to remain some days longer in camp at Ballinrobe, and if the Commander-in-Chief on military grounds thinks this course is desirable, I think it had better be done'. Also with the convoy was Mr Robinson, the proprietor of the Dublin *Daily Express* and organiser of the expedition's supplies, who had descended from Dublin during the last few days. Mr Robinson wore his habitual tam o'shanter, a mode of headgear that had earned the expedition a new name locally, 'the Tam o'Shanter brigade'.

On the return journey the *Express* man noted a marked change in the behaviour of the local population – 'No one touched his hat or wished you good morning: so great a change has been effected in a people by nature kindly and good-natured by the teaching of the Land League'. This statement allowed *The Nation* to indulge in irony – 'This is really awful! Think of the number of country people passing by the correspondent of the *Express* – passing also, perhaps, Mr Robinson himself, habited in his Tam o'Shanter – without touching their hats!' In more serious vein, the *Express* man's observation underlined the myths that had emerged about the simple, courteous, dignified, humorous peasant, who would be all those things if only he were left to himself. When it was discovered that some Irish peasants could be rude, stupid, cunning or totally lacking in humour, the blame was laid on malign outside influence. One aspect of change in the peasant outlook, on which nearly all observers agreed, was that they had ceased to be wholly subservient; it could be said that Michael Davitt's 'gosepel of manhood' was taking effect.

By Thursday, November 25, after a night of torrential rain and gale force winds, words failed to describe the condition of the camp. Walking round with Boycott's friend, Ashton Weekes – whom, incidentally, most correspondents describe as being beloved of the peasantry, in contrast to their feelings towards Boycott himself – the *Express* man visualised himself disappearing into the Mayo mud, but Weekes cheered him up by saying there was a strata of solid rock beneath the ground, so they could only sink to their knees. All the tasks required of the Ulster volunteers had been virtually completed, and preparations were under way to strike camp as rapidly as possible. During the day, Mr Wynne, a photographer, arrived from Castlebar and in torrential rain took photographs of the expedition. One Monaghan man who insisted on wearing his Orange scarf, was told to remove it by Captain Somerset Maxwell, and refused, whereupon the whole Monaghan contingent threatened to withdraw from the proceedings, but were eventually cajoled into posing, without scarves, and 'oblingingly allowed their faces and figures to be handed down to posterity'.

Father O'Malley had also been busy preparing for the departure, and placards were posted in Ballinrobe and the neighbouring villages bearing the message:

Men of Mayo – in the name of the Lough Mask tenants, for the sake of the cause which they are so manfully upholding, you are earnestly entreated to permit the Orangemen and the English army to take themselves away out of your outraged county unmolested and unnoticed.

November 25 1880   JOHN O'MALLEY P.P.

The press still speculated on whether what loyalists described as 'the pent up wrath of the defeated Mayomen' would exhibit itself during the next forty-eight hours, despite O'Malley's appeals. There was also much speculation about Boycott's future. It was agreed that feeling against him in the area was so high that he could not remain at Lough Mask House once the military had departed. The loyalists emphasised that he had not announced his intention of leaving Ireland permanently, but was merely going to England for a well-earned rest; they also insisted that there was no confirmation of a rumour that Lord Erne had relieved him of his job as land agent.

Despite the continuing animosity towards Boycott, a great deal of magnanimity was suddenly being shown towards the Ulster volunteers, and there was even talk of providing carriages for the return journey to Claremorris. Many nationalists had decided that the volunteers were not riff-raff from the Belfast slums – on the contrary the majority had proved to be as decent a group of men as the labourers of Mayo themselves, and they had merely been misled by their own landlords, without understanding the true situation at Lough Mask. In local circles, it was said that now they did understand the situation they had been converted and, disgusted by their reception at Boycott's hands, were returning north as ardent Land Leaguers. Loyalists said they were *not* disgusted by their reception (a view the scenes at the departure would seem to uphold) and the Land League conversion wish was doubtless father to the thought.

Before the final departure from Lough Mask, the Press Association correspondent took the opportunity of interviewing the man whose name and influence had been so much in the news, Father O'Malley. With the actual Boycott affair, O'Malley dealt but briefly, concentrating his attention on what boycotting was about, a lever which the tenant farmers of Mayo, and Ireland in general, could use to extract a good land Bill from the Liberal administration. O'Malley said that what the tenant farmers required was what had become widely known as 'the three F's', fixity of tenure, fair rents and free sale. (In loyalist circles they were interpreted as fraud, force and folly.) Fair rents and fixity of tenure were intertwined; rents must be regulated by government valuation subject to periodic reassessment, and a legal registration must be made when a tenant took over a holding – it could be done at the post office – which guaranteed fixity of tenure providing he paid his rent regularly and farmed his land suitably. Free sale explained itself; when a tenant wished to sell a holding he must be recompensed for the goodwill and the improvements effected during his tenure. Father O'Malley concluded the interview by saying he felt certain Mr Gladstone intended to introduce a Bill that would settle the Irish land question for many years to come, and that both the Prime Minister and Mr Forster were sincere in their desire to benefit Ireland and her people. However, the past history of his country had forced him to the conclusion that unless attention were directed towards Ireland 'by some extraordinary event like the Boycott expedition', the genuine grievances would go unremedied. In general, O'Malley showed himself to be far more of a Fabian than a Fenian, believing that the condition of Ireland could only be rectified by a slow and gradual process of reform.

CHAPTER 16

'There was Much that was Ridiculous in the Whole Business'

On Friday, November 26, just two weeks from the day they had set foot on Lough Mask estate, the members of the Relief Expedition and their large escort prepared to leave. That night, as if to uphold the nationalist joke that the clerk of the weather had joined the Land League, the worst storm that Mayo had endured in years burst over the area. In the early evening inky black clouds shrouded the mountains of Maam Turk, then the fury of the storm was unleashed, screaming winds and lashing rain swept across Lough Mask, whipping the water into huge white-crested waves, uprooting trees and hurling them across roads, tearing the roofs from houses, ripping some of the tents in the encampment to pieces, carrying others bodily away. It was after a sleepless night, spent battling with the elements and the tents, that the volunteers and troops greeted a calmer morning, while 'the more privileged occupants of the boathouse', namely the expedition leaders, discovered that a large boat had been lifted from the Lough and pitched on to the shelving floor. The storm had also broken the telegraph wire between Ballinrobe and Tuam, which meant that the press correspondents were forced to transmit to Dublin via an unprepared Claremorris. As the *Express* man noted: 'It is an unfortunate coincidence that the arrival and departure of the expedition should have been marked by hitches in the telegraphic arrangements,' adding that he had no idea whether the despatch he was now composing would get through. In fact his did and he had the distinction of being one of the few correspondents whose copy appeared the next day – most newspapers had not received the despatches in time and were forced to hold over the news of the departure until Monday.

The knowledge that they were leaving must have helped counteract the fatigue induced by the restless night, and when the order was given to be ready to depart at two o'clock, volunteers and troops enthusiastically embarked on the task of striking camp. The Army Service Corps wagons rumbled up, baggage and implements were loaded into them and, within a very short time, the camp was down, leaving only the tents of the Hussars, who were staying on to protect Boycott and his family until the next morning, and the ground strewn with 'cannisters, boxes and other debris of the commissariat'. When it was time to fall in, the volunteers marched to the front of Lough Mask House, headed by Captain Somerset Maxwell, Mr Goddard, Mr Manning and Mr Robinson in his tam o'shanter. On the steps of the house stood Captain Boycott, his wife and niece while around them and behind them were the officers and some of the troops, the press correspondents and the artists from the weekly illustrated papers, the latter busily sketching. Boycott had discarded his rifle, carrying instead a sheep hook. He handed a letter to Captain Somerset Maxwell which this gentleman proceeded to read to the assembly:

My Dear Captain Maxwell and Gentlemen: As leaders of the Boycott Relief Expedition, I cannot allow you to depart from Lough Mask without expressing to you and the brave men who have so nobly accompanied you to my relief, my deep and heartfelt gratitude for the generous and timely aid you have one and all rendered to me by saving my crops, and for the many sacrifices of comfort and convenience you have endured on my behalf. The difficult and unsolicited task you undertook, and have so fully and ably carried out in the face of many and great difficulties, would to men not possessed of your unflinching determination have proved insurmountable. With you and your worthy band of stalwart labourers, whose untiring exertions, good conduct, and self-sacrifice I cannot too highly praise, I

am compelled, for reasons now well-known, to quit with my
wife a happy home, where we had hoped, with God's help, to
have spent the remainder of our days. Mrs Boycott joins me in
again thanking you all from our hearts for the signal service you
have rendered us. Believe us, my dear Captain Maxwell and
gentlemen, Yours very faithfully,

C. C. Boycott.

After a brief silence, a great cheer suddenly rent the air and, once
started, the men went on cheering for Captain Boycott, then they
cheered Captain Somerset Maxwell and the other leaders, and
everybody was shaking hands with everybody else and congratulating themselves on the success of the mission, and, in the
emotion of the moment, even Boycott's 'rigid reserve and
depression', as *The Times* described it, melted. He came down the
steps and mingled with the throng, shaking hands with each
volunteer in turn, personally thanking each for his effort, receiving
the replies: 'You're welcome, your honour' and 'You know where
to find us again when you want us'. After the emotion had subsided, the volunteers formed back into line and, giving a further
cheer for Captain and Mrs Boycott, started to march away from
the open ground in front of the house, down the long avenue that
leads to the front gates. As the *Belfast News-Letter* commented:
'The parting was certainly very much warmer than the meeting'.
The military escort was already drawn up along the edges of the
avenue close to where the main encampment had been, and the
volunteers halted as they approached the troops. In the churned-
up parkland, surrounded by the debris of the expedition, ensued a
scene of even greater enthusiasm than that just enacted before the
house. The volunteers shook hands with the troops, cheers were
given for the Orangemen and caps were flung into the air, cheers
were given for the Hussars, the 84th Regiment, the press, the
magistrates and the officers (the long-suffering RIC appear to
have been omitted) and, according to the man from the *News-
Letter*, 'a crisis in the outburst of sentiment was reached when

Lieutenant Freeman of Her Majesty's 19th Hussars and Captain
Maxwell, the leader of the Boycott expedition, rushed into each
other's arms and hugged each other with vigour'. Then everybody started singing 'For auld lang syne' and 'For they are jolly
good fellows', while the regimental cook, in full working attire,
borrowed a scabbard from a Hussar's sabre and proceeded to
wield it as a baton, a cause of much merriment. Eventually the
bugle sounded and, with a further hearty cheer, the cavalcade was
under way.

A fifty-strong escort of constabulary was in the van, with the
wagons following them, then the volunteers, surrounded by the
84th Regiment, while at the iron gates to the estate they were
joined by a further escort of 1st Dragoons. After the night's
storm, the skies were clear and the march into Ballinrobe was
undertaken in as fine weather as the expedition had experienced.
There was hardly a soul on the roads to witness the departure of
'the queerest menagerie that ever came into Connaught', only a
few noisy children, the odd head raised from behind a stone wall
and – according to Michael Davitt – Father O'Malley and an old
lady. Davitt reported that when O'Malley espied her he advanced
and said, 'Did I not warn you to let the British army alone? How
dare you come to intimidate Her Majesty's troops? For shame!
Be off now, and if you dare to molest these two thousand heroes
after their glorious campaign I'll make an example of you. Be
off!'

As the convoy neared Ballinrobe, the Dragoons closed in round
the Ulstermen, and as it turned a corner, a shot was heard from
near-by woods and a momentary tension ran through its length.
Nothing further was heard, and the cavalcade moved into the main
street, which was lined with spectators, but the verbal uproar that
had greeted the arrival was absent, and the members of the cavalcade quickly disappeared into the infantry barracks where they
were to spend the night before embarking on the last lap of the
return journey

At 3 a.m. the next morning, November 27, reveille sounded in the Ballinrobe infantry barracks; at 4 a.m. troops and volunteers breakfasted, and, just before 6 a.m., they left the barracks and wheeled into the streets of the town that probably none of them wished to see again. The long procession moved through the greyness of the early morning light, with only the tramp of feet, the rattle of the wagons wheels, the snorting of the horses and the jingle of the Hussars' accoutrements breaking the silence. Troops of dragoons patrolled the roads from Ballinrobe through Hollymount to Claremorris, but the only incident concerned an accident to a Hussar's horse, as it had, coincidentally, on the inward march with Major Coghill's steed.

In the meantime Captain Boycott, his wife and niece had left Lough Mask House, at an early hour, in an ambulance wagon escorted by twenty troopers of the 19th Hussars and accompanied by Mr Hamilton, one of the resident magistrates. Previously Mr McSheehy, the Ballinrobe magistrate, had tried to hire a carriage for Boycott and although the owner of the Valkenburgh Hotel had offered to loan his, no driver could be found to undertake the journey. Consequently, Mr McSheehy had applied to Colonel Bedingfield who had placed an ambulance wagon at Boycott's disposal. (No mention was made of Mr Ashton Weekes or Arthur St John Boycott, so they must have left earlier by alternative transport.) The estate was not left unguarded, as Mr McSheehy reported: 'It was deemed advisable not to remove all the military and police from Lough Mask on the same day, so there remain some fifty men of the 84th, an equal number of the police until Tuesday, Mr Harrell, R.M., remains in charge'.

The Boycotts' transport caught up with the main body of the convoy about a mile outside Claremorris, and a passage was made for it through the sprawling convoy, which Boycott acknowledged by raising his hat to the labourers and troops. According to loyalist sources the effect of this flying cavalcade on the watching labourers was immense; they saw a fugitive, hunted and persecuted, driven from his home, his future uncertain, escaping from the wrath of his enemies in an army ambulance under cavalry escort, and that the scene they had just witnessed was the direct outcome of the Land League's teachings was not lost upon them. At Claremorris station the Boycotts were not subjected to a hostile display, although Mr Nally – the local Land League leader who had penetrated the heart of the camp – was on the platform to witness their departure. Just before 10.50 a.m. the scheduled train from Westport to Dublin steamed in, the Boycotts took their seats in a first class compartment accompanied by Mr Hamilton and Colonel Bruce of the RIC, the whistle blew, the Ulstermen who had by now also arrived at the station doffed their caps, and the train departed. Thus Boycott left the county in which he had lived for nearly thirty years, a notorious man, the possessor of verbal immortality.

The advent in Claremorris of the main cavalcade had likewise occasioned no hostile demonstrations. Loyalist sources attributed their absence, in sharp contrast to the hostility shown at their arrival, to the fact that the men of Mayo had learned that the government intended to maintain law and order; that their evil policy of boycotting could and would be defeated by military force if necessary. Nationalist sources attributed it to the fact that the people knew they had won, that there were not sufficient numbers of Queen's horses or Queen's men to prevent boycotting if the tenant farmers of Ireland pursued it relentlessly. Shortly after the Boycotts' train had disappeared into the distance, two special trains steamed into the station, one to carry the labourers, the returning troops and the immediate baggage, the other for the heavier baggage and supplies. The labourers helped load the latter before taking their seats, and correspondents noted that the soldiers appeared to have suffered more from the fortnight at Lough Mask than the labourers. At 11.30 a.m. the first train bearing the volunteers and their leaders, the men of the 84th Regiment and their officers, drew out of Claremorris station preceded by a pilot engine. At about 12.30 the second special train left, an exceptionally long one as, in addition to Colonel Twentyman, the Hussars, Mr Robinson, and the baggage wagons, it included the cavalry horse boxes. Thus the Boycott relief expedition departed from Mayo.

In the meantime, the Boycotts' train proceeded towards Dublin without incident; at one or two stations people called out to ask whether he was on it but when he showed himself, boldly, according to loyalist sources, they failed to recognise him. At the Broadstone terminus in Dublin, Boycott's arrival attracted some attention but there were no demonstrations hostile or otherwise, and he, his wife and niece were escorted to the Hamman Hotel in Upper Sackville Street by detectives, who stayed to protect them, while a constable was posted at the door of the hotel. Later the same night, Broadstone terminus was the scene of greater excitement when the special train bearing the horses and baggage arrived after a long slow journey from Claremorris. A much larger crowd turned out to witness the disbandment of the relief expedition than had gathered to see the Boycotts' arrival, but again there were no demonstrations.

The special train with the volunteers and troops had travelled to Athlone without incident, and at Athlone the men of the 84th Regiment bade farewell to the Ulstermen and returned to their barracks at the Curragh. The train steamed on towards Cavan, encountering a mild outburst of booing on Mullingar station, and, at Ballywillan, Captain Somerset Maxwell and ten of his men left and proceeded under constabulary escort to their near-by homes. At Cavan, the remainder of the men detrained, those who lived in the immediate area went home, while the Monaghan contingent boarded another special train which took them to Clones. There they joined the mail train from Dublin, arriving in Monaghan at 9.45 p.m. to be greeted by a large crowd, the Constitutional Brass Band and a strong force of police in case of Land League disturbance and the over-exuberance of the rapturous crowd. They were then entertained at a sumptuous feast by Colonel Lloyd. After the meal there were speeches and toasts – to the successful accomplishment of the mission, the exemplary conduct of the contingent, and the excellent organisation provided by Colonel Lloyd throughout. It was then announced that the men would be further entertained to a public dinner in the town during the course of the next week by the nobility and gentry of the neighbourhood.

The organisers of the relief expedition had every reason to be pleased with themselves. They had propelled a reluctant Liberal administration into a show of armed force in the name of law and order; they had entered Mayo without incident; they had accomplished what they had set out to do with a display of industry and cheerfulness under the worst possible conditions; all this, for them if not for others, spelled the intimidation of the Land League and a successful confrontation with lawlessness. However, the persecution of the man they had gone to save did not end with his arrival in Dublin. Boycott had intended to stay in the Irish capital for about a week, but on the Tuesday after his arrival, he was subjected to the same sort of treatment he had received in Mayo, being followed by a hissing and hooting mob. He was by now accustomed, if not inured, to such receptions and it is doubtful whether a hostile crowd would have driven him from Dublin before he wished to leave. But the proprietor of the Hamman Hotel had received threatening letters, two of which were published and read as follows: 'I am giving you notice that if you keep him I will Boycott you. A Straight Tip', and, 'We warn you that if you keep Mr Boycott in your hotel another day your life is in danger. As a friend I give you warning. You are marked for vengeance already; and as for Boycott he need not crow till he gets out of the wood. There were closer watched men than he shot in Dublin: and I do not think he will bring his life out of it. Rory'. *The Times* commented that it was only too true that people had recently been shot in the area of the Hamman Hotel, in the very centre of Dublin, and it was believed that Fenians likely to commit such outrages lived in the surrounding streets. The hotel proprietor certainly took the letters seriously, and it was at his request that the Boycotts suddenly packed up and left for England, by the Holyhead mail boat, on the morning of December 1. It was a sudden departure as a banquet had been arranged in their honour by the Dublin promoters of the Relief Expedition at the Shelbourne Hotel that same evening, but doubtless the proprietor's fears proved to be the final straw, and to the nationalists' delight, the Boycotts removed themselves from the wood, leaving the country 'to the blarsted Irish' as the *Irish World* gleefully reported.

CHAPTER 17

'The Moral Force Artillery of the Land League – Better than Any 81-ton gun'

The assessments and analyses of the implications of boycotting had started almost as soon as the incident had become news, and once the relief expedition was over, they gathered momentum. There was much amused comment over the recent spectacles of crack troops guarding cattle down deserted Mayo roads and patrolling while labourers dug up mangolds. The *Nation* added its poetic contribution to the chorus of amusement thus:

BYCUT'S VOLUNTEERS OR THE RELIEF OF LOUGH MASK
To Crichton of Fermanagh,* thus 'twas Buckshot Forster spoke:
'I find, my lord, upon my word, this business is no joke:
To gather in your agent's crops bring Orange Ulster down,
And we'll defend the diggers with the army of the Crown.'

Thus from Monaghan and Cavan the valiant volunteers,
Protected by revolvers from the country people's jeers,
With spade and sned, and mate and bread, and knives and forks
    and spoons,
Surrounded by bould infanthry and peelers and dhragoons.

When Bycut his deliverers so brave and martial saw
Arrayed in might and majesty for order and for law,
His spirit wance down-hearted, ruz, and moving towards the ranks,
With accents of emotion he thus expressed his thanks:

'Hail, champions of the loyal North! hail warriors of the Queen!
To you a long-afflicted man now welcome bids serene;

* Crighton was Lord Erne's family name.

Long may your praise in thrilling lays to times unborn go down,
Brave sons of Orange Ulster, brave defendhers of the Crown!'

They dug out all his praties and they thrashed out all his corn,
His turnips and his mangels saved, that long had lain forlorn:
And nothing interrupted their intherprising work
But the pouring rain from Heaven and the wind from Maam Turk.

And whin those noble hayroes to their own firesides go back,
And suffer from ague's chills or rheumatisms's attack,
They'll proudly boast on Ulsther's coast throughout the coming
    years,
Of their campaign 'gin wind and rain, as Bycut's Volunteers.

But 'tis said that his purtectors have put Bycut to great cost;
With trampled lawns and trees cut down and much good substance
    lost:
The throopers of her Majesty made free with his young lambs,
And ate his mutton and his ducks, and thanked him with G-d d-s.

The gallant Colonel Twentyman will get his K C B,
And Coghill (wounded by his horse) resave his due V C;
And the Queen, in gratitude to aich, for his triumphant task,
Will make Gladstone Duke of Dullsig-no* and Fosther Lord
    Lough Mask.

But boycotting, as *The Nation* intimated, was no joke. Even as
Boycott himself left Ireland, the weapon was being turned on a
more prominent figure, William Bence Jones, the Cork landlord
we met in an earlier chapter, of whom *The Nation* said, 'the plain
fact of the matter is that Captain Boycott did not merit his
Boycotting half as well as Mr Bence Jones'. The latter's difficulties
started towards the end of November when his tenants refused to

* Dullsig-no was a reference to the Eastern Question. In October 1880
Gladstone had threatened force against the Turkish Sultan unless he ceded
Dulcigno to Montenegro and thus implemented one of the conditions of the
Congress of Berlin. At the eleventh hour the Sultan had capitulated, but in the
meantime Dulcigno had come a close second to the Boycott Relief Expedition
in newspaper space and popular interest.

pay the rents demanded and insisted on Griffiths' Valuation. By early December a grave had been dug in front of his house, he had received the usual threatening letters and a full boycott was in swing, while his labourers were supported by local Land League funds. A contingent of marines and dragoons was duly sent to protect him, but the pressures were extended beyond the confines of his estate. The Land Leaguers prevented the sale of his oats at the local fair, they blocked a shipment of cattle to Bristol for the Christmas market, and when he managed to get the cattle to Cork under a constabulary escort, they were successfully boycotted in the market and refused shipment from the docks. These by-then notorious cattle were next sent by train to Dublin under heavy escort, with lively scenes at all stations along the route, but once having arrived in the capital, they were again boycotted, and when Bence Jones eventually managed to get them to Liverpool the Irish influence there succeeded in having them declared black and they were finally sold privately at a loss.

By the end of the year, newspapers were filled with accounts of boycotting in every county of Munster, Leinster and Connaught and the practice was extending into Ulster where the appeal of the Land League, if not of outright nationalism, was gaining ground. When the Relief Expedition was still at work Joseph Chamberlain wrote, 'You might arrest half the country and still Captain Boycott's position would be as intolerable as ever', while after it was over, *The Times* said: 'The impossibility of keeping intimidation at bay by the use of troops to protect individuals was strikingly demonstrated'. Mr Forster's biographer wrote: 'boycotting had grown up with the suddenness of Jonah's gourd and was now a weapon of the most formidable kind, all the more formidable because it could not be touched by ordinary laws', and Randolph Churchill pithily assessed it as 'better than any 81-ton gun'. Even had the Liberal administration wished to use troops to succour beleaguered individuals, the expenditure would have been prohibitive, and the cost of the actual relief expedition was the subject of much comment. While the volunteers were still at

Lough Mask, Parnell sent a telegram to America estimating that each turnip dug from Boycott's land had cost the government a shilling, and the *Irish World* elaborated on the theme thus: 'The cost of gathering Boycott's crops is estimated at £3,000 (15,000 dollars) a day, the total amount not far under a quarter of a million of money. . . . There are thirteen other landlords in the neighbourhood of Lough Mask who are now being Boycotted. If one Boycotted man cost the government 15,000 dollars a day, what will thirteen such men cost? What will two thousand cost?' In circles other than the *Irish World*'s it was generally agreed that the enterprise had totalled £10,000, which remains a fair sum and was then an enormous amount, and a question was asked in the House of Commons about the cost to the government and the taxpayers of the whole affair.

It had, ironically, been the relief expedition that had focused attention on the situation at Lough Mask, serving, as the *Annual Register* said, 'the purpose of a gigantic advertisement for the system henceforward known as boycotting'. Boycotting was the ideal weapon for a semi-revolutionary, semi-constitutional agitation, a method whereby the legal administration could be brought to its knees by fierce, but non-violent, means; in Davitt's words it provided 'the moral force artillery of the Land League warfare'. It had also assisted the position of the man who was generally credited with having instigated it, in his Ennis speech – Parnell. While Captain Boycott was enduring his plight, first in obscurity then in the glare of publicity, the power of the Land League had increased immeasurably and Parnell had reached what was probably the peak of his success as a popular leader, a position of near-idolatry, the undoubted 'uncrowned King of Ireland'. For the mass of peasants it was a euphoric fact that they now had a leader who could twist John Bull's tail, who would obtain for them the Land Bill to solve their immediate problems. However, Parnell himself made his ultimate objective clear; in October 1880 he said he would not have taken off his coat over the land war unless he had thought it would lead to the independence of

Ireland. He, as much as anybody on the government side, wanted a solution to the land question, for with that successfully tucked under his belt he could then proceed, from an infinitely stronger position, with the main battle for Irish self-government.

Gladstone also wanted a just land settlement, and at the end of November he was writing: 'the subject of the land weighs greatly upon my mind and I am working upon it to the best of my ability'. Gladstone had another problem weighing just as heavily upon his mind, the question of law and order which, as Prime Minister, it was his duty to implement and maintain. By the end of 1880, the ultra-Tory gentlemen were outraged by the level of Irish lawlessness, and their fears and apprehensions were shared by many moderates. While, as a result of the Land League's activities, evictions had sharply decreased – 2,110 for the whole of the year of which only 198 took place in the last three months – agrarian outrages had as sharply increased – 2,590 for the whole year, with 1,700 of them committed in the last quarter. These latter figures were given by Mr Forster; Gladstone himself was to speak of crime dogging the footsteps of the Land League, and at the end of 1880, the Dublin *Evening Mail* published its own figures linking the League with the increase of crime thus:

	LAND LEAGUE MEETINGS	AGRARIAN CRIMES REPORTED
Jan	26	114
Feb	15	97
March	22	83
April	4	67
May	18	88
June	17	90
July	17	84
August	38	104
Sept	32	168
Oct	77	268
Nov	119	561
Dec	190	867

These figures covered everything, from murder and wounding to the slaying and maiming of animals, from the sending of threatening letters to the implementation of the boycott. On the subject of cruelty to animals, English public opinion waxed particularly passionate, and before the end of 1880, *The Times* reported that the stage had already been reached of branding cattle 'with the Boycott stamp – a hot iron with the letter B on its point'. The image of the English as animal lovers was a recently acquired one as the proliferation of societies to protect our dumb friends would indicate, for if the English had loved animals as much as all that, there would have been no need for these numerous groups. However, by the 1880s, it was established and accepted, and the innumerable reports of cruelty to animals reinforced the view that the Irish were a barbarous race who could not be dealt with by the processes of ordinary civilised law. Sir Charles Dilke, who was no ultra-Tory, bent so far towards the swell of public opinion as to suggest that fresh coercive measures must be introduced into Ireland because of the widespread killing and maiming of animals. And the Irish nationalists themselves took the outcry sufficiently seriously for Tim Healy to issue a pamphlet, a section of which was devoted to the statistics and analysis of cruelty to animals in England. This contained cited instances of the pouring of turpentine on dogs, pulling out the tongues of horses, burning cats alive, and included the case of a Major in Southampton, in whose house nine cats had been found nailed to a board, as the *pièce de résistance*.

Whether or not cruelty to animals was a side-issue or whether it was a barometer of a society's degree of civilisation, it was not denied that there had been the most serious increase in crimes of all kinds throughout rural Ireland, which meant most of the country, in the last three months of 1880. The *Connaught Telegraph*, not among the more moderate of nationalist organs, admitted that 'the system of social ostracism, known as boycotting ... has been considerably ill-used ... the majority of the boycotting being carried on is at the instance of irresponsible parties

who, to satisfy a private spleen, ape the position of leaders . . .
ruining the whole movement and bringing it into ridicule'. The
Irish World, from a distance of a few thousand miles, wrote,
'Outrages! Outrages! They haven't begun yet! Out ye vipers of
darkness! Out ye hungry wolves! Ye bloodhounds! Out from
God's holy isle ere ye are overtaken by that punishment which
caught the wicked land-wolves of France from 1779 to 1793'.
(1779 was, presumably, a misprint for 1789.) These two comments illustrated the split in nationalist thought and action; on one
side there was Michael Davitt and all who followed him, believing
that any agitation against England must go to the limit, but must
be restrained from actual violence – as it had successfully been in
the Boycott affair – because violence was a weapon that destroyed
the user as much as the victim; while on the other side, apart from
'the irresponsible parties' who would always implement private
vengeance or advantage in the name of patriotism, there were those
who failed to recognise any limit once a campaign against English
domination had been set in motion. Davitt's side had the additional difficulty of needing to go to the limits of verbal violence,
both to ensure that enthusiasm was kept on the boil among a
population not noted for its response to pure reason, and to forestall any accusations that it was failing in its task or becoming
anglicised. The constant outpouring of violent rhetoric was
recognised by some of its scribes – and even among some, though
fewer, of its recipients – as an evil political necessity, not to be
treated at face value, but to its more excitable and less sophisti-
cated readers it was taken as an encouragement to actual violence;
a view which such poems as 'Hold the Harvest' written by Fanny
Parnell, and hailed as the 'Marseillaise of the Land League', did
nothing to lessen.

Now are you men, or are you kine, ye tillers of the soil?
Would you be free, or evermore, the rich man's cattle toil?
The shadow on the dial hangs that points the fatal hour –
Now hold you own! or, branded slaves, for ever cringe and cower.

The serpent's curse upon you lies – ye writhe within the dust,
Ye fill your mouths with beggar's swill, ye grovel for a crust;
Your lords have set their blood-stained heels upon your shameful heads,
Yet they are kind – they leave you still their ditches for your beds!

Oh, by the God who made us all – the seignior and the serf –
Rise up! and swear this day to hold your own green Irish turf;
Rise up! and plant your feet as men where now you crawl as slaves,
And make your harvest fields, your camps, or make of them your graves.

Miss Parnell continued with three more verses in similar vein,
including a reminder of the famine years – 'Your butchered sires;
your famished sires, for ghastly compost spread' – finishing thus:

The hour has struck, Fate holds the dice, we stand with bated breath;
Now who shall have our harvests fair – 'tis Life that plays with Death;
Now who shall have our Motherland? – 'tis Right that plays with
   Might;
The peasant's arm were weak indeed in such unequal fight.

The peasant's arm had been considerably strengthened by the
introduction of 'boycotting'. But the actual or threatened mis-use
of the new weapon, together with the outpourings of verbal
violence, posed as great a problem for the Irish leaders as it did
for Gladstone. They recognised the new militant Irish mood as an
essential ingredient in any struggle against England – indeed they
had helped create it – but would they be able to control it?
Gladstone himself saw the lawlessness – of which boycotting was
only a symptom – as a factor which had to be curbed. This was not
merely to placate outraged right-wing feelings, but because he
himself believed in the necessity of law and order as a framework
for any society. For the nationalist in Ireland, as in other countries
before and since, it was a question of whose laws? – and for the
Irish as for others the justification for breaking them lay in the
answer that they were an alien imposition. But for Gladstone there
was already a set of laws in existence, and like most Englishmen he
sincerely believed they were as good as any the world had seen –
which is not to say he thought they were perfect – and that

England's great gift to civilisation was the supremacy of her law as established, with her other great concept, parliamentary democracy, ensuring it did not atrophy. Gladstone was therefore in a position where emotionally, rationally, and politically, he needed to enforce the law in those parts of Ireland from which it was currently conspicuous by its absence, and Captain Boycott's was but one of the smaller voices telling him so. Equally, he believed that Ireland had suffered grave injustices at England's hands, his long-stated and now-remembered mission was to heal the wounds and place Ireland happily within the safe, prosperous harbour of the British Empire. Thus, on the one hand he needed to make concessions to those outraged gentlemen who were fulminating against the breakdown of law and order; while on the other he wanted to amend certain laws so that the process of healing the Irish wounds could be accelerated. He was in the classical cleft stick of the ruling political power: which should come first, the reinforcement of existing laws to show that authority must be respected for everybody's sake, or concessions towards the unrest which might reduce it but, equally, might encourage the more anarchic elements?

Before the Relief Expedition presented him with fresh problems in the shape of 'the boycott', Gladstone had taken one step which he faintly hoped might lessen his dilemma regarding the enforcement of law and order and the necessary concessions towards Irish grievances. He had agreed to the prosecution of the Land League leaders on the charges of conspiracy to prevent the payment of rent. If Parnell and the nationalist leaders could be convicted, Westminster's authority would be partially restored, and then he could introduce his remedial measures from a stronger position. But the success of the prosecutions was a big 'if'. When Forster had first suggested them at the beginning of October he had listed the pros and cons to Gladstone thus: on one side he said that by prosecuting they would be doing the only thing they could without fresh legislation, they would prove they did not fear the agitators, make it clear they were not in league with them and did not intend to let Parnell's law be put in place of *the* law. On the other side, he admitted that great enthusiasm would undoubtedly be engendered for Parnell, subscriptions would flow in from America, moderate Home Rulers would be tempted to join him in the face of British pressure, in Ireland ranks would close and there would probably be no conviction, the best the government could hope for would be a hung jury. In nationalist circles the prosecutions were regarded more as an introduction to further coercion; when they failed, as they undoubtedly would, the government would be able to say that stronger measures had to be taken. From the moment the prosecutions were publicised, in early November, Forster's predictions started to come true. Subscriptions poured into the Parnell defence fund, not only from England and Ireland, from John Devoy and the Clan na Gael, Patrick Ford and the *Irish World*, but from a wide variety of less committed American sources (the considerable overflow found its way into the nationalist coffers), while all shades of nationalist opinion in Ireland united behind Parnell.

When the trial opened in Dublin on December 28, 1880, thousands thronged the streets outside the court, while inside the spectacle reminded the *Daily Express* reporter 'more of the stalls of the theatre on opera night' than of a state prosecution, with ladies in their best attire bringing bouquets and throwing flowers at the defendants. The defence lawyers took the opportunity to remind the watching and listening world of England's past misdemeanours in Ireland – Daniel O'Connell's prosecution, the history of the famine years, Gavan Duffy's Tenant Right League, and Isaac Butt's attempts to amend the 1870 Land Act were recounted at length. When the prosecution read recent Land League speeches to illustrate the validity of the charges and the generally lawless and conspiratorial nature of this organisation, the defence countered by reading passages from the writings of such a mixed bag as Gladstone himself, John Bright, the historian Froude, John Stuart Mill and the economist Ricardo in which all had admitted England's mishandling of the Irish land question. And when the prosecution made the fatal mistake of reading aloud Fanny Parnell's 'Hold the Harvest' as an example of pernicious Land League literature, virtually the entire court burst into prolonged applause. A. M. Sullivan, the barrister brother of the celebrated nationalist poet in the dock, delivered the longest speech for the defence, in which he passionately declaimed that the wrong men were being indicted, that the true culprits were in Downing Street, and that if the conquerors did not assimilate themselves, their position was 'simply that of an arrow-head buried in the human flesh – the hateful source of a festering sore and a fatal wound in an otherwise wholesome body'. Generally as splendid a time was had by the nationalists as they had enjoyed over the Boycott relief expedition, and news of the trial was of consuming interest, at least until January 5, 1881. After that date interest waned because on that day the MPs among their number – Parnell, Joseph Biggar, Thomas Sexton, John Dillon and T. D. Sullivan – travelled to England for the new session of Parliament. Interest re-awakened on January 24 when Parnell returned to hear the judge address the jury 'through a clatter of china and teaspoons', according to *The Times*, the Dublin society ladies having thoroughly organised themselves in respect of refreshments. The jury retired at 12.30 p.m. and at 7 p.m. they were dismissed having, as Mr Forster had forecast, failed to agree, being ten to two in favour of an acquittal.

Parnell was able to cable his supporters in New York: 'The Land League has scored a victory', while more exuberantly Michael Davitt had already claimed: 'We have beaten the Government to smithereens in the affair so far', and that nothing had contributed to the victory more forcefully than boycotting.

CHAPTER 18

'I am Unable to See that We Can Get on Without the Suspension of Habeas Corpus'

As 1881 dawned, the Irish situation was the dominant issue in British politics; boycotting loomed large in the public mind, though it was not the sole preoccupation of the politicians. Much attention focused on what manner of Land Bill Mr Gladstone intended to introduce into the new session of Parliament; and whether he would first satisfy the demand of the British majority for the reinforcement of law and order in Ireland. Another result of the success that Parnell, Davitt and the Land League had achieved, in forcing attention on to Ireland, was the proliferation of pamphlets on the subject. In the era when the printed word was the only medium of mass communication, pamphlets on every conceivable subject abounded; in the late 1870s and early 1880s the Irish Land question and Irish nationalism became the chief preoccupation of the pamphleteers. There were serious dissertations on both sides, dealing with the historical background, the rent statistics, eviction and land tenure. On the one side, the authors urged the necessity of 'the three F's' as a short-term measure, peasant proprietary as the long-term answer; on the other side, they refuted this need, arguing that free contract allied to better farming and more capital investment was the solution, laying stress on the unlikelihood of thousands of small peasant landlords making Irish agriculture a better or more viable proposition than hundreds of larger ones.

One person who did not join the rush into print was Captain Boycott. It is probable that he was asked to record his version of the affair that had given a new weapon to the Land League and a new word to the dictionary, and assuredly, had he wanted to write a first-hand account there would have been no difficulty in finding a publisher. It is also fairly certain that a pamphlet written by Boycott himself would have brought in a reasonable sum of money, and he needed money, since at this point in time he was uncertain whether he would be able to recuperate his losses in Mayo. But he did not publish a pamphlet and this would seem to uphold the contention that he disliked his notoriety. Having power, fighting to retain that power on Achill, or fighting for his rights when isolated at Lough Mask, was one matter; trading upon world-wide notoriety was another. One gains the strong impression that he wanted to forget the affair, which is understandable, but mainly for the reason that it was not the sort of enterprise with which an English gentleman would wish to be associated. Boycotting, however, remained headline news, the repercussions of the relief expedition were still being felt and the time had not yet come for Boycott to ease himself from the limelight. Nor did he yet wish to do so, because one aspect of the repercussions, the financial side, was of great importance to him.

Shortly after his return to England, he had written what was for him a very long letter to Mr Gladstone on the subject of his present situation and government compensation. He started by saying he had settled in the West of Ireland some thirty years earlier when he was assured by the British government that the land laws had been simplified and capital might safely be invested. He outlined his early struggles on Achill Island, then the purchase of the thirty-one year lease on Lough Mask estate and the undertaking of the agency for Lord Erne, and said he had sunk his entire capital of £6,000 into stocking and supplying the estate. (This was not strictly true, as he had also purchased the Kildarra property, but without doubt he had put much of his money into Lough Mask.) He stated his belief that he had been denounced and victimised by the Land League solely as a result of having to serve eviction notices in the course of his duties as Lord Erne's agent, saying it was unnecessary for him to refer other than briefly to subsequent events, namely the despatch of the relief expedition. However, he continued, it was necessary for him to state his present circumstances, for when the military withdrew he was compelled to leave with them, for his life would not otherwise have been safe for an hour. To emphasise the continuing harassment, he referred to his forced departure from the Hamman Hotel.

He ended by saying that, though innocent of wrong-doing, he was a ruined man, the owner of a house and an estate in Mayo that was utterly valueless; the house full of furniture he could not remove and the land going to waste. Those same circumstances that had compelled him to leave also prevented his return, because lawlessness held sway in Mayo. Having stated these facts, which he would only too gladly verify further if required, he ventured to think they entitled him to assistance from Her Majesty's Government and wished to ascertain whether Her Majesty's Government would assure him that the matter of assistance would be recognised. Though Boycott did not state explicitly that Her Majesty's Government was supposed to be the upholder of the law and was correspondingly responsible for its breakdown in Mayo and his subsequent ruination, the inference was clear. A week later, a reply came from Downing Street in which Mr Gladstone's secretary said the Prime Minister was not sure 'in what way he is to understand your request for assistance from Her Majesty's Government'. Mr Gladstone had thought that considerable assistance had already been afforded in the shape of military force, and had nothing further to suggest, beyond assuring Captain Boycott that it was the duty of any government to enforce the law, or if necessary, to ask the Legislature to amend or enlarge it, the former of which tasks the present administration was endeavouring to perform, the latter being a matter of much importance 'on which you can, of course, only receive information together with the public generally'.

To this unencouraging missive Boycott replied immediately, saying he was sorry his meaning had been unclear but he had lost

£6,000 and he wished to know whether the government would compensate him for the loss, and to what extent? With reference to the military force, he had from the start of his unfortunate situation been in contact with the Irish Executive, asking them to afford protection to twelve labourers whilst they harvested his crops. Instead of receiving the requested protection, a relief expedition was sent into Mayo accompanied by an army, whose aim was not to assist him, but to preserve the peace. As for prospective alterations in the law he had no interest in them, as they would neither restore his property nor protect his life, and he deeply regretted that Her Majesty's Government, having itself failed to protect him, now refused to compensate him. This correspondence had appeared in *The Times* on December 18, 1880, together with a letter from a Major-General Burnaby and a Mr Day. These two gentlemen had said they were publishing it to show that Mr Gladstone had refused to assist a noted victim of the Land League, and to appeal to the public to come to Captain Boycott's aid. A committee was being organised to administer a Boycott Fund, and in the meantime donations could be sent to Messrs Hoare of Fleet Street or Messrs Dimsdale and Fowler of Cornhill.

As events transpired, Boycott was not to receive what he considered adequate financial aid from either the public or the government. Mr Gladstone adhered to his view that the government had already expended more than sufficient money on Captain Boycott – and having unwisely undertaken the job of Chancellor of the Exchequer as well as Prime Minister in this administration Gladstone felt the expenditure of £10,000 the more keenly. But after the publication of his correspondence in *The Times*, and the accompanying letter announcing the setting-up of a Boycott Fund and its criticism of the government's meanness, Gladstone dictated yet another letter. In this he emulated Parnell, leading the reader to believe what he wanted him to believe, without committing himself to a firm course of action. He expressed his approval of the public sympathy which had already been shown towards Boycott and said he was referring the subject of compensation to the Irish Executive for serious consideration. The result of this was that, just as the Fund was getting into its stride, those who were prepared to make contributions were given the impression that the government was taking care of the matter, and subscriptions dwindled away.

Boycott realised that compensation from Her Majesty's Government, as presided over by Mr Gladstone, was extremely unlikely when a further letter came from Downing Street on January 20, 1881. This brief letter said that Mr Gladstone was not to be understood as having made any admission on the subject, and would Captain Boycott kindly address further correspondence direct to the Chief Secretary for Ireland, Mr Forster, as the whole matter had, as intimated, been referred to his office. Boycott tried to continue the fight by having this letter published but it was by then too late, as he himself more or less admitted in his reply:

It was evidently thought that I should be compensated by the Government, and therefore there was no need of any other aid. The submission of my case to a specified department and the expression of Mr Gladstone's approval of the sympathy I had met with, in the minds of ordinary men could lead to no other conclusion. And now, after allowing that opinion to obtain universal currency, your second letter informs me that no such meaning is to be attributed to your words, and having thus lost my hold on the generosity of my countrymen, I have gained nothing from the Prime Minister save a barren expression of sympathy accompanied by a delusive hope of substantial assistance.

This diagnosis proved correct and sympathy was the limit of Mr Gladstone's further interest in the matter. Boycott, however, was not entirely friendless – he had his family in Norfolk and there were plenty of English gentlemen outraged by his treatment at the hands of the Land League, enough, in fact, to ensure that he did not lack material comfort or consolation. On January 15, 1881, Boycott was observed being entertained at the House of Commons, where he had the privilege of witnessing Mr Parnell in some angry parliamentary scenes. Later Boycott admitted that the public subscription had amounted to £2,000 which, though not measuring up to £6,000 lost in Mayo, was a good sum of money in the 1880s. Incidentally, Boycott was not the only person who attempted to obtain recompense from the government on account of the relief expedition. As late as June, 1882, Mr Harrell, one of the resident magistrates who had been drafted into the area and was left in charge of Lough Mask House after the expedition and the Boycotts had departed, was still trying to claim for the expenses he had incurred. Whether his attempts finally proved more successful than Boycott's remains unknown.

Before Boycott received his financial *coup de grace* from Mr Gladstone, indeed before the new session of Parliament opened on January 6, 1881, the government had come to a decision, namely that coercive measures must be introduced to re-establish Westminster's authority in Ireland before reforms could be augmented. The prime mover behind the decision was Mr Forster, whose morale, judgement and ability to weigh the salient factors in a confused situation had been increasingly shattered by the Land League's activities in the past year. The thoughts, assessments and recommendations in his innumerable memoranda, letters and reports to Gladstone were endlessly qualified. At one moment he seemed to have a clear picture of the situation; the next he was filled with doubts and fears about the advisability of taking any course of action at all. On the one hand, he admitted the power and effect of the Land League, while on the other, he put forward the extraordinary proposition that the League was basically formed of 'old Fenians and Ribbonmen or *mauvais sujets*' who would slink into their holes if a few more were arrested'. His general state at the end of 1880 was graphically described by a fellow-liberal thus: 'Forster is so worried and ill as to be likely to break down altogether. In fact I fancy he is like the Yankee General after Bull's Run – "Not just afraid but dreadful demoralised".'

Despite his demoralisation, Forster was still sufficiently liberal to believe that a good land Bill was necessary, and to accept the recommendations of the Bessborough Commission which the cabinet had in its possession before the end of December 1880 (large scale Commissions worked much more quickly in those days). The Commission had consisted of Lord Bessborough himself, accounted one of the best landlords in Ireland; William Shaw, the ex-Home Rule leader; O'Conor Don, also known as an excellent and liberal landlord; Richard Dowse, a judge; and Arthur Kavanagh, a conservative landlord. Its recommendations came down strongly in favour of major land reforms including the legal recognition of dual ownership in Ireland and the implementation of 'the three F's'. (In fact, Arthur Kavanagh refused to sign the final report, considering its recommendations went too far, but O'Conor Don contributed a supplementary report in which he said peasant proprietary was the only long-term solution.) Forster agreed that the recommendations should be implemented, but only after the introduction of new coercive measures, a view he was able to impress on the majority of the cabinet, although the considerable divergence of opinion was still much in evidence. Joseph Chamberlain argued that this time the carrot in the shape of the land Bill should come before the stick in the shape of coercion, because a progressive Act would cool passions, and outrages would die down, further stern coercive legislation would be unnecessary and a new wave of Irish co-operation would be engendered. Eventually Gladstone succumbed to the proposition that coercion must come first, although, after the decision was taken, he was described as 'downright piteous – his wrung features, his strained gesture, all the other signs of mental perturbation in an intense nature'.

The new session of Parliament therefore opened with the news that Mr Forster intended to secure special powers to deal with the agrarian violence in Ireland; in other words a new Coercion Act which would inevitably include the suspension of Habeas Corpus, an announcement which gladdened the hearts of many moderates as much as Captain Boycott or the ultra-Tories. Parnell, who was obviously of Chamberlain's opinion that reform would obviate the necessity for coercion, swung into immediate obstructive action, doggedly supported by many of the sixty-odd Home Rulers. They succeeded in stretching the debate on the address in reply to the Queen's Speech for eleven nights – and it was one of these sessions, involving angry interchanges between Parnell and the government, that was witnessed by Captain Boycott, the man who more than any other single individual represented the need for the new Coercion Bill. But it was when Forster finally sought leave to introduce his Protection of Persons and Property (Ireland) Bill, on January 24, that obstruction was brought to its peak as a method of wrecking procedure in the House of Commons. The majority of the Irish members showed little finesse in obstructing, they did not possess Parnell's skill or adeptness in utilising the forms of the House against itself, but by sheer persistence and weight of numbers they forced the House into a twenty-two-hour sitting on January 25–26 and on January 31 they prolonged a sitting until February 2, forty-one hours in all. This was the swan-song of obstruction for, in the early hours of Wednesday morning, February 2, the Speaker intervened; thereafter the closure was introduced. This gave control of the House to him if members should vote by three to one that business was urgent; thus, for the first time in British parliamentary history, a check was put on debates; and many English parliamentarians never forgave Parnell for the tactics that had led to this curtailment. A more immediate consequence was that Forster's Coercion Bill could be introduced for its First Reading and its passage was then ensured.

The excitement and uproar had not finished, for the day after the closure was introduced, the news of Michael Davitt's arrest was given to Parliament. Why Davitt was not charged with the other Land League leaders at the Dublin trial is an interesting question, since he was the man who had founded and organised the League; but the answer would seem to be that the Liberals were in a quandary over him because he was an ex-convict on a ticket-of-leave. Forster had earlier given his opinion that, although Davitt was 'a most mischievous not to say dangerous agitator', it was not possible to revoke his licence unless he clearly broke the law. But Davitt had technically been breaking the terms of his parole for a long time by failing to report monthly at the police office, as Forster admitted in the same letter, and it would not have been difficult to find illegal matter in virtually any of his speeches, if the government had so desired. The problem was that once they did arrest Davitt on a serious charge, they had to send him back to prison for violating the conditions of his parole. In the autumn months of 1880, they had not decided on coercion, therefore Davitt was left alone, but once they had embarked upon this policy he had to be arrested.

As soon as the news of the arrest was given to the House of Commons there were scenes of indescribable confusion, with some English members cheering, Irish members shouting and stamping, Gladstone 'up and down between his seat and the table like a hen on a hot gridiron', John Dillon refusing to recognise the authority of the Speaker and being suspended, Parnell, not to be outdone, interrupting Gladstone with the outrageous proposal that he be no longer heard, and likewise being suspended; the whole wild, noisy, ugly episode lasting three and a half hours and culminating in the suspension and expulsion of thirty-six Irish members. Incidentally, prior to his arrest, Davitt made a speech which rightly gave the opposition a good deal of amusement. He said, 'If your patience becomes exhausted by government brutality and every right, privilege, and hope which is your god-given inheritance be trampled upon by vindictive power, the world will hold England and not you responsible if the wolf-hound of Irish vengeance bounds over the Atlantic at the very heart of that power from which it is now held back by the influence of the League'. After commenting on the loss to litera-ture Davitt's arrest would occasion, the Dublin *Evening Mail* said, 'the wolf-dog of Irish vengeance bounding over the Atlantic would be a sight even England would put up with a great deal to

see'. If Davitt unfortunately sounded hilarious, the threat of
Irish-American vengeance was one which many Englishmen took
seriously when Parnell and his fellow nationalists were expelled
from Westminster.

In effect, there were three courses open to Parnell after the
expulsion from Westminster; he could return to Ireland, set up a
parliament there and declare what would virtually have been a
unilateral declaration of independence from Great Britain. (The
idea of secession went back into Irish history, Parnell himself had
occasionally threatened its use, and Michael Davitt had been an
enthusiastic advocate, given the right moment and circumstances.)
Or he could follow the more dispersed course of action, actually
advocated by Davitt, when the crunch came. This included
Parnell's going to America to raise money and support there,
while other Home Rulers stayed at Westminster, and the Land
League fought the battle against coercion in Ireland. Apart from
these two courses, both of which would harness the revolutionary
fervour of the Land League and have the whole-hearted backing
of the Irish-Americans, there was a third possible path for Parnell
to follow: he could return to the House of Commons and
continue to fight for Ireland's independence by constitutional
means.

It was this third course he chose, the moment when he proved
that he was a constitutionalist rather than a revolutionary.
However, there were those who said that the decision only proved
that Parnell was, above all, a realist; he knew Ireland was geo-
graphically too close to England for a gesture such as setting up
an independent parliament because the weight of military force
was on England's side. Moreover he knew that neither the
Catholic hierarchy nor the moderate Home Rulers would support
him in a secessionist venture.

When Parnell and the other expelled members all returned to
Westminster, they continued to harass the passage of the Coercion
Bill to the best of their ability, but their basic weapon was gone.
The Bill was passed by the House of Commons on February 28

and quickly became law; its terms included the suspension of Habeas Corpus in Ireland and the right to arrest and imprison suspected persons without trial. Shortly afterwards it was followed by another, the Peace Preservation (Ireland) Bill, which was concerned with the illegal possession of weapons and the use of arms. There was considerable reaction in both England and Ireland to the passage of the Bills. In England there were radical protest meetings in all the major cities – Birmingham, Leeds, Newcastle, Manchester and, of course, London – and an Anti-Coercion Association was founded which proved to be a precursor of the Labour Party. In Ireland itself, reaction was naturally greater and Parnell had a hard time keeping in check the more extreme elements, both in his party and the Land League. However, he had one factor on his side, and that was the knowledge that Gladstone intended to introduce a Land Bill, for the Queen's Speech had also contained information of fresh land legislation. How radical this would in fact be – whether the recommendations of the Bessborough Commission would be implemented, whether it would take account of recent events in Ireland, such as boycotting, and popular feeling there – remained a matter for speculation. As a tense Ireland awaited the introduction of the Land Bill, the knowledge that it was coming helped Parnell keep in check those of his supporters who were demanding immediate revolutionary action.

CHAPTER 19

'A Great Benefit for which Gratitude is Due to Mr Gladstone'

While Ireland waited for the Land Bill, Boycott visited America, a journey indicating that the dire financial straits he had so loudly proclaimed in January were not as severe as all that, although doubtless the visit also presented an excellent opportunity to help erase recent unhappy memories of 'boycotting'. He was not to escape from his immediate past without recognition, however, despite being entered on the passenger list of the steamship *Italy* as Mr Charles Cunningham. The *nom de voyage* was easily penetrated and the visit earned banner headlines and many column inches in the New York papers – 'Boycotted Boycott', read the *Herald*, 'Arrival of the Isolated Man of Lough Mask on American soil'; while the *Tribune* said, 'The arrival of Captain Boycott, who has involuntarily added a new word to the language, is an event of something like international interest'. He was accompanied by 'the same little band as held the fort at Lough Mask', his wife, his nephew Arthur St John Boycott who, bearing the well-known name, travelled as Mr A. St. John, and Ashton Weekes, whom Boycott described as 'late of the Thirteenth Hussars, an old and well tried friend, though, as you may see, a much younger man than myself'. The *Tribune* said he was also accompanied by his brother, but the *Herald* made no mention of the Reverend Edmund Boycott, who was certainly not a member of the little band that had endured the vicissitudes of Lough Mask.

The *Italy* docked in New York in the early hours of April 5, 1881, and, as the saloon passengers were taken off by tender, there was an outburst of hissing from the steerage passengers – many of whom were Irish – which was directed towards 'the thick-set, middle-aged gentleman standing on the upper deck of the tender', but this brought an immediate counter-response of 'Three cheers for Captain Boycott'. The *incognito* had obviously been penetrated long before he set foot on American soil, where he proceeded to be interviewed as a celebrity. His appearance was noted – 5 ft 7½ in. tall, muscular build, broad-shouldered, upright as a dart, partially bald; the once dark whiskers, moustache and beard liberally flecked with grey. His speech was said to be polished (he would certainly have had an upper-class English accent), his manner jovial, and, according to the *Herald*, he 'appeared to be on excellent terms with himelf and the world'. His normal self-confidence had obviously returned after the rigours which had led observers to comment on his strained and careworn appearance. The *Herald* reporter also noted that the key to Boycott's character was to be found in the small grey eyes in which firmness and determination were visible. In his long interview in the *Herald* Boycott admitted that upwards of £2,000 had been gathered by public subscription in England, although at this point in time he was correct in emphasising that the £6,000 invested in Mayo could be written-off. For, as he told the *Herald* man, Lough Mask House remained under constabulary protection, nobody could be found to work the farm and, during the previous month, the house had been twice fired into, one bullet lodging in a lintel, one in the hall door. He was then asked his opinion of the trustworthiness of the RIC, and Irish soldiers within the armed forces, should the situation within Ireland deteriorate; what the prospects for a peaceful solution were; whether Mr Gladstone's proposed Land Bill would do much towards ameliorating conditions; what other remedies were possible; and, finally, for his views on Mr Parnell.

Boycott was emphatic that Irishmen within the armed forces had in the past remained loyal to the monarch and would continue to do so, although he was less certain about the reliability of the RIC. (Other sources considered Irish members of the army might be suspect in certain circumstances but that the RIC would always be reliable.) He did not commit himself to a prognostication on Ireland's future, but his views on Gladstone's proposed Land Bill and Ireland's past and present situation were firm, English and conservative. He thought the Land League would never have grown so powerful had the Liberal administration shown a strong arm from the start, and while conceding that some revision of the land laws in favour of the small tenant farmer was desirable, he did not believe that implementation of 'the three F's' would in any way solve the problem. For it remained a simple one – 'the insane desire to farm the land at all hazards. The demand is greater than the supply, and that is all about it'. The only answers were emigration and industrialisation, and the solution lay in the Irish people's own hands. If sufficient numbers could be persuaded to emigrate, or move to the towns, then those left on the land would be able to farm at a profit, but those who went to the towns would also have to prove they were capable of hard work, for-getting past or imaginary grievances and observing the laws, otherwise no capitalist would be willing to invest in the country. He believed that the Irish mania for the land, laziness, harping on past grievances, and contempt for the law were the reasons capital and industry had not previously been attracted to the country. With regard to Mr Parnell he thought he was 'a good leading man', undoubtedly backed by the masses, but lacking the support of the country's intellectuals. The *New York Daily Tribune* considered these views 'on the heroic order', but on the whole more moderate than might have been expected 'from a man who has rubbed against the roughest edges of the Irish character'.

Boycott was asked if he intended to settle in the United States and replied that the sole object of his visit was to see friends in Virginia, although he hoped to have the opportunity of viewing Brooklyn Bridge, New York's elevated roads and 'other big things in America' before returning to England. The friend he went to see in Virginia was Mr Murray McGregor Blacker, his old confederate from the days of salvage battles on Achill Island. Blacker was by now resident in the United States, although he still owned the estate near Claremorris, and when James Redpath heard of Boycott's visit and read the interview in the *New York Herald* he immediately had himself interviewed, lambasting Boycott and Blacker as 'birds of a feather'. He had obviously not read the *Connaught Telegraph*'s allegations about Boycott and Blacker dangling poor Irishmen over the cliffs of Achill as he never mentioned this or anything of their Achill litigation, and he had a good nose for dirt. But he managed to produce evidence that Murray McGregor Blacker had taken out long distance eviction notices against his famished peasants in Claremorris from Haw Branch, Amelia Court House, Virginia, U.S.A. He asserted that Blacker's tenants lived in wretched hovels, their rents were extortionate, and that if ever a man deserved to be boycotted, it was Blacker himself, and he stated that 'since the yellow fever met the cholera at New Orleans a few years since, there has never been such an illustration of the law that like seeks like' than the meeting of Boycott and Blacker.

The 'Interview with James Redpath', ten times the length of any given by Boycott, presented him with the opportunity to review the whole Boycott affair in not too accurate detail, and then refute Boycott's opinions as stated in the New York papers. Redpath claimed that statistics proved that Ireland could comfortably support a population of fifteen millions from the land, if only all the good land were not in the possession of Englishmen or their agents like Boycott. He made the valid point that Irish industry had been suppressed by English legislation after the Act of Union, and that the British government had done nothing to encourage investment in Ireland. Another valid point was his comment on Boycott's statement that some revision of the land laws in favour of the tenants was desirable, particularly in respect of the improvements made on property. Redpath said that this admission coming from such a man as Boycott was the strongest proof he had yet heard of the effect and influence of the Land League. It could be so viewed because Boycott had never given any indication that he considered the land laws in need of amendment prior to the Land League's dissemination of literature and its attacks upon landlordism.

Boycott stayed in America a couple of months, before returning to England to follow the battle for Gladstone's Land Bill. It was in April, while he was in Virginia, that Gladstone introduced the Bill, and if it was not the final solution of the Irish land question, it was a massive, radical step forward and fulfilled most of the peasant's immediate demands. As the Bessborough Commission had recommended, 'the three F's' were to be legalised, officially recognising the dual ownership of land in Ireland. Fair rents were to be achieved by the establishment of a Land Commission by which tenants would have their rents judicially fixed for a period of fifteen years; fixity of tenure would be guaranteed by the Commission, provided that the tenant regularly paid the agreed rent; free sale gave the right to sell at the best price, taking into account the improvements made by the tenants. There were still loopholes in the Bill – there was no provision for leaseholders or tenants already in arrears with their rents, and a fair rent still had to be defined. As with all Gladstonian legislation, the Bill was immensely complicated (apart from Gladstone himself, Tim Healy was said to be the only man who fully understood it). Piloting it through the House of Commons against the Opposition, which said it struck at the rights of property and had bowed to the lawless and unholy pressures of the Land League, needed all Gladstone's parliamentary skill and massive physical and mental energy. The *Annual Register* was not exaggerating when it said that the Land Act was 'probably the most important measure introduced into the House of Commons since the passing of the Reform Bill', nor was Lord Hartington when he declared 'The parliamentary history of the year was the history of a single measure carried by a single man'.

Ironically, the introduction of the Bill put Parnell into a difficult position. He had fought for a good Bill, both because it would benefit his country and so that he could claim the major credit for having forced Gladstone into a position where he could not withhold it. Thus far, he had carried with him the Catholic hierarchy and the moderate nationalists, but they were more than satisfied with the results of the campaign – 'A great benefit,' said the *Freeman's Journal*, 'for which the gratitude of the country is due to Mr Gladstone' – and would be unlikely to lend their support to a further campaign based on semi-revolutionary methods and the threat of violence. The militant nationalists and the Irish-Americans did not view the Bill as a great benefit kindly bestowed by Mr Gladstone – they saw it only as a sop, induced by the effects of boycotting and other Land League activities. Some of them insisted that landlordism must go and peasant proprietary be established, while all of them insisted that the semi-revolutionary fervour of the last twelve months must be sustained and the battle continued on similar lines until England was forced to grant Ireland independence. As an immediate measure, they became increasingly fervent advocates of the no-rent campaign, since, if all the Irish tenants refused to pay their rents, it would bring economic chaos, at the same time demonstrating Irish determination to fight until they had achieved their goal.

When John Dillon was arrested early in May, 1881, Parnell was put into an even more difficult position, because he had earlier vowed that if any of the League leaders were arrested under the Coercion Act he would implement the no-rent campaign. But he had no enthusiasm for this project, and he circumvented his failure to implement his promise by focusing attention on his parliamentary intransigence, urging the other Home Rulers to vote against the Second Reading of the Land Bill. Although some of his supporters followed his example which kept the militants happy, several Home Rulers disobeyed their leader's instructions and voted in favour, thus reinforcing Parnell's awareness of moderate feeling. He proceeded to work hard on the Bill in the committee stages and allowed his party a free vote on the Third Reading. Once the Bill had safely passed the Commons and was on the way to becoming law, the moderates were happy, so Parnell immediately adopted his revolutionary stance to keep the extremists in line.* At the beginning of August he made an outrageous speech in the Commons for which he was suspended, and was thereby able to return to Ireland to take a firm grip on the situation there. At an important Land League meeting in Dublin in September, Parnell produced a formula that he hoped would keep contented both the moderates who wanted to accept the Act, and the militants who wanted to embark on the no-rent campaign. He proposed that they test the Act by submitting selected cases to the new Land Commission, a procedure that would stop everybody rushing to the courts simultaneously, thus placing the courts in the position of needing the tenants' support, and possibly exposing the hollowness of the Act. This ingenious solution did not appease the extremists, particularly the Irish-Americans who continued to urge resistance to the new law and the start of the no-rent campaign. In order to placate them, Parnell embarked on a series of highly militant, inflammatory speeches.

These speeches became too much for Gladstone to bear and indeed, although one can admire, in retrospect, Parnell's skill in keeping his disharmonious team on the rein, his tactical finesse in maintaining a balance was not nearly so apparent at the time. Gladstone knew he had succeeded in piloting through both Houses a bitterly opposed Land Act which was of benefit to Ireland, he could see that a considerable section of the Irish population wanted to accept those benefits, but from Parnell's actions and speeches he could only conclude that this man was bent on using the Land League as a means of frustrating them. On October 7 Gladstone was in Leeds, and that evening, from 'an extemporised hall in the old cloth-yard' he let himself go on the subject of Ireland in general and Parnell in particular, delivering one of his most famous speeches. A good part of it was devoted to a panegyric on Daniel O'Connell – whom he had long admired.

* A parliamentary observer had earlier commented on Parnell's ability to change roles from fiery revolutionary to reasoned constitutionalist thus: 'Mr Irving's success in the dual character of the Corsican brothers palls before Mr Parnell's assumption of his new personality'.

He drew a portrait of O'Connell the Irish patriot, but devoted constitutionalist and believer in law and order, that contrasted with the current stance of the Member for Cork, Mr Parnell, allegedly an Irish patriot, but seemingly bent on destroying all that was of value in English and Irish society by preaching a doctrine of public plunder.

With specific regard to the Land Act Gladstone suggested that Parnell desired 'to arrest the operation of the Act – to stand as Moses stood, between the living and the dead, but to stand there, not as Moses stood, to arrest, but to spread the plague'. Towards the end of the speech he said that what he had stated was merely opinion, but it was opinion based on the recent words and actions of Mr Parnell, and if his view was correct and a great crisis was impending between the body Mr Parnell represented and the body he represented, then he could only tell the world, '... we are determined that no force and no fear of force and no fear of ruin through force shall ... prevent the Irish people from having the full and free benefits of the Land Act. ... And if ... it should then appear that there is still to be fought a final conflict in Ireland between the law on one side and sheer lawlessness on the other ... then I say, gentlemen, without hesitation, the resources of civilisation are not yet exhausted'.* Parnell not only ignored this warning but deliberately insulted Gladstone in a speech made two days later at Wexford, when he spoke of the Prime Minister as 'this masquerading knight-errant, this pretending champion of the rights of every nation except those of the Irish'. Finally on October 13, convinced that Parnell's intention was to wreck the Land Act and generally spread lawlessness and disorder, Gladstone ordered his arrest and Parnell was duly lodged in Kilmainham jail with the other imprisoned nationalist leaders.

It has since been generally agreed that, by arresting Parnell, Gladstone extricated him from the difficulties of a situation that

* Gladstone succumbed to a severe cold immediately afterwards, the result, in his opinion, of 'excessive exertion of the throat in the Cloth Hall at Leeds, the greatest physical effort I ever made'.

had become overwhelming even for such a tight-rope walker and juggler of divergent views as Parnell was. At the time, observers considered Parnell had deliberately courted arrest; Forster, for example, was of the opinion that he was being 'moved by his tail' and that the Wexford speech would inevitably be a treasonable outburst. But he also believed that action must be taken, as he wrote in a letter to Gladstone: 'Unless we can strike at the boycotting weapon, Parnell will beat us. If we strike a blow at all it must be a sufficiently hard blow to paralyse the action of the League, and for this purpose I think we must make a simultaneous arrest of the central leaders and the local leaders who conduct the boycotting . . . I see no alternative unless we allow the Land League to govern Ireland'.

Parnell himself was clear that the incarceration in Kilmainham was opportune, although he had a different view of the Land League's current standing. He wrote to Katharine O'Shea, 'Politically it is a fortunate thing for me that I have been arrested, as the movement is breaking fast and will be quiet in a few months, when I shall be released'. He knew the Land League was being killed by its own success and Gladstone's Act, and he had no desire to be in at the death throes, nor did he want to watch the extremists try to resurrect the corpse. After the death of the League, he could emerge from prison crowned with martyrdom, having had no hand in the demise, and all sides would only be too eager for him to reshape the tactics of the Home Rule movement.

The operation, in practice, was by no means as clear or as simple as that – for one thing, Parnell had no idea how long Gladstone would keep him in prison and he could not afford to be absent too long or others might do the reshaping.

Parnell made one last gesture towards the extremists when, a few days after his imprisonment, he and other nationalist leaders issued a manifesto calling for a no-rent strike.* There is evidence

* The manifesto read, 'Every tenant-farmer of Ireland is today the standard-bearer of the flag unfurled at Irishtown, and can bear it to a glorious victory. Stand together in the face of the brutal and cowardly enemies of

that Parnell signed the manifesto reluctantly, as did its formerly enthusiastic advocate, John Dillon, both considering it would be a dangerous move when the Irish peasants were leaderless. The campaign, from the start, was a fiasco. The clergy were against it, the moderate nationalists considered it irresponsible, while the peasants who should have implemented it were much too busy discovering the benefits of Gladstone's Land Act to do so.

The government viewed the manifesto as an indication of Parnell's deliberate intention to wreck the implementation of the Act and to further his own lawless aims, and consequently took the opportunity to suppress the Land League. This left the field clear for the Central Land League of the Ladies of Ireland, which had been founded early in 1881 by Parnell's formidable sister, Anna, who had by then returned from the United States. The idea behind the formation of the Ladies Land League, apart from the fact that Anna Parnell and her supporters believed that women had an active role to play, was that they should be prepared for just such a moment – to take control of the campaign should the men be arrested. Unfortunately for the ladies, they met with fierce opposition from most of the male nationalists, including Parnell, and from the Catholic Church, which considered that the existence of a Ladies League threatened the modesty of Irish womanhood. Michael Davitt was one of the few leaders who gave women his blessing, but then he was ahead of his time generally, and certainly in Catholic Ireland, in that he believed in the right of women to be more than merely child-bearers and housekeepers. More serious than the male opposition was the fact, clearly recognised by Parnell if not his sister Anna, that circumstances had changed

your race. Pay no rent under any pretext.' The defiant signatories gave their present abodes even more defiantly – 'Charles S. Parnell, President, Kilmainham Jail; A. J. Kettle, Hon. Sec, Kilmainham Jail; Michael Davitt, Hon. Sec, Portland Prison; Thomas Brennan, Hon. Sec, Kilmainham Jail; John Dillon, Head Organiser, Kilmainham Jail; Thomas Sexton, Head Organiser, Kilmainham Jail; Patrick Egan, Treasurer, Paris'. (Egan had taken the Land League funds to Paris, where they remained, to forestall possible confiscation by the British government.)

and the League was no longer necessary. The ladies battled bravely on, but the organisation was beyond control and, consequently, in the autumn of 1881, it became the province of the dark forces of extreme men, of secret societies and private vendettas. While Anna Parnell tried unsuccessfully to control the dying League, her sister Fanny lent her talents to the opponents of the Land Act and to the proponents of the ill-starred no-rent campaign. Two verses will indicate her opinion of the former and its progenitors:

> Tear up that parchment lie!
> Scatter its fragments to the hissing wind –
> And hear again the People's first and final cry;
> No more for you, oh lords, we'll dig and grind;
> Nor more for you the castle and for us the sty!
>
> Tear up that parchment lie!
> You, Gladstone, sunk supine to quivering slush;
> You, Forster, with the sign of Cain in breast and eye;
> You, Bright, whose slopping tongue can gloze and gush,
> You, puppet brood, the lesser legislative fry
> A people's wrath your grinning cozenage defy
> We will not loose the land, we will not starve or fly;
> Tear up that chartered lie.

While another of her poems *Coercion – Hold the Rent* ran thus:

Keep the law, oh, keep it well – keep it as your rulers do;
Be not righteous overmuch – when they break it, so can you!
As they read their pledge and bond, rend you, too, their legal thongs;
When they crush your chartered rights, tread you down their chartered
  wrongs;
Help them on and help them aye, help as true brethren should, boys.
All that's right and good for them, sure for its right and good, boys.

Its chorus ran:

> Hold the rents and hold the crops, boys;
> Pass the word from town to town;

Pull away the props, boys,
So you'll pull coercion down.

For many British sources these sentiments represented the elements they must suppress in Ireland, as did 'the regimental orders' of one of the proliferating secret societies which were printed as follows:

(1) James Sullivan, to be shot in the leg. Mother and daughter to be clipped for dealing at Heggarty's.
(2) John Linehan, for story telling to Father F. clipped also.
(3) Dennis Coakley, for turning out his labourers, clipped also.
(4) John Murphy, shot in the leg for paying his rent.
(5) Another man, name unknown, to be shot in the leg for paying his rent. And Mary Coakley to be clipped for speaking to the police at Macroom.

(*signed*) Captain Moonlight

This, for many British people and some Irish ones, was what the Land League meant – mob law, intimidation, maiming and killing, a reign of private and individual terror untouched by public and collective law. To say that Parnell, Davitt and the other imprisoned leaders had formerly restrained the outrages was nonsense; their speeches, their organisation, their introduction of the vile boycotting weapon, their violent language, their constant threats of physical violence had inevitably created a climate where actual violence, indiscriminate and undirected, thrived. The only answer was coercion, until ordinary civilised law was re-established.

In some respects the situation in rural Ireland had changed for the better – at least a more tolerant attitude had become prevalent. One area where it had changed notably was in Mayo, for, on September 19, Captain Boycott returned to Lough Mask House. It was exactly a year to the day after Parnell's Ennis speech that he descended from the train in Claremorris. He was met by three policemen, but when the small party travelled along the route followed by the relief expedition and its escort, there were no demonstrations. Even when the news of the return spread round Ballinrobe and among the Lough Mask tenants there was no harassment or overt hostility. However, Boycott claimed that when, at the end of the month, he went to a cattle auction in Westport, he was subjected to treatment similar to what had taken place in the autumn of 1880. He said that he was surrounded by a mob which hooted and groaned, that he had to be rescued from the crowd by the police, and that later his effigy was hoisted up in the market square and finally burned. This appears to have been the last angry outburst of the Mayo population against him, and the local papers, although noting his return, failed to report the demonstration in Westport. After that, apparently, what was past was past and Boycott was left in peace to resume his role as a landlord, although whether he also resumed his job as land agent for Lord Erne, whether the hated tyrant, who had been subjected to so much abuse and ill-treatment, and the tenantry found a real *modus vivendi*, remains obscure.

During this period, articles about Boycott still appeared in the newspapers from time to time – the *Irish World* ran one on him in October 1881, written by a Mrs McDougall, a lady of Irish birth who now lived in Canada and was doing a journalistic tour of her native land. The article was headed 'At Lough Mask House', with the sub-heading, 'A Visit to the Home of Captain Boycott. A Universally Detested Man. Instances of his Cruelty and Despicable Meanness'. Before arriving at Lough Mask, Mrs McDougall had visited Achill Island, where she found 'the people did not hold his name in much reverence'. Her tour of the estate took place before Boycott's return because she wrote of the empty house and the iron huts of the constabulary, who were still patrolling the grounds and using the stable loft as their head-quarters. She mentioned that his return was expected; according to her informant, he could not find anyone but the Irish to put up with him. The article was chatty in tone – the reader also learned that Mrs McDougall had had neuralgia in Ballinrobe – and did not contain much new information, being mainly a rehash of the stories of Boycott fining his labourers, of his being justifiably boycotted because he was 'the height of a great tyrant', and being equally mean and unkind to the soldiers and volunteers. She elicited the information that nobody had a bad word to say against Mrs Boycott, and indulged in some philosophic musings – did Boycott think he was doing right in imposing his system of fines? Did he think that increasing their hunger pains would make the tenants more orderly? Would he have acted differently if he had been 'suddenly brought to change places with the serf?'. The questions were rhetorical, and Mrs McDougall moved on to bring her journalistic talents to bear on a visit to the house of the murdered Lord Montmorres.

Even if the situation had calmed down at Lough Mask, in other areas 'Captain Moonlight' and the forces of intimidation reigned supreme, as Parnell had predicted they would if he were arrested. Much of British public opinion was able to enjoy a gloomy satisfaction over the scene, not because it thought Parnell was right, but because it justified the continued use of coercive measures. Mr Gladstone had not the same belief in the effects of repressive measures on a hostile population, he was well aware that they could also serve to stiffen resistance. Increasingly if slowly, he was being driven to the conclusion that the periods of Irish unrest were not passing phases, that although they subsided from time to time, they were always linked to dissatisfaction with English rule as such, whether it was progressive or coercive. But by late 1881 and early 1882 he had not yet reached his final conclusion that Irish nationalism was a steady flame, that the demands for some form of self-government were justified, and that Parnell was the man who could lead a partly autonomous Ireland. Even at this time he did not suffer from the common English disease of hating Parnell personally and therefore failing to understand what he represented and why. Although, like Forster, he had no direct contact with the Irish leader, he was impressed by the manner – if not the methods – with which Parnell had fought and forged a political party from the supposedly undisciplined Irish, and he recognised in Parnell real qualities of leadership which might one day mature into statesmanship. Furthermore he could not, temperamentally or politically, allow the current situation in Ireland to continue, and was therefore prepared to negotiate with the imprisoned Irish leader.

Parnell's need for a solution was as great as Gladstone's; indeed he had banked upon a compromise being reached. Eventually, after much secret and tortuous negotiation, one was agreed upon which has gone down into history as 'the Kilmainham treaty'. Parnell came to an understanding with Gladstone that, in return for amendments to the Land Act which would deal with the arrears question and include leaseholders in the Act, and the abandonment of coercion at the earliest opportunity, he would use all his influence in Ireland to restrain violence and outrage, and would 'co-operate cordially for the future with the Liberal party in forwarding Liberal principles and measures of general reform'. On this understanding, Parnell and the other imprisoned leaders were released at the beginning of May, 1882. Queen Victoria was horrified by one release – 'Is it possible that M. Davitt, known as one of the worst of treasonable agitators, is also to be released?' she wired Home Secretary Harcourt, 'I cannot believe it.' Mr Forster was also appalled and, as Parnell came out of Kilmainham, he resigned. In part he considered the negotiations, in which he had not directly participated, a blow to his authority as Chief Secretary, but he objected to the idea of the treaty even more; negotiating with Parnell was, in his opinion, a surrender of England's authority and a direct submission to lawlessness and outrage. If he had hoped that those who shared his opinion would rally to his side, he was disappointed; a political reputation built up over twenty years had been shattered during his two years as Chief Secretary for Ireland and, although he remained in Parliament, he never regained his former prestige. Within four years he was dead, another casualty, perhaps, of the bitterness of Anglo-Irish relations.

What happened after Kilmainham is, in detail, another book, a story that has already been written from many angles and doubtless will be covered in the future from as many more, for it remains perennially fascinating. One thing assuredly killed by the Kilmainham treaty – by what was known in some nationalist circles as 'Parnell's one man new departure' – was the Land League. It was in its death throes as Parnell lay in Kilmainham, but after his release he proceeded to suppress the Ladies League with as much vigour as Gladstone had suppressed the original one – an act for which his sister Anna never forgave him – and to turn his attention to a different approach.

The Land League had been the most unified and disciplined agrarian movement in Irish history. It had welded together, as Fintan Lalor had long ago predicted that agitation based on the land question would, virtually all the disparate elements of Irish nationalism and discontent, and thereby produced the essential social revolution. Gladstone was in no doubt as to the effectiveness and achievements of the League when, in April 1882, he said, 'The government had to deal with a state of things in Ireland entirely different from any that had been known there for fifty years ... a social revolution. ... The seat and the source of the movement ... is to be looked for in the foundation of the Land League'; and, later, in 1890: 'Suppose I told you that without the agitation Ireland would never have had the Land Act of 1881, are you prepared to deny that? I must record my firm opinion that it would not have become the law of the land if it had not been for the agitation with which Irish society was convulsed.' If the League had not survived, this was because it was, basically, a short-term organisation which must die once its objectives (or most of them) had been achieved, but its short life had proved that the Irish peasants could be effectively organised and provided a spring-board for Parnell. The man who saw the potential in Fintan Lalor's ideas and harnessed it was Michael Davitt, who deserves a credit Irish history has not accorded him. The man who utilised the ready-made engine once Davitt had set it on the rails was, of course, Parnell, who, more clearly than Davitt, realised where the engine could go if properly driven. Just as Davitt was incapable of furthering a coherent, long-term, political campaign, Parnell was incapable of organising grass-roots agrarian agitation, and for a brief, vital period, the two men complemented each other.

The single most effective weapon forged by the Land League was boycotting, as its use in subsequent land agitation and its later world-wide application, proved. In 1882, as the Land League itself was being helped on its way to oblivion by Parnell, the subject of boycotting was discussed in the House of Commons. During a debate on the latest Prevention of Crime Bill for Ireland, John Dillon defended the practice as a means whereby the people 'could protect their rights more effectually than by murder or incendiarism, and other processes familiar in the history of Ireland'. He said it had kept the roofs over the heads of hundreds of poor families in Mayo, that when the choice lay between 'Captain Moonlight' and boycotting, it was the lesser of the two evils, and had become a proper and legitimate weapon in circumstances where the people remained without governmental protection from the worst evils of eviction. In reply to Dillon's defence, Gladstone asked and answered the question, 'What is meant by Boycotting? In the first place it is combined intimidation. In the second place, it is combined intimidation made use of for the purpose of destroying the private liberty of choice by fear of ruin and starvation. In the third place, that being what Boycotting is in itself, we must look to this – that the creed of Boycotting, like every other creed, requires a sanction; and the sanction of Boycotting, that which stands in the rear of Boycotting, and by which alone Boycotting can in the long run be made thoroughly effective – is the murder which is not to be denounced'. There were loud cries of 'No' from the Home Rulers at this interpretation, and later, when the subject was again in the spotlight, William O'Brien said, 'In a country like Ireland there was nothing like boycotting for keeping down outrages'; by boycotting he meant 'an expression of organised public sentiment and opinion, without admixture of intimidation', and that, in his view – and he quoted criminal statistics to uphold his view – boycotting was indubitably 'the peacemaker of Ireland'.

William O'Brien also asserted: 'The two master keys to Parnell's success were obstruction in Parliament and Boycotting in Ireland'. Undoubtedly they were the keys that unlocked the door of popular success, that helped turn Parnell into the leader whom first the Fenian element, then the mass of Irish peasants and Irish-Americans followed (although O'Brien was too intelligent to think they explained the whole of Parnell's success; that being a more complex, subtle business). But to have attracted and fired the popular imagination in the Irish situation of 1880, a politician needed a flamboyant personality or spectacular powers of oratory, qualities which Parnell lacked. Boycotting filled the gaps and helped put the seal on his position as 'the uncrowned King of Ireland'.

'The Death of the Gentleman with Whom the Never-to-be-Forgotten Term "Boycotted" Originated'

Boycott himself made one last, brief appearance in the limelight when he gave evidence before the Parnell Special Commission in 1888. In February, 1886, he had returned to England, taking up an excellent position as agent for Sir Hugh Adair's large Flixton estate which lay on the Suffolk border, not far from his birthplace at Burgh St Peter. Exactly when he sold the lease on the Lough Mask estate is uncertain, but it is probable that too much acrid water had flowed under the bridge for him to resettle in Mayo permanently, and that he sold at the first favourable opportunity. It also is probable that in the end he emerged from Ireland without too great – if any – financial loss, for he did manage to sell the lease and there was also the £2,000 raised by public subscription. He left Ireland without bitterness, holding on to the Kildarra estate and frequently spending his holidays there.

The Parnell Special Commission was one of the most extraordinary and remarkable events in British parliamentary history, with an equally remarkable and extraordinary background. After the defeat of Gladstone's first Home Rule Bill in 1886, Parnell, whose health had suffered under the strain of the recent fight, decided to set up house with Katharine O'Shea. He went into semi-hibernation, while Lord Salisbury's new Tory administration addressed itself to the task of twenty years resolute government as the first step towards the peaceful integration of Ireland into the United Kingdom. It was in early March, 1887, as the new Chief Secretary, Arthur Balfour, was piloting through Parliament a particularly fierce Coercion Bill, that *The Times* printed a series of articles entitled 'Parnellism and Crime'. These articles were aimed partly at making clear to all but the wilfully blind the necessity for Balfour's measure, partly as an attack on Gladstone whom the editor of *The Times* hated, and finally to discredit Parnell.

The first article claimed that the Irish leaders, whose chief was Parnell, were in fact 'in intimate, notorious and continuous relations with avowed murderers'; that their power initially came from the Land League, a movement based on 'a scheme of assassination, carefully calculated and coolly applied' organised by known Fenians. It threw his speeches back at Gladstone, including the ones in which he had claimed that crime dogged the footsteps of the Land League and that 'that which stands in the rear of boycotting . . . is the murder that is not to be denounced'. An accompanying leader stated that *The Times* was embarking on the long overdue exposé of Land League tactics to help shake off the flabby tolerance of evil currently pervading the English people and convince them that defiant attacks upon the State by 'a contemptible minority of a minority' could no longer be permitted. This first onslaught was followed by another, which dealt with 'the Parnellite paymasters', generally the Irish-Americans, specifically the *Irish World*. It was not difficult to provide examples of the *Irish World*'s virulent anti-British, pro-Parnell, extremist attitudes, nor to enumerate its financial support. Ominously, however, the article continued by linking the Irish-Americans and a well-known Land League leader, and therefore, by implication, Parnell himself, with the Phoenix Park murders which had occurred immediately after the Kilmainham treaty in 1882, in which the newly arrived Chief Secretary, Lord Frederick Cavendish, and the permanent Under-Secretary, Thomas Burke, had been brutally stabbed to death. The third article was again concerned with the supposedly constitutional organisation founded by Irish Fenian brains, backed by American Fenian money, enforced by bullet and knife, and it, too, linked Parnell to the Phoenix Park murders. This was followed by a leading article demanding that Parnell reply to the serious charges levelled against him, and asking whether Mr Gladstone, in the light of the startling facts accumulated and laid bare in the articles, was prepared to continue his shameful association with the nationalists. If Parnell himself was prepared to let judgement go by default, *The Times* appealed to honest Liberals to save the honour of their party and the honour of Parliament by answering the charges, and denouncing them if necessary.

Letters poured into *The Times* offices, congratulating the newspaper on its masterly exposé, but no reply came from Parnell, other nationalist leaders or the Liberals. In mid-April there was a further article followed by the publication of the *pièce de résistance*, a secret letter supposedly written by Parnell. This letter was admittedly not in Parnell's hand but the signature was undoubtedly his, according to *The Times*, and it intimated that Parnell had only denounced the Phoenix Park murders because of political expediencey while privately condoning them. To this accusation Parnell did reply in the House of Commons, briefly and coldly stating that the signature bore no resemblance to his, the subject matter was preposterous, the phraseology absurd, and that he would have gladly stood between the daggers of the assassins and Lord Frederick Cavendish and even Mr Burke. He finished: 'Now, Sirs, I leave this subject. I have suffered more than any other man from that terrible deed in Phoenix Park, and the Irish nation has suffered more than any other nation.'

The Times had no intention, however, of leaving the subject, and it published further articles demanding that Parnell refute the terrible implications of the letter in a less off-hand manner, and making further accusations of his links with those who had perpetrated the murders. But Parnell had no intention of demeaning himself or the Irish nation by further interest, and the matter might have hung fire – with some damaging results to Parnell's reputation in England if not in Ireland – but for the intervention of Frank Hugh O'Donnell who issued a writ against one of the proprietors of *The Times* and its printer, claiming very large damages for libel. O'Donnell had barely been mentioned in any of the lengthy articles and this seems to have been his main reason for bringing the libel action. He felt he should have been mentioned more; he, who had played such an important role in the early days of obstruction and the fight for Home Rule; he, who knew so many distinguished people. The writ was issued on the claim that *The Times* had linked him, as an early Home Ruler, with the activities of the Land League and the agrarian outrages, and thereby libelled him because he had never supported or condoned Parnell in this phase of his campaign. When the case finally came to court in July 1888, the result was that further evidence was produced against Parnell and Michael Davitt, for during the course of the proceedings, fresh letters were introduced. One, in particular, supposedly written by Parnell to Patrick Egan, the Land League treasurer, ran as follows:

KILMAINHAM, JAN 9/1882.

Dear E.

What are these fellows waiting for? This inaction is inexcusable; our best men are in prison and nothing is being done.

Let there be an end to this hesitency. (*sic*) Prompt action is called for.

You undertook to make it hot for old Forster and Co. Let us have some evidence of your power to do so.

My health is good, thanks.

Yours very truly,
Charles Stewart Parnell.

This extraordinary letter, more damning than the original one published in *The Times* because it inferred that Parnell had precipitated the Phoenix Park murders by his call for prompt action, was produced in court with great solemnity and accepted with equal solemnity as genuine beyond any shadow of doubt. Indeed nobody asked where *The Times* had obtained it – or the other incriminating letters ; or whether it had verified its sources.

Some Irish nationalists claimed that O'Donnell had only initiated the libel action because he hated Parnell and wanted the further damaging evidence, in the shape of the additional letters, to be produced, and that he had been supported by *The Times* and the government in his endeavour. This seems far-fetched, even in the context of the bitter political climate, and when O'Donnell inevitably lost the case, he gave his opinion that it had been deliberately sabotaged by his own counsel so that Parnell would not have to give evidence and could discover what material *The Times* had against him, which would enable him to decide whether to bring an action himself!

It was true that, by now, even Parnell had decided judgement could not be allowed to go by default, and he asked for a Select Committee to be set up to enquire into the authenticity of the letters produced in evidence during the O'Donnell suit. For he – and everybody else – realised that the O'Donnell case had thrown up the old accusations, that the new letters, coming on top of the earlier one printed in *The Times*, had seized the attention of the country, and that by them he could well be damned. As an honourable Member of the House of Commons, he was entitled to a Select Committee but he did not get it, because Lord Salisbury was among the many convinced that *The Times* would not have published or produced the letters without incontrovertible proof of their authenticity, and considered Parnell guilty of the charges made against him. Salisbury consequently took what seemed a golden opportunity to bring Parnell and his whole movement to trial (in fact, if not officially) and condemn them in the eyes of the country and the world. He asked for the establishment of a Special Commission to enquire, not into the authenticity of the letters, but into the entire range of charges and allegations made against certain Members of Parliament in the articles 'Parnellism and Crime' and during the recent proceedings of O'Donnell v. Walter and another. It required a special Act of Parliament to give statutory authority to the Commission and this was introduced at midnight on July 16, 1888. It was bitterly condemned and opposed by Gladstone and other Liberals but it was passed by Parliament. The terms of reference of this novel, and quite extraordinary, Commission were indeed wide; the Land League was charged with promoting and inciting boycotting and other outrages, with collecting funds for agrarian crimes; with making payments to persons injured in the commission of such crimes; with holding meetings inciting the boycott and general intimidation; with disseminating similar literature; with advocating resistance to the law and duly constituted authority; with impeding the detection of crime and making payments to persons guilty of boycotting for their legal defence. The Members of Parliament scheduled in the indictment – all the leading Home Rulers – were charged that by their acts and conduct they had led people to believe that they approved of boycotting and other outrages, with attending meetings and making speeches encouraging this belief, with making payments of money for the above purpose, with receiving large sums of money from America for the same, with expressing little or no disapproval when crime followed their speeches, or, if they did express faint disapproval, with letting it be known this was not their real opinion but a political ploy. Then there were the specific charges against Parnell himself arising from the letters; that he had incited, or connived at, and approved of, the Phoenix Park murders.

It was on Monday, September 17, 1888 that the initial sitting of the Special Commission took place in Number One Probate Court of the Royal Courts of Justice, but the proceedings were then adjourned until October 22, from which date the commissioners heard evidence with what became monotonous regularity. The Attorney General appeared for *The Times* (as he had in the O'Donnell suit), which, through him, was given access to government papers, while Sir Charles Russell and the young Herbert Asquith appeared for Parnell. The crucial matter for the country at large was whether Parnell had written the letters linking him with the Phoenix Park murders; on these, his reputation as a responsible leader of constitutional agitation would stand or for ever be discredited. However, the government, *The Times* and the Attorney General were interested in blasting his reputation, and thereby the credibility of the Home Rule movement, by more detailed methods. The extraordinary personal hostility Parnell had engendered in England was apparent in the setting-up of the Special Commission, and it included a widespread belief that he was chiefly motivated by a hatred of England, an unedifying, base and destructive reason for leadership. Another belief which was also widely held by 1888, in anti-Parnell circles, was that if Parnell himself was destroyed, the Home Rule movement would automatically collapse, and this reasoning can be discerned in the initial publication of the articles in *The Times* and in the instigation of the Special Commission.

As a result of the government's desire to expose and ruin Parnell, witnesses in their scores appeared through October, November and December, to catalogue the major crimes of the Land League, but no mention was made of the letters. One of the worst crimes of the Land League, as emphasised in the indictment, had been the introduction of boycotting, and a great deal of time was devoted to tracing its origins, from Michael Davitt's speech at Knockaroo in January 1880 to Parnell's Ennis speech, and all those early Land League speeches which had foreshadowed the policy. Discussions took place as to whether it was a legitimate and proper process, tolerable within certain limits, or whether it was an intolerable form of terrorism. It was on December 12, 1888, that Captain Boycott appeared in the Probate Court – 'the gentleman who has added the verb "boycott" to the English vocabulary, and whose name is, in consequence, as widely known over the habitable globe as the names of Homer, Moses, Dickens, or Parnell'. The same commentator noted that Boycott was 'a shortish man, with a bald head, a rim of white hair, and a heavy white moustache, and a patriarchally rich and flowing white beard'. Boycott related the sequence of events leading up to his isolation, told of his being forced to leave Mayo, of being similarly forced to quit the Hamman Hotel in Dublin, produced some of the threatening letters he had received, and said he knew of no cause whatever, beyond the matter of collecting rents, for his ill-treatment. Boycott emerged from his recent anonymity, without pressure and with pleasure, to give this evidence, for he was among those who believed in the validity of the Commission and expected Parnell and the Home Rule movement to be finally and justly discredited.

This was Boycott's last appearance on the national stage, but the Special Commission reassembled after a Christmas recess and ploughed manfully on through January 1889, with never a mention of the letters. Early February was enlivened by the appearance of Henri le Caron, the English spy whom Davitt had encountered in Chicago in 1880, and who treated the court to a lurid account of the anti-British activities of the Fenians in the United States. However, the denouement was at hand, for on February 19, 1889, John Cameron Macdonald, the manager of *The Times*, appeared and admitted that, although he knew the source of the letters, namely Richard Pigott the former Irish nationalist and journalist, he had not bothered to enquire how or where Pigott had obtained them in the first place. The next day Edward Caulfield Houston, an ex-reporter on the Dublin *Daily Express* and latterly secretary of the Irish Loyal and Patriotic Union (a strongly anti-Parnell and anti-Home Rule organisation), took the stand. Caulfield was the man who had originally obtained the letters from Pigott in a series of cloak-and-dagger meetings in Paris, and had eventually sold them to *The Times*, but he also admitted that he had taken no steps to check their authenticity but, in his enthusiasm to discredit Parnell, had accepted Pigott's word that the letters were genuine. On February 21, Pigott himself appeared in the witness-box and, subjected to merciless cross-examination by Sir Charles Russell, started to crumble, one of the highlights of the highly dramatic scene being when he was asked to spell 'hesitancy' and proceeded to spell it 'hesitency', as in the letter supposedly written by Parnell from Kilmainham. (Parnell, not noted for an overall love of literature or language was noted for meticulousness in spelling, a fact as well-known in Irish nationalist circles as was the reputation of Pigott as a blackmailer, sponger and pornographer.) After the week-end, Pigott failed to appear in court and Sir Charles Russell was able to announce that he had fled the country, leaving behind a confession that he had forged the letters. The final sensation occurred later in the week when the news arrived from Madrid that Pigott had committed suicide there, and that, as far as the majority of the inhabitants of the United Kingdom of Great Britain and Ireland was concerned, was the end of the Special Commission.

Parnell had been more than exonerated, he had been proved to be the victim, if not of a conspiracy – nobody actually accused *The Times* of commissioning the forgery of the letters – at least of a blind desire to vilify him at any cost. The pendulum of public opinion, compounded of regret, shame and sympathy, swung violently in his favour and he became the idol of England, lionised in Liberal society, given a standing ovation in the House of Commons. The Commission continued to sit until November 22, 1889, by which time 98,000 questions had been put to 450 witnesses, all the Irish leaders had appeared and made their speeches, and thousands of pounds had been spent. The speeches included Parnell's own testament, cool and trenchant; Michael Davitt's impassioned defence of the Land League, and a magnificent address by Sir Charles Russell in which he said that what the Commission was attempting was the impossible, for it was attempting to put on trial the Irish nation. The findings were eventually published at the beginning of 1890, by which time most people had lost interest, and the conclusions were that the Irish MPs were not members of a conspiracy to establish an independent Ireland, but that some of them did help establish the Land League with Michael Davitt; that they did enter into a system of coercion and intimidation to promote agrarian agitation, but that there was no ambivalence in their public and private statements; that they did disseminate the literature of the *Irish World* and other extremist newspapers, but did not directly incite people into crime or make payments for the encouragement of crime, on the contrary, many of the respondents, particularly Davitt, had tried to prevent violence; that they did help defend people charged with agrarian crimes but were not intimate with notorious criminals; they did obtain support from men who advocated violence such as Patrick Ford and John Devoy but that it was not proven that their actions were influenced by these men. The specific charges against Parnell, that he had known the Phoenix Park murderers, made payments to them, encouraged their heinous crime or been insincere in his denunciation of it, were unconditionally withdrawn. Parnell's comment on the findings was, 'Well, really, between ourselves, I think it is just about what I would have said myself.'

By the beginnings of 1890 there was a general atmosphere of Anglo-Irish, or more accurately Liberal–Home Rule euphoria, induced not so much by the Commission's findings but by the Pigott episode and Parnell's nation-wide vindication. Parnell had visited Gladstone at Hawarden, each had been impressed with the other (although Gladstone more with the Irish leader than he with 'the grand old spider'), and the shape of a new Home Rule Bill had been cordially discussed. Gladstone was not then in office, but the Conservative administration was coming towards the end of its term and the likelihood of the Liberals being returned at the next general election, with a mandate from the country to implement Home Rule (which they had not possessed in 1886) was high. The successful culmination of Parnell's leadership was within reach, the tactics of his campaign forgotten or accepted as necessary and justified, and the winds stood fair for a peaceful solution of Anglo-Irish relations and fruitful future co-operation. But the storm warning had already been hoisted. At the end of 1889, Captain O'Shea filed a suit for divorce against his wife Katharine, citing Parnell as co-respondent, and a tragedy of classical Greek proportions lay ahead. The suit came to court in December 1890 and Parnell did not defend it. The image of a man who had cuckolded his friend's wife was presented to the world,

O'Shea was granted his divorce and the English noncomformist conscience demanded Parnell's head. Gladstone was faced with the agonising problems of condemning a man for his private life (a pastime of which he did not approve), of believing that man to be the only one who could, and should, lead Ireland to Home Rule, but of knowing that his party, and the majority of the country, would no longer tolerate Parnell's leadership. Eventually he issued what amounted to an ultimatum – either Parnell went or he could not carry Home Rule. The Irish nationalists, who at first had stood firm behind their leader, were then faced with their agonising choice between loyalty to the man who had brought Home Rule to within inches of success, or the destruction of the movement – for it was by then accepted that only the Liberals would implement Home Rule. They ousted Parnell from the chairmanship of the party. With the decree absolute granted in June 1891, Parnell married Katharine O'Shea, and the Irish Catholic conscience rose in outrage. With his back to the wall, but believing that time was on his side and that if he stood firm he must eventually regain the uncontested leadership, Parnell fought three by-elections in Ireland, but his candidates lost disastrously. Then, in October 1891, came the final, unbelievable curtain, beyond the bounds of melodrama; Parnell, aged only forty-five, died in England in his wife's arms, exhausted by the physical exertions of the bitter campaigns of the last few months, torn by the emotional pressures, partly killed by the qualities that had made him the leader he had been, the fierce pride and the unqualified belief in the motto 'to thine own self be true'. Parnell's body was taken to Ireland for burial in Dublin's Glasnevin cemetery, in pouring rain and to the lurid accompaniment of a falling comet. It was an occasion for mass mourning such as Ireland had never before witnessed. Perhaps Gladstone's words remain the best summary of Parnell's death: 'Dear, dear, what a tragedy! A marvellous man, a terrible fall'.

Boycott outlived the man who had helped catapult him into notoriety by six years. Undoubtedly he was of the opinion, shared by many Englishmen, that the manner of the Irish leader's fall vindicated the intention, if not the methods, of *The Times* articles and the Special Commission. Parnell, in his private life, had been shown as a treacherous, deceitful fellow, and, concomittantly, was not to be trusted in public life; while the behaviour of his lieutenants and followers after the divorce and after his death, with the continuation of bitter, unedifying, internecine warfare, reinforced the contention that the Irish were emotionally and politically immature, a self-destructive, violent race who needed to be governed by the British. The other effects of Parnell's leadership were overlooked: that he had married the forces of agrarian unrest to parliamentary pressures; that he had forged an adult parliamentary party (however infantile its behaviour in the years after his death); that he had forced Britain to examine its past record in Ireland, and convinced at least half the country that Home Rule was justified.

Boycott remained as agent for Sir Hugh Adair's Flixton estate, continued to indulge his lifelong passion for horses and racing by becoming secretary of the local Bungay Race Committee, and to be active in local politics as a staunch upholder of the Union. His health had not been good for some years, but at the beginning of 1897 it began to cause concern, and he and his wife embarked on a cruise for Malta, in the hopes of improving his condition. He was taken seriously ill at Brindisi and had to return to Suffolk. Early in June he collapsed, and on the night of June 19, 1897, he died peacefully at his home, The Hollows, on the Flixton estate, aged sixty-five.

His death was noted not only in the local papers but in several London ones including the *Standard* and *The Times*. All the obituaries mentioned that he was the gentleman with whom the term 'boycotting' had originated and gave accounts of the Land League's campaign against him, and of the relief expedition. The local papers were equivocal in their assessment of his manner and behaviour during the trying times of depression through which agriculture in East Anglia had recently passed. The *Norfolk News* said he was 'stern and brusque of manner', while the *Norfolk Chronicle* wrote: 'Those who knew him thoroughly, appreciated his very business-like methods, and he was as popular as it was possible for any man to be who desired to do justice as between landlords and tenants.' Appropriately, for a man who believed in the concepts of Empire and England's inherent racial superiority, Boycott died in the week of celebrations for Queen Victoria's Diamond Jubilee, the apotheosis of the Imperial dream and reality. He was buried in the churchyard of Burgh St Peter, the funeral service being conducted by his nephew, Arthur St John Boycott, who had shared the vicissitudes of the siege of Lough Mask. His grave lies to the left of the church and its famous red-brick tower (in the 1970s it is overgrown with weeds), while on the pulpit inside, surrounded by other Boycott plaques, is one bearing the words: 'Charles Cunningham Boycott, elder brother of the above, who died June 19, 1897, aged 65 years'.

Boycott made his last will and testament on May 31, 1897, bequeathing 'all his real and personal estate whatsoever and wherever to his dear wife, Annie', and appointing her sole executrix. Whatever the *Norfolk Chronicle* might have stated about his business-like methods, the disarray in which he left his affairs upheld the earlier Mayo contention that he was a poor business-man. In November 1897 Annie Boycott, sued by creditors, was forced to appear in the chambers of the High Court of Justice, Chancery Division. The judge ordered that an account of the testators personal estate be rendered and applied to payment of the funeral expenses and debts, and if this proved insufficient, that further enquiries be instigated into the real estate owned by the testator at the time of his death, plus the encumbrances attached thereto, and that part or if necessary the whole of the real estate be sold. Accordingly, further legal proceedings were instituted in Dublin, the Kildarra estate in Mayo was duly sold to meet Boycott's debts, and the last links with Ireland were severed.

Michael Davitt, who had been as responsible as Parnell for the introduction of boycotting, lived into the twentieth century.

After the Kilmainham treaty, disapproving of Parnell's 'one man new departure', he continued to concentrate on solving the land question finally and absolutely, but as the land campaign had ceased to be the major issue, he consequently slipped from the centre of power. Later, briefly, he became an MP, but passionate campaigning for a single issue was Davitt's strength, not the compromise, the negotiating, the tactical finesse required in politics, and he was not a success. He spent much of his later years in England, associated with Keir Hardie and the rising Labour movement, interested in the wider platform of the rights of the working man, championing the underdog everywhere (he campaigned for Jewish rights and against the pogroms in Russia). In the last years of his life he became involved in a movement for non-sectarian education in Ireland, believing this to be essential for solving the religious and racial bitterness of his native land. This was a single subject to which he could have brought his capacity for passionate organisation, but he came to it too late in life to make any dent in the equally passionate Catholic belief that Catholic children must have a Catholic education. When he died, he was buried at Straide, the tiny Mayo hamlet of his birth, and inside the church was erected a plaque which bears the words, 'Pray for the soul of Michael Davitt, Untiring benefactor of the Irish Catholic tenantry who died 30 May, 1906', while in the graveyard, his wife erected a memorial stone with two verses from St Matthew carved thereon: 'Blessed are they that suffered persecution for justice sake, for theirs is the kingdom of heaven', and, 'Blessed are they that hunger and thirst after justice for they shall have their fill'.

Of the four main protagonists of this story, Parnell and Gladstone retain their stature, Davitt has never been properly accorded his, but the name known to more people, in more constant usage, is, ironically, that of Boycott.

Notes and Sources

A considerable amount of material with reference to Boycott, the relief expedition and its military and policing arrangements is listed in the index of the correspondence emanating from the Chief Secretary's Office, Dublin Castle (now in the State Paper Office at the Castle). Much of this material was sent to London at the time of the Parnell Special Commission in 1888, not all of it was returned to its source, and there was considerable misfiling of the material eventually reclaimed by the Irish State Paper Office. When I found difficulty in tracing some of the correspondence, Mr Mac Goilla Choille, the Keeper of the Manuscripts, kindly allowed me to search through boxes at random, by which process I was able to trace more material, but I was not always clear what the proper index number was and when doubtful I have given the box number for those interested.

Abbreviated titles for the sources are used here, the fuller titles are given in the bibliography.

Chapter 1: 'A RESPECTABLE GENTLEMAN, FORMERLY AN OFFICER IN HER MAJESTY'S 39TH REGIMENT'

The chapter heading is taken from counsel's description of Boycott when he appeared in the libel suit at the Mayo Assizes: 'a respectable gentleman living in this country, and was formerly an officer in Her Majesty's 39th Regiment'. (*Mayo Constitution* 13.3.1860.)

Page 13: With reference to Boycott's Huguenot ancestry there is a note in the Burgh St Peter parish register, thus: 'Samuel Boycott (came '64, lived 33 years) died aged 73 in 1797 (therefore was 40 years of age on coming) therefore was born in 1724. Revocation of Nantes 1685 – 39 years before – I think it was not his father but his g.father who was the French refugee – nay I am *sure* from other circumstances.'

Page 17: The explanation about the cypresses and the red brick tower was taken from the *Raveningham Group Magazine*, June 1971. This in its turn was taken from an article by a former vicar of Burgh St Peter in the *Beccles and Bungay Journal*, October 1949.

Page 19: James Redpath's comment on Boycott's fraudulent use of the title of Captain appeared in the article 'An Exile of Erin – An Interview with James Redpath', reprinted in his book *Talks About Ireland*.

Page 25: Gladstone's view that the Encumbered Estates Act was passed with lazy, heedless uninformed good intentions is quoted from Morley's *Life of Gladstone*.

Page 25: It was William Cobbett who said that the ever-damned potato was the curse of Ireland. It appears in Desmond Ryan's *The Phoenix Flame*.

Page 26: The letter in which James Fintan Lalor wrote that the land question contained the material from which victory could be manufactured and that it could be a self-acting engine once fired was written on 25.1.1847, but not published in the *Irish Felon* until 24.6.1848.

Page 27: Charles Gavan Duffy's remark that there seemed no more hope for the Irish cause than for the corpse on the dissecting table is quoted from *Devoy's Post Bag 1871–1928*.

Chapter 2: 'OUT AND MAKE WAY FOR THE BOLD FENIAN MEN'

The chapter heading is taken from the famous Fenian ballad.

Page 29: Boycott said that only after a long struggle did he become prosperous on Achill in his letter to *The Times*, 18.12.1880.

Page 30: The incident involving Boycott and Thomas Clarke is reported in the *Mayo Constitution*, 29.1.1856.

Page 30: The magistrates adjudging no assault had been threatened or committed, *ibid.*

Page 32: Carr's letter to the Receiver of Wrecks was given in evidence during the libel action, and reported in the *Mayo Constitiuton*, 13.3.1860.

Page 33: That the defence occupied the greater part of the day, *ibid.*

Page 33: Boycott was noted as being among the gentlemen present at the proceedings against the Achill Poor Law Guardians in the *Mayo Constitution*, 30.6.1863.

Page 34: The allegation that Walter Bourke had called Boycott a hairy beggar when he prosecuted him for having a poor man dragged to the Achill cliffs was made in the *Connaught Telegraph*, 27.11.1880.

Page 36: The amended IRB path of 1859 is quoted from P. S. O'Hegarty's *A History of Ireland Under the Union*.

Page 37: That an Irish-American vowed never to forgive the bloody English government which had treated him worse than a dog is quoted from Richard Pigott's *Personal Recollections of an Irish Journalist*. This was published in 1882, before his ultimate notoriety.

Page 37: Harcourt's comment about the power of the Irish in the United

States was made in a letter to Lord Hartington, 24.12.1885, and is quoted from Gardiner's *The Life of Sir William Harcourt*.

Page 39: Isaac Butt said that Fenianism had taught Gladstone the intensity of Irish disaffection at the Home Rule Conference of 1873. The remark is quoted from Davitt's *The Fall of Feudalism*.

Page 39: William O'Brien quoted Gladstone as saying that Fenianism had acted as the chapel bell to rouse the conscience of England in his *Recollections*.

Page 40: Gladstone's comment on the burden of becoming Prime Minister is quoted from Philip Magnus's *Life of Gladstone*.

Page 40: Disraeli's cynical comment, *ibid.*

Page 40: That Gladstone received the news of the Queen's summons to form a cabinet while chopping trees at Hawarden, and commented that his mission was to pacify Ireland, was printed in the *National Review* in 1898, and is quoted from Morley's *Life of Gladstone*.

Page 40: Gladstone told the House of Commons that it was only since the onset of Fenianism that the country had taken note of Irish affairs on 30.3.1868 (Hansard, vol. 191).

Page 40: (footnote) Lord Granville's comment about envying Gladstone's wonderful body is quoted from G. W. E. Russell's *Portraits of the Seventies*.

Chapter 3: 'HOME RULE KEEPS A LITTLE CAULDRON
SIMMERING'

The chapter heading is from the comment made on the movement in the *Annual Register*, 1875, as in the text (page 52). The exact quote was 'Home Rule still keeps a little cauldron simmering'.

Page 47: Isaac Butt was described as the very type of ultra-domineering, narrow-minded Protestant Ascendancy by his first biographer, Sir William Gregory. The remark is quoted from the more recent book by David Thornley, *Isaac Butt and Home Rule*.

Page 49: The comment on the lack of generalship and organisation in the 1874 elections appeared in *The Nation*, 11.7.1874.

Page 50: It was George Bryan of Kilkenny who made the statement that a man should be a gentleman first and a patriot afterwards. The remark is quoted from Michael MacDonagh's *The Home Rule Movement*.

Page 51: It was T. P. O'Connor who described Joseph Biggar as the Belfast Quasimodo to the Irish Esmeralda in his *Memoirs of an Old Parliamentarian*.

Page 51: T. P. O'Connor said that Biggar possessed the true Ulster nature in *The Parnell Movement*.

Page 52: Disraeli said that the Home Rule movement would bring about the disintegration of the Empire during a debate on Butt's motion to introduce a Home Rule Bill, 2.7.1874. (*Hansard*, vol. 222.)

Page 52: Gladstone spoke of the ridiculousness of disintegrating the capital institutions of the country at an earlier date, in a speech made at Aberdeen, 24.9.1871.

Page 52: Joe Ronayne's suggestion regarding obstruction is quoted from Michael J. McCarthy's *The Irish Revolution.*

Page 55: Davitt's remark that Parnell frequently quoted two lines from Shakespeare inculcating fidelity to oneself is from his book *The Fall of Feudalism.*

Page 55: It was Davitt who described Parnell as the very picture of manly strength, *ibid.*

Page 55: Dozens of people commented on Parnell's extraordinary eyes, but it was Justin McCarthy who described them as especially remarkable, penetrating and magnetic in *The Story of an Irishman.*

Page 56: It was Joe Ronayne who said that Parnell was barely able to utter three consecutive sentences at the start of his career. The observation is quoted from William O'Brien's *Recollections.*

Page 56: Isaac Butt's comment that Parnell was a splendid recruit, likely to prove an ugly customer for the Saxon, is quoted from Barry O'Brien's *The Life of Charles Stewart Parnell.*

Page 56: A journalist told T. P. O'Connor that Parnell was a frightful duffer as a candidate, and the remark is quoted from his book *Charles Stewart Parnell – A Memory.*

Page 56: It was Richard Pigott who said Parnell's English accent was a serious disqualification for an Irish patriot in his *Personal Recollection of an Irish Journalist.* T. P. O'Connor also wrote of Parnell's 'fatal and obtrusive English accent' in his memoir of Parnell, but it was not generally regarded as a grave handicap.

Page 57: Joe Ronayne's comment that Parnell would tread on John Bull's toes harder than Napoleon did is quoted from William O'Brien's *Recollections.*

Chapter 4: 'LONG LIFE AND GOOD HEALTH TO BOWLD PARNELL'

The chapter heading is taken from a poem of T. D. Sullivan's (not one of his best) written in the early days of obstruction:

> Long life and good health to bowld Parnell and Biggar
> For they have hearts like the heart of a mouse;
> They're fighting for Ireland with courage and vigour
> And don't care a hang for 'the tone of the house'. . . .

Page 59: Boycott stated that family circumstances placed him in possession of further capital in his letter to *The Times,* 18.12.1880.

Page 60: George Moore's description of the typical Irish country house, a box with stone steps, is quoted from his book *Parnell and his Island.*

Page 60: Boycott said there was an amicable agreement between Lord Erne and his previous tenant, and that it was not as the result of an eviction that he obtained the lease of Lough Mask in his evidence to the Bessborough Commission, given at the Railway Hotel in Galway, 22.10. 1880.

Page 62: Parnell's maiden speech in which he said Ireland was not a geographical fragment but a nation was made during a debate on the Peace Preservation (Ireland) Bill, 26.4.1875. (*Hansard*, vol. 223.)

Page 62: His intervention on the subject of 'the Manchester Martyrs' occurred during a debate on Isaac Butt's motion for a Select Committee to enquire into an Irish Parliament on 30.6.1876. (*Hansard*, vol. 230.)

Page 62: Henry Lucy's comment that Biggar was the head and Parnell the tail of a new Irish party is quoted from his *Diary of Two Parliaments vol 1, 1874–1880.*

Page 62: Lucy's question as to why Parnell wasn't the biggest bore in the House was asked on 30.5.1877 and is similarly quoted.

Page 62–63: The poem on Parnell and Biggar was written by Sir Wilfrid Lawson and printed by Henry Lucy, 2.8.1877, *ibid.*

Page 63: The observer who said that Parnell's name was little known to Irish peasants was Michael J. McCarthy in *The Irish Revolution.*

Page 64: Gladstone's comment on Parnell's ability to say what he meant is quoted from T. P. O'Connor's *The Parnell Movement.*

Page 64: Parnell's assertion that he cared not for the English parliament, its outcries or its existence, was made at a meeting in Dublin on 21.8.1877.

Page 64: It was Michael Davitt who described Parnell as an Englishman of the strongest type moulded for an Irish purpose in *The Fall of Feudalism.*

Page 65: It was James Redpath who wrote of the sore-hearted Irish exiles, the missionaries of hatred, in the article 'Between Two Lords Slain' in his *Talks About Ireland.*

Page 66: It was Henri le Caron, the famous British spy, who described John Devoy as forbidding of aspect, in his book *Twenty-five Years in the Secret Service.* Even those who admired Devoy admitted he was not lovable.

Page 67: Devoy's dismissal of the Home Rule movement as a miserable caricature of Grattan's Parliament was made in a letter written to Dr Carroll on 16.11.1877. It is quoted from *Devoy's Post Bag 1871–1928.*

Page 67: His hope that a young man of spirit might emerge, *ibid.*

Page 67: J. J. O'Kelly's letter in which he reported on Parnell's character and his uncertainty of direction is also contained in *Devoy's Post Bag.*

Page 68: It was Barry O'Brien, whose biography remains one of the best on Parnell the man and contains much first-hand material, who wrote of his extraordinary silence in his *Life of Charles Stewart Parnell.*

Chapter 5: 'IT IS TIME WE CAME OUT OF THE RAT-HOLES
OF CONSPIRACY'

The chapter heading was Devoy's slogan for the New Departure. It is quoted from Desmond Ryan's essay on Devoy in *The Shaping of Modern Ireland*.

Page 73: The man who said the Fenian conspiracy could boast of no more interesting personality than Michael Davitt was Robert Anderson, the Assistant Commissioner of the Metropolitan Police in his book *Sidelights on the Home Rule Movement*.

Page 73: Davitt said that being forced to sit upright on a bucket ten hours a day was very distressing on the chest in his evidence to the Penal Reform Commission, 20.6.1878.

Page 75: Nearly all observers agreed that Davitt's Lancashire accent overlay his native Irish accent, although when, in 1906 John Devoy published a seventeen-part assessment of Davitt's career in the *Gaelic American* (9.6.1906 to 27.10.1906) he wrote that Davitt 'never acquired, nor tried to acquire an English accent'. It is possible that Devoy's ability to distinguish between one British accent and another was not great.

Page 75: Davitt's comment that 8 stone 10 lbs was not the proper weight for a man 6 ft in height and thirty years old is quoted from Sheehy Skeffington's *The Life of Michael Davitt*.

Page 76: Davitt said that the peasant's hatred of landlords was a vast untilled field of popular force in his *The Fall of Feudalism*.

Page 77: Parnell's speech refuting the policy of conciliating England was made at a Fenian meeting in Manchester in July 1877, and is quoted from Barry O'Brien's *The Life of Charles Stewart Parnell*.

Page 79: It was William O'Brien who described Patrick Ford as a small, dingy, silent man in his *Recollections*.

Page 80: Davitt wrote of the Fenian-constitutional merger as bringing the advanced nationalist spirit into Irish politics in his *The Fall of Feudalism*.

Page 80: That the only solution to the Irish land question was the abolition of landlordism was one of the resolutions passed at a Clan na Gael meeting at the Cooper Institute in New York in the autumn of 1878. It is quoted from John Devoy's *The Land of Eire*.

Page 82: Devoy's comment that his supporters no longer believed in little insurrections that England could crush in a few weeks appeared in the lengthy article on the New Departure in the *New York Herald*, 27.10.1878. The crucial telegram to Parnell was published in the *Herald* on 25.10.1878.

Page 83: That Davitt disapproved of the fate of Ireland dependent on the impression conveyed to the deaf Kickham was stated by John Devoy in article VII of his series published in the *Gaelic American* in 1906.

Page 85: Devoy wrote of his belief that Parnell was prepared to go more than half-way to meet the Fenians on 7.3.1879. The letter appears in *Devoy's Post Bag 1871–1928.*

Page 85: Devoy wrote of Davitt's lack of tact and social standing in article XIV of his series in the *Gaelic-American* in 1906.

Chapter 6: 'THE ONLY ISSUE UPON WHICH IRELAND CAN BE UNITED IS THE LAND QUESTION'

The chapter heading is my transposition into the present tense of a statement made by Michael Davitt in the *Irish World* in 1882: 'When I was in prison I spent my time thinking of what plan could be proposed which would unite all Irishmen upon some common ground. ... The only issue upon which ... each and every shade of opinion existing in Ireland could be united, was the land question.'

Page 88: William Bence Jones wrote of the stupidity of preferring boggy, rocky Connaught to the magnificent lands of North America in his book *A Life's work in Ireland of a Landlord who tried to do his Duty.* Published at the end of 1880 as he was being boycotted, it was an unremitting, repetitive attack upon the Irish.

Page 89: The drunkenness, indolence and ignorance of the Irish, *ibid.*

Page 89: The Irish ability to bargain, *ibid.*

Page 89: Ireland as a backward, barbarous country, *ibid.*

Page 90: The description of the peasant cabins in Mayo as being the very worst dwellings the reporter had seen appears in an article in the *Daily Telegraph*, 14.11.1880.

Page 90: The construction and dimension of the Connaught hovels is quoted from Daniel Grant's *Land Tenure in Ireland.*

Page 90: The officer who had lately served with honour in Zululand made his comments about the conditions of the Mayo peasants to the *Daily Telegraph* reporter, 14.11.1880.

Page 91: The purpose of the Irishtown meeting was printed in the *Connaught Telegraph*, 19.4.1879.

Page 91: It was Tim Healy who said that Davitt would have been the Father of the Land League had he not missed the train in his *Letters and Leaders of my Day.*

Page 91: The resolution that the tenant farmers were determined to resort to every lawful means to regain their inalienable rights was printed in the *Connaught Telegraph*, 26.4.1879.

Page 92: That Irishtown was a neat little hamlet on the borders of Mayo, Galway and Roscommon, *ibid.*

Page 93: Davitt's belief that a commonsense plan of semi-revolutionary action was the most that could be expected from a Fenian-constitutional merger was stated in *The Fall of Feudalism.*

Page 94: The Archbishop of Tuam's letter in which he said that an Irish MP had unwittingly expressed his readiness to attend the Westport meeting was printed in the *Freeman's Journal,* 6.6.1879.

Page 95: Parnell's telling Davitt he would certainly attend the meeting because he had promised to do so is quoted from Davitt's *The Fall of Feudalism.*

Page 95: Davitt's opinion that it was the most courageously wise act of Parnell's whole political career, *ibid.*

Page 96: The description of the central procession of young men wearing green scarves, and of the banners carried, was reported in the *Connaught Telegraph,* 14.6.1879.

Page 96: Davitt's general resolution on Irish self-government, *ibid.*

Page 96: His calling the Zulus a race of savages, *ibid.*

Page 96: (footnote) Parnell's remark about Davitt being stoned by the farmers if they had understood him was made to William O'Brien and is quoted from his *Recollections.*

Page 97: His urging the crowd never to forgo their hereditary rights to the soil, *ibid.*

Page 97: His statement that no power on earth could stand in the way of victory if the Irish remained faithful to their principles, *ibid.*

Page 97: The voice calling from the crowd that the Archbishop of Tuam had never written the letter is from the *Connaught Telegraph,* 14.6.1879.

Page 98: His definition of a fair rent, *ibid.*

Page 98: His call to the tenant farmer to keep a firm grip on their homesteads, *ibid.*

Page 98: That the meeting had been a glorious triumph, *ibid.*

Page 98: That it should be viewed as evidence of communism in Connaught was stated in the Dublin *Evening Mail,* 10.6.1879.

Chapter 7: 'COMMUNISM IN CONNAUGHT'

The chapter heading was the Dublin *Evening Mail's* view of events in Connaught, as above, 10.6.1879. The Communism it had in mind was that of the Paris Commune in 1870, but the connotation was the same as if written today in a right-wing paper.

Page 100: Davitt stated that the gospel of manhood was as vital to the success of the Land League as the cry 'the land for the people' in *The Fall of Feudalism.*

Page 101: That Boycott played the tyrant in every shape and form was stated in the tenants' letter to Lord Erne, 25.9.1880, and is quoted from *Lord Erne and his Lough Mask Tenantry: Correspondence in Reference to the Agency of Captain Boycott*, a pamphlet produced in 1880.

Page 103: Details of the Kildarra estate and Boycott's purchase of it are contained in the document entitled 'Abstract of the title of Annie Boycott to Kildarra, Barony of Costello, Co. Mayo, with map from and L.E.C. rental' (MG 123 LA 23 and 29, Public Records Office, Dublin). I am grateful to Mr Mac Giolla Choille, the Keeper of Manuscripts at the State Paper Office in Dublin for bringing this particular information to my attention.

Page 104: Davitt wrote to Devoy that the Home Rulers were alarmed by the new agrarian movement and that Parnell was afraid to lead it on 23.8.1879. The letter is quoted from *Devoy's Post Bag 1871–1928*.

Page 105: Parnell's Limerick speech was reported in *The Times*, 1.9.1879.

Page 105: Davitt said that he had a long conversation with Parnell about the desirability of forming a National Land League in his evidence to the Special Commission, 2.7.1889.

Page 105: Devoy's belief that Davitt wanted Parnell as leader of the Land League and not seeing himself as titular head is quoted from *Devoy's Post Bag*.

Page 105: His further conviction that Davitt saw himself as the power behind the throne and resented Parnell's usurpation of the leadership, *ibid.*

Page 106: Davitt stated that it was necessary for the Land Leaguers to accept Parnell's parliamentary platform because the extremist Irish leaders would have nothing to do with the New Departure in *The Fall of Feudalism*.

Page 107: That the latest Sunday afternoon amusement in Ireland was attending Land League meetings was stated in *The Times*, 6.10.1879.

Page 108: Davitt's assertion that the Ballinrobe meeting was the greatest honour he had received in Mayo is from the *Connaught Telegraph*, 11.10.1879.

Page 108: Davitt said his Sligo speech was very violent and not very wise in his evidence to the Special Commission, 2.7.1889.

Page 108: Davitt was referred to as a convict at large on a ticket-of-leave in the House of Commons, 26.6.1879. (Hansard, vol. 247.)

Chapter 8: 'FORTY MILLION WELCOMES TO THE IRISH PEOPLE'S CHAMPION'

The chapter heading is from the headline of the *Irish World* of 10.1.1880, an issue devoted to Parnell's arrival in the United States. The full headline ran: 'Forty million welcomes to the Irish people's champion of land and liberty!'

Page 111: Davit wrote to J. J. O'Kelly about the urgent need for money on 22.10.1879. The letter appears in *Devoy's Post Bag*.

Page 112: That Parnell replied to the address of welcome in a brief and appropriate manner was recorded in the *Irish World,* 10.1.1880.

Page 112: That he was greeted by multitudinous *cead mille failthes* at the Fifth Avenue Hotel, *ibid.*

Page 113: The *Daily News* comment on Parnell's being invited to address the House of Representatives was reprinted in the *Irish World,* 14.2.1880.

Page 114: The *New York Herald* accused Parnell of stalking around the country preaching treason against his native government on 20.2.1880.

Page 114: Parnell's retort that the *Herald* had embarked upon a much harder task than the discovery of Livingstone in choosing to support Irish landlordism was made at a speech in Rochester, New Jersey, 28.1.1880. It was printed in the *Irish World,* 7.2.1880.

Page 114: The speech in which he said that Irishmen should be prepared to shed the last drop of their blood, *ibid.*

Page 114: Parnell's famous last link speech was made in Cincinatti on 23.2.1880, and published in the *Irish World,* 6.3.1880.

Page 115: Healy's description of Parnell as the uncrowned King of Ireland was reported in the *New York Herald,* 10.3.1880.

Page 117: Devoy's comment that the Irish-Americans were looking for the qualities of mind and leadership to cope with the hard-hearted Englishman and thought they saw them in Parnell is quoted from *Devoy's Post Bag.*

Page 117: Tim Healy described the Parnell family as the most extraordinary he had come across in *Letters and Leaders of My Day.*

Page 118: His belief that Mrs Parnell was a little off her nut, *ibid.*

Page 118: The family's apparent indifference to each other, *ibid.*

Page 118: Parnell's religious beliefs or lack of them, *ibid.*

Page 120: Davitt's early boycotting speech at Knockaroo on 22.1.1880 is quoted from the evidence given to the Special Commission, 7.11.1889.

Page 120: That there were signs of the wild waves of democracy surging round Ireland's shores was stated in the Dublin *Evening Mail,* 23.3.1880.

Chapter 9: 'CIVIL WAR AND ANARCHY WILL END THE DRAMA'

The chapter heading is from an article in the *Connaught Telegraph,* 7.8.1880. Commenting on the rejection of the Compensation for Disturbance Bill by the House of Lords it said: 'Civil war, and anarchy, with defeat to the accursed system of landlord atrocity, which is based on their alleged rights to the privileges and liberties of the people, will end the drama. Who will be responsible? The so-called Lords who comprise the Upper Chamber of the modern Babylon.'

Page 121: Gladstone confessed that he had been unaware of the severity of the Irish crisis during a speech made at Edinburgh, 1.9.1884.

Page 123: Parnell's phenomenal flight among the Irish constituencies in March

1880 was described in an anonymous pamphlet *Parnellism* by 'An Irish Nationalist' – nationalist in this case meaning an upholder of the Union.

Page 126: (footnote) It was T. P. O'Connor who said the Tory Chief Secretary Lowther had a mind of medieval and impenetrable ignorance in *The Parnell Movement.*

Page 126: (footnote) Lowther's opinion that the depression in Connaught was not as acute as existed in other parts of the United Kingdom, *ibid.*

Page 126: (footnote) Lowther said that the land laws had no connection with the present state of Ireland in a speech made on 6.2.1880. The remark is quoted from Tim Healy's *A Word for Ireland.*

Page 127: Gladstone's statement that a sentence of eviction was near to a sentence of death for Irish peasants was made in the House of Commons during a debate on the Compensation for Disturbances Bill, 5.7.1880. (Hansard, vol. 253.)

Page 127: Lord Randolph Churchill stated that the Bill was 'the commencement of a campaign against the landlords; it was the first step in a social war; it was an attempt to raise the masses against the propertied classes' in the same debate, 5.7.1880. (Hansard, vol. 253.)

Page 128: Forster's letter hoping that Gladstone would show the necessity of doing something about Ireland was written on 25.6.1880. (Gladstone Papers, add mss 44157, British Museum.)

Page 128: Queen Victoria's comment on the Liberals in the House of Lords voting against their party is contained in *The Letters of Queen Victoria*, 2nd series, edited by G. E. Buckle.

Page 128: John Bright's comment that the House of Lords appeared to be declaring war on Ireland is quoted from Davitt's *The Fall of Feudalism.*

Page 128: Joseph Chamberlain's comment that the rejection of the Bill meant the declaration of civil war is quoted from N. D. Palmer's *The Land League Crisis.*

Page 128: It was Chamberlain's friend and biographer, J. L. Garvin, who said that no more foolish vote than the rejection of the Bill was recorded in the annals of the Lords, in his biography *Joseph Chamberlain.*

Page 128: Davitt called it the House of Landlords in *The Fall of Feudalism.*

Page 129: That Forster undertook the post of Chief Secretary in the spirit of a soldier sent to the front was observed by T. Wemyss Reid in his *Life of W. E. Forster.*

Page 129–130: Randolph Churchill's more malicious assessment of the spirit in which Forster undertook the task is recorded in Winston Churchill's *Lord Randolph Churchill.*

Page 130: That Forster was the best stage Yorkshireman currently on the scene was stated by Frank H. Hill in his essay on Forster in *Political Portraits.*

Page 131: Forster's unfortunate reference to the humaneness of buckshot which earned him his nickname was made in a debate on the state of Ireland on 23.8.1880. (Hansard, vol. 255.)

*Chapter 10: '*WHAT MR PARNELL MEEKLY DESIGNATES
SOCIAL OSTRACISM*'*

The chapter heading is from the Dublin *Daily Express*, 18.10.1880. It was commenting on Parnell's Ennis injunctions, with specific reference to Lady Montmorres, who was being subjected to a mild form of ostracism.

Page 134: That the members of the Ennis crowd shouted 'Shoot him' when asked what to do with a land-grabber was reported in *The Times*, 20.9.1880.

Page 134: Parnell's instructions on the better, more charitable, more Christian way to treat a land-grabber, *ibid.*

Page 135: Frank Hugh O'Donnell said that boycotting had been invented by Michael Davitt in his Knockaroo speech in *A History of the Irish Parliamentary Party*.

Page 135: Forster's belief that the policy of deliberate, merciless boycotting dated from Parnell's Ennis speech is quoted from T. Wemyss Reid's *The Life of W. E. Forster*.

Page 137: The sudden impulse that made the crowd rush to Lough Mask House was commented upon in the *Connaught Telegraph*, 25.9.1880.

Page 138: Father O'Malley urging the journalists to partake of whiskey so early in the day was recorded in the *Illustrated London News*, 11.12.1880.

Page 139: James Redpath wrote of the ruined cabin in Straide where Davitt threw out the flag of the land war and prophesied that in time to come it would be regarded as the Runnymede of the Irish People in the article 'Welcome to an Irish Statesman' in his *Talks About Ireland* which he dedicated to Davitt.

Page 139: Boycott said that his servants left under threat of ulterior consequences in his letter to *The Times*, 18.10.1880.

*Chapter 11: '*A SIGHT UNPARALLELED IN ANY CIVILISED
COUNTRY*'*

The chapter heading is my adaptation of Bernard Becker's description of his first sight of Captain and Mrs Boycott as they tried to herd their sheep: 'I came upon a sight which could not be paralleled in any other civilised country at the present moment.' It is quoted from his first despatch on 24.10.1880.

Page 144: That Lord Montmorres in his more intoxicated moods arrived at decisions that astonished even his brother magistrates was reported in the *Connaught Telegraph*, 2.10.1880.

Page 144: That the Montmorres murder was an act of intimidation against the landlords was reported in *The Times*, 1.10.1880.

Page 144: The Dublin *Evening Mail*'s assertion that it was the coping stone of an edifice of lawless outrage appeared on 27.9.1880.

Page 145: James Redpath recorded the conversation with Father O'Malley which brought the word 'boycott' into being in the section 'An Exile of Erin' in his *Talks About Ireland.*

Page 145: It was Michael Davitt who called Father O'Malley the neologist of an immortal term in *The Fall of Feudalism.*

Page 146: That Boycott used the timber freely for his own use was stated in the tenants' first letter to Lord Erne, 25.9.1880, reprinted in the pamphlet *Lord Erne and His Lough Mask Tenantry.*

Page 146: The postscript requesting an early reply addressed to Mr David Connor but not to Boycott, *ibid.*

Page 149–50: Bernard Becker's description of the shepherd and shepherdess inexpertly trying to herd their sheep appeared in his first despatch to the *Daily News* entitled 'The Isolation of Captain Boycott', written on 24.10.1880. All his articles on Ireland were later published in book form under the title *Disturbed Ireland.*

Page 150: Becker's description of the wretched Connaught hovels which would bring down a torrent of indignation on an English landlord's head is similarly quoted.

Page 154: The *Freeman's Journal* denounced the promoters of warlike expeditions in Ulster in 5.11.1880.

Chapter 12: 'A NARROW ESCAPE FROM AN ORANGE INVASION'

The chapter heading is from Forster's letter to Gladstone of 9.11.1880, in which he said: 'We have had a narrow escape from an Orange invasion of Connaught which would have been civil war.' (Gladstone Papers, add mss 44157, British Museum.)

Page 157: That the honest Ulstermen were picturing Boycott holding Ekowe against bloodthirsty Connaught Zulus was stated in the *Freeman's Journal*, 5.11.1880.

Page 158: The information about Boycott's race with Mr Nally appeared in *Vanity Fair*, 29.1.1881.

Page 159: That the town of Ballinrobe presented an untoward appearance on the day Boycott attended the Petty Sessions was admitted in the *Ballinrobe Chronicle*, 6.11.1880.

Page 160: The *Belfast News Letter* quoted Boycott as saying that the spirit of terrorism towards him was increasing on 6.11.1880.

Page 160: Forster wrote to Gladstone on 8.11.1880 that he had obtained information 'that large bodies of men were going from the North to Captain Boycott's farm' and that if they were allowed to do so the result would be civil war because the whole countryside would be up against them. (Gladstone Papers, add mss 44157, British Museum.)

Page 160: He further wrote in the same letter 'We send down to Boycott's district tonight 500 infantry and 3 squadrons of cavalry, and we tell Boycott that we will do what we have always promised to do etcetera.'

Page 161: Forster's memo requesting that the military stations at Ballinrobe be instructed to patrol the roads near Boycott's house was sent on 4.11.1880. (CSO RP 1880/27094, State Paper Office, Dublin Castle.)

Page 162: Mr Forster's statement that it was not usual for the government to communicate matters of news to the press is from the *Freeman's Journal*, 9.11.1880.

Page 163: Forster's reference to the unfortunate event of Captain Boycott, *ibid.*

Page 163: His allusion to the very strong collision the descent of armed men would occasion, *ibid.*

Page 164: That the government had done nothing to suppress the malignant power of the Land League was stated in the Dublin *Daily Express*, 9.11.1880.

Page 164: The government's unexpected resolution in thwarting the benevolent purpose of the relief expedition, *ibid.*

Page 165: That the arrangements for a relief expedition could not be made in a day, *ibid.*

Page 165: The newspaper which most notably coined the phrase 'the invasion of Mayo' was the *Freeman's Journal*, using it as the heading for all its reports on the Boycott expedition.

Page 167: The unusual scene on Broadstone terminus was described in the *Irish Times*, 9.11.1880.

Page 167: The poor soldiers standing in the rain at Claremorris was described in the *Connaught Telegraph*, 13.11.1880.

Page 167: The conglomeration of redcoats, baggage and general disarray on arrival, *ibid.*

Page 167: The inefficiency of the Army Service Corps and the commissariat, *ibid.*

Page 168: The story of the colonel of Hussars lying on the ground all night is from the *Freeman's Journal*, 12.11.1880.

Page 168: That the Boycott expedition was the most exciting topic of the day was reported in *The Times*, 10.11.1880.

Page 168: Ballinrobe was described as the headquarters of the nearest approach to any army since 1793 in the *Freeman's Journal*, 11.11.1880.

Page 169: The lusty cheers of the harvesters for Parnell, scotching the rumour of two thousand Ulstermen arriving in Claremorris, *ibid.*

Page 170: The Ulstermen in the role of armed filibusters, *ibid.*

Page 170: The placard in Claremorris urging the men of the barony to march on Lough Mask, *ibid.*

Page 171: Bernard Becker wrote of hearing the news that the Boycott brigade was actually going to invade Lough Mask on 10.11.1880, and the article was reprinted in his book *Disturbed Ireland*.

Page 171: His description of the army camp at Ballinrobe, *ibid.*

Page 171: His description of the slight, spare figure of Boycott, *ibid.*

Page 171: The text of the tenants' letter to Boycott, *ibid.*

Page 172: That the tenant's action in offering to pay the disputed rents should be viewed as an act of hostility rather than as a surrender was reported in the *Freeman's Journal*, 12.11.1880.

Page 172: Becker's hearing the expedition described as 'the Ulsterior force' was reported in his despatch on 10.11.1880, reprinted in *Disturbed Ireland*.

Page 172: His belief that the descent of the Ulster volunteers was a hideous infliction on Boycott, *ibid.*

Chapter 13: 'THE QUEEREST MENAGERIE THAT EVER CAME INTO CONNAUGHT'

The chapter heading is a comment made to *The Times* reporter about the relief expedition and its accompanying army: 'Bedad, Sur, it's the queerest menagerie that ever came into Connaught,' printed in *The Times*, 15.11.1880.

Page 175: The Monaghan contingent was said to be composed of stout, respectable young men in the *Belfast News-Letter*, 11.11.1880.

Page 175: Colonel Lloyd's speech in which he referred to the bludgeon men of Mayo was reported in the *Belfast News-Letter*, 11.11.1880.

Page 176: That the Monaghan contingent had been given an ample quantity of tobacco to consume during their sojourn in Mayo, *ibid.*

Page 176: The Cavan volunteers were described as stalwart, respectable and quiet in the Dublin *Daily Express*, 12.11.1880.

Page 176: The report that a high official of Dublin Castle had permitted the men to travel with revolvers, *ibid.*

Page 177: The list of supplies for the expedition, *ibid.*

Page 178: The Ballyhaunis crowd hooting at the train with perfect impartiality, *ibid.*

Page 178: The shouts asking why the blackguards did not come out of the train were reported in *The Times*, 12.11.1880.

Page 178: The instructions for the extra cavalry and infantry escort from Castlebar are contained in CSO RP 1880/27728 (State Paper Office, Dublin Castle).

Page 179: That Major Coghill was the uncle of the Lieutenant Coghill slain on the retreat from Isandula was reported in the *Freeman's Journal*, 11.11.1880.

Page 180: The description of the relief expedition looking as if it had stepped from the Belfast slums is from the *Freeman's Journal*, 12.11.1880.

Page 180: The volunteers were described as looking as nervous as half-hanged dogs in the *Connaught Telegraph*, 13.11.1880.

Page 180: The labourer asking James Daly what sort of man Boycott was and Daly's reply that he was not worth all the fuss, *ibid.*

Page 180: That Mr Manning and Captain Somerset Maxwell were got up in campaigning frieze was reported in the *Freeman's Journal*, 12.11.1880.

Page 180: The Claremorris women describing the volunteers as 'Boycott's angishores', *ibid.*

Page 182: The men of the 76th Regiment calling out 'Charge him' during the altercation about the carriages, *ibid.*

Page 182: The news that the relief column was three miles behind eliciting responses more suitable to bird-cage walk was recorded in the *Belfast News-Letter*, 12.11.1880.

Page 183: Bernard Becker said that the labourers looked terribly knocked-up in his despatch written on 12.11.1880 and reprinted in *Disturbed Ireland.*

Page 183: The uncomplimentary remarks made to the cavalcade as it passed through Ballinrobe was noted in the Dublin *Daily Express*, 13.11.1880.

Page 184: The cries of the onlookers were reported in the *Connaught Telegraph* 20.11.1880.

Page 184: Bernard Becker described the convoy as being like a huge red serpent with black head and tail in his despatch of 12.11.1880, reprinted in *Disturbed Ireland.*

Page 184: The reception of the Ulster party by Boycott was described as the tamest and most unemotional possible in the *Connaught Telegraph*, 20.11.1880.

Page 185: It was noted that the men slept with their feet pointing towards the centre tent pole in the Dublin *Daily Express*, 13.11.1880.

Page 185: Becker described his Mayo friend's mouth watering at the prospect of Cavan and Monaghan fighting over the tents in his despatch of 12.11.1880, reprinted in *Disturbed Ireland.*

Chapter 14: 'THEY DUG OUT ALL HIS PRATIES AND THEY THRASHED OUT ALL HIS CORN'

The chapter heading is from the poem 'Bycut's Volunteers' printed in *The Nation*, 20.11.1880, as in the text.

Page 189: The editorial urging the people of Mayo to be cool, calm and resolute and to show the world that they were worthy of their traditions appeared in the *Connaught Telegraph*, 13.11.1880.

Page 189: That it was not due to the gentle persuasion of the Land League but to the government's firm action that peace had been maintained, was the view expressed in *The Times*, 13.11.1880.

Page 190: *Le Figaro* devoted its 'Correspondence Anglaise' column to 'Incident Boycott' on 17.11.1880.

Page 190: The *Freeman's Journal* complained about the wretched telegraph wire on 12.11.1880.

Page 190: The Dublin *Daily Express* made its comment about the difficulty of telegraphic communication on the same date.

Page 190: The absence of more startling news leading the correspondents to dilate minor matters was admitted in the Dublin *Daily Express*, 15.11.1880.

Page 191: The soldiers doing Gladstone, chopping down trees and being cheered as true sons of Hawarden Castle was reported in the *Ballinrobe Chronicle*, 20.11.1880.

Page 191: That the rumour that hundreds of armed men were *en route* from Tipperary would doubtless prove as baseless as other rumours was stated in the Dublin *Daily Express*, 15.11.1880.

Page 192: That the special war correspondents were full of anecdotes of Plevna, Zululand and the Franco-German war, *ibid.*

Page 192: Bernard Becker described the scarcity of accommodation in Ballinrobe in his despatch of 10.11.1880, reprinted in *Disturbed Ireland*.

Page 193: The war correspondents were described as thirsting for blood in the Dublin *Daily Express*, 16.11.1880.

Page 193: Father O'Malley's long poster in which he appealed for funds for the counter-expedition to Fermanagh was reprinted in the Dublin *Daily Express*, 16.11.1880.

Page 195: The text of O'Malley's second telegram to Brennan saying how disappointed the Mayo men were by Brennan's disapprobation was printed in *The Times*, 17.11.1880.

Page 196: The Land League committee's resolution urging that action be taken against the landlord organs of slander, *ibid.*

Page 196: The telegram advising the tenants to stay at home and let the landlord come looking for his rent was printed in the *Freeman's Journal*, 17.11.1880.

Page 196: The expedition to round up Boycott's missing herd of cattle was reported with great enthusiasm in the *Freeman's Journal*, 17.11.1880.

Page 197: That the sight of half a troop of Hussars guarding cattle was certainly unusual was noted in the Dublin *Daily Express*, 17.11.1880.

Page 197: Mr Nally and Mr Joyce's penetration of the camp was called an attack in the Dublin *Daily Express*, 18.11.1880.

Page 197: It was described as 'an irruption' by the *Freeman's Journal*, 18.11.1880.

Page 197: Mr Goddard treating the proposal to address the Ulsterman about the true gospel *au grand serieux*, *ibid.*

Page 198: Nally and Joyce being led back to the gates under escort after a lively exchange of compliments, *ibid.*

Page 199: Boycott's letter to the gentleman in Dublin in which he said he was in no mental state for active duty was published in the Dublin *Daily Express*, 18.11.1880.

Page 199: His comment that ruin faced him, *ibid.*

Page 199: The anonymous letter from Hebburn, *ibid.*

Page 200: That Colonel Twentyman was a good-hearted, gallant but choleric officer was stated in the *Freeman's Journal*, 19.11.1880.

Page 200: That no news of the smallest interest had emanated from Lough Mask was reported in the *Freeman's Journal*, 19.11.1880.

Page 201: That '*les gais irlandais*' had invented a new word, '*boycotter*', was stated in *Le Figaro*, 24.11.1880.

Chapter 15: 'AND NOTHING INTERRUPTED THEIR ENTER-
PRISING WORK BUT THE POURING RAIN FROM HEAVEN
AND THE WIND FROM MAAM TURK'

The chapter heading is from the poem 'Bycut's Volunteers' printed in *The Nation*, 20.11.1880, as in the text. The only amendment is the 'enterprising' straight rather than in dialect form.

Page 203: Davitt said he arrived back in Ireland in time to witness the discomfiture of Mayo landlordism in *The Fall of Feudalism*.

Page 203: His comment on the personality of Major Henri le Caron, the British spy, *ibid.*

Page 203: His meeting with J. W. Mackay, 'the Silver King', and the proposition Mackay put to him about settling the Irish nation in Nebraska or Colorado, *ibid.*

Page 206: That Captain Somerset Maxwell's presence at Lough Mask should be regarded as an electioneering manoeuvre appeared in the *Penny Pictorial*, 20.11.1880. Bernard Becker was among others who made this assertion.

Page 206: The charge against fifteen local inhabitants for unlawfully assembling and obstructing Captain Boycott is from the Dublin *Daily Express*, 23.11.1880.

Page 207: Mr Forster's memorandum regarding the use of army wagons for transporting Boycott's corn was written on 18.11.1880. (Box 2701, State Paper Office, Dublin Castle.)

Page 207: That none of the population touched his hat or wished the *Express* man 'Good morning', and the general change wrought in the Mayo population by the effects of the Land League, *ibid.*

Page 207: The ironic comment that this was an awful state of affairs appeared in *The Nation*, 27.11.1880.

Page 207: That the Ulstermen eventually allowed their photographs be taken for posterity was reported in the Dublin *Daily Express*, 26.11.1880.

Page 208: The words of Father O'Malley's poster urging the inhabitants to let their invaders go without interference are taken from *The Times*, 26.11.1880.

Page 208: Whether the pent-up fury of the defeated Mayomen would burst forth at the last minute was a question asked by the PA correspondent and reported in the *Freeman's Journal*, 26.11.1880.

Page 210: Father O'Malley's interview with the PA correspondent in which he said attention was only ever focused on Ireland by extraordinary events such as the Boycott expedition was printed in the *Freeman's Journal*, 26.11.1880.

Chapter 16: 'THERE WAS MUCH THAT WAS RIDICULOUS IN THE WHOLE BUSINESS'

The chapter heading is taken from an early assessment of the expedition in the *Penny Pictorial*, 20.11.1880.

Page 211: The more privileged occupants of the boathouse discovering the boat had been lifted from Lough Mask by the storm is from the Dublin *Daily Express*, 27.11.1880.

Page 211: The unfortunate coincidence of the hitch in the telegraphic arrangements, *ibid.*

Page 212: That the ground was strewn with the debris of the commissariat was noted in *The Times*, 29.11.1880.

Page 212: Boycott's letter of thanks as read aloud by Captain Maxwell, *ibid.*

Page 213: The disappearance of Boycott's rigid reserve and depression was noted in *The Times*, 29.11.1880.

Page 213: The replies of the volunteers after he had shaken hands with them is from the Dublin *Daily Express*, 27.11.1880.

Page 213: That the parting was considerably warmer than the greeting was noted in the *Belfast News-Letter*, 29.11.1880.

Page 214: The crisis in the outburst of sentiment, with Captain Maxwell and the Hussar lieutenant hugging each other, *ibid.*

Page 214: The departure of the queerest menagerie that ever came into Connaught is taken from the comment made to *The Times* reporter, 15.11.1880.

Page 214: Davitt related the story of Father O'Malley marching in front of the departing relief expedition and upbraiding the old lady in *The Fall of Feudalism*.

Page 215: Mr McSheehy's report on the departure, informing Dublin Castle that some troops and constabulary had been left at Lough Mask, was written on 30.11.1880. (CSO RP 29558, Box 2702, State Paper Office, Dublin Castle.)

Page 218: The threatening letters received by the proprietor of the Hamman Hotel were printed in the Dublin *Daily Express*, 2.12.1880.

Page 219: That Boycott would 'go 'ome and leave the country to the blarsted Irish' was a wish expressed in the *Irish World*, 13.11.1880. I have transposed it to the slightly later date as it undoubtedly still expressed their view.

Chapter 17: 'THE MORAL FORCE ARTILLERY OF THE LAND
LEAGUE – BETTER THAN ANY 81-TON GUN'

The chapter heading is an amalgamation of Michael Davitt's statement that Boycotting was the 'moral force artillery of the League warfare afterwards', and Randolph Churchill's assessment that it was better than any 81-ton gun, as in the text.

Page 221–22: The poem 'Bycut's Volunteer's' appeared in *The Nation,* 20.11.1880.

Page 222: The assertion that Boycott did not merit boycotting half as much as Bence Jones was printed in *The Nation,* 25.12.1880.

Page 223: Chamberlain wrote to Gladstone on 16.11.1880 saying that Boycott's position would be as intolerable as ever even if half the country was arrested. The letter is quoted from his book *A Political Memoir.*

Page 223: The impossibility of keeping intimidation at bay by means of military force was noted in *The Times* survey of the year's events which devoted considerable space to the Boycott affair, 31.12.1880.

Page 223: That boycotting had grown up with the suddenness of Jonah's gourd was stated by T. Wemyss Reid in *The Life of W. E. Forster.*

Page 223: Randolph Churchill's pithy assessment of boycotting as better than any 81-ton gun is quoted from Winston Churchill's *Lord Randolph Churchill.*

Page 224: The estimate of the cost of the Boycott relief expedition appeared in the *Irish World,* 4.12.1880.

Page 224: Davitt described Boycotting as the moral force artillery of the League warfare in *The Fall of Feudalism.*

Page 225: Gladstone said the subject of the land was weighing heavily on his mind in a letter written to Forster on 29.11.1880. (Gladstone Papers, add mss 44544, British Museum.)

Page 225: The figures showing Land League meetings and agrarian crimes were published in the Dublin *Evening Mail,* 27.1.1881.

Page 226: The use of Boycott branding irons for cattle was noted in *The Times,* 30.12.1880.

Page 226: The *Connaught Telegraph*'s view that boycotting was being considerably ill-used was reprinted in the *Ballinrobe Chronicle,* 15.1.1881.

Page 227: That the outrages had not yet begun and the hungry wolves of landlords should leave Ireland's holy isle immediately was the view expressed in the *Irish World,* 18.12.1880.

Page 227–28: Fanny Parnell's 'Hold the Harvest' was originally published in the *Boston Pilot,* and had appeared in most Irish nationalist papers by the autumn of 1880. It was reprinted in *Lays of the Land League.*

Page 230: That the court had seemed more like an opera house for most of the trial was a comment made in the Dublin *Daily Express,* 21.1.1881.

Page 231: A. M. Sullivan's statement that the position of the conqueror who did not assimilate himself was that of an arrow-head buried in human flesh is quoted from his *Speeches and Addresses.*

Page 231: That the judge addressed the jury through a clatter of teacups was noted in *The Times,* 26.1.1881.

Page 231: Parnell's cable to New York claiming victory for the Land League is quoted from Davitt's *The Fall of Feudalism.*

Page 231: Davitt's own claims that the League had beaten the government to smithereens was made in a long letter to John Devoy written on 16.12.1880. It is quoted from *Devoy's Post Bag.*

Chapter 18: 'I AM UNABLE TO SEE THAT WE CAN GET ON WITHOUT THE SUSPENSION OF HABEAS CORPUS'

The chapter heading is from Forster's letter to Gladstone, dated 26.11.1880, in which he said: 'On Thursday I shall bring before the cabinet my draft coercion, or, as it may be called, Protection Bill. I am very anxious not to insist upon more than is absolutely necessary but I am unable to see that we can get on without the suspension of the Habeas Corpus Act'. It is quoted from T. Wemyss Reid's *The Life of W. E. Forster.*

Page 234–35: Boycott's first long letter to Gladstone was written on 1.12.1880 and printed in *The Times* on 18.12.1880.

Page 235: Gladstone's reply asking in what way H.M. Government was expected to assist Captain Boycott was written on 14.12.1880 and published in *The Times* 18.12.1880.

Page 236: Boycott's reply saying he had lost £6,000 and wanted compensation was written on 16.12.1880 and appeared in *The Times* 18.12.1880.

Page 237: The final letter in which Boycott said he had been deluded by the government into thinking it was going to compensate him was printed in the *Ballinrobe Chronicle,* 5.2.1881.

Page 238: It was in a letter written to Gladstone on 8.11.1880 that Forster first put forward the view that old Fenians and Ribbonmen were the planners of the Land League. (Gladstone Papers, add mss 44157, British Museum.)

Page 238: Harcourt wrote to Joseph Chamberlain about the dreadfully demoralised Forster on 11.12.1880. The letter is quoted from Gardiner's *The Life of Sir William Harcourt.*

Page 239: Gladstone was described as being downright piteous after the decision to bring in coercion in a letter Joseph Chamberlain wrote to John Morley on 31.12.1880. It is quoted from Garvin's *The Life of Joseph Chamberlain.*

Page 241: Forster described Davitt as a most mischievous and dangerous agitator in a memorandum written on 19.1.1881. (Gladstone Papers, add mss 44158, British Museum.)

Page 241: Gladstone was described as leaping up and down from his seat like a hen on a hot gridiron in *Punch.* The quotation is taken from J. L. Hammond's *Gladstone and the Irish Nation.*

Page 241: Davitt's unfortunate metaphor of the wolf-hound of Irish vengeance bounding over the Atlantic was made in a speech in Kilburn and was printed in the Dublin *Evening Mail.* 17.1.1881.

Page 241: The Mail's ironic comment on the loss to literature Davitt's arrest would occasion, and the wolf-dog bounding over the Atlantic being a sight worth seeing, *ibid.*

Chapter 19: 'A GREAT BENEFIT FOR WHICH GRATITUDE IS DUE TO MR GLADSTONE'

The chapter heading is taken from the *Freeman's Journal*: 'A great benefit... for which the gratitude of the Irish nation is due to Mr Gladstone', as in the text.

Page 245: The arrival of the boycotted Boycott on American soil was reported in the *New York Herald,* 6.4.1881.

Page 245: That his arrival was an event of international interest was a comment in the *New York Daily Tribune,* 6.4.1881.

Page 245: Boycott's being accompanied by the same little band that held the fort at Lough Mask House is from the *New York Herald,* 6.4.1881.

Page 245: His description of his friend Ashton Weekes, *ibid.*

Page 246: The thick-set, middle-aged man in the tender and the three cheers for Captain Boycott, *ibid.*

Page 246: That he appeared on excellent terms with himself and the world, *ibid.*

Page 247: Boycott's view that the insane desire to farm the Irish land at all costs was the root cause of the trouble, *ibid.*

Page 247: His view of Parnell as a good leading man, *ibid.*

Page 247: That his views were on the heroic order but more moderate than might have been expected from a man who had rubbed shoulders with the roughest edges of the Irish character is from the *New York Daily Tribune,* 6.4.1881.

Page 247: That Boycott hoped to see Brooklyn Bridge and other big things in America is from the *New York Daily Herald,* 6.4.1881.

Page 248: James Redpath described Boycott and Blacker as birds of a feather in 'An Interview with James Redpath' which was reprinted in *Talks About Ireland.*

Page 248: His statement that the meeting of Boycott and Blacker was the best illustration of the law that like seeks like since the yellow fever met the cholera in New Orleans, *ibid.*

Page 249: Lord Hartington's remark that the parliamentary history of the year was the story of a single measure carried by a single man was printed in *The Times*, 27.8.1881.

Page 250: The great benefits of Gladstone's Land Bill were noted in the *Freeman's Journal*, 27.9.1881.

Page 251: (footnote) The parliamentary observer who compared Parnell's ability to change roles with Henry Irving's success in the dual roles of the Corsican brothers was Henry Lucy. It was actually made in September, 1880, but remained valid in August, 1881. It is quoted from *The Diary of Two Parliaments*, vol 1.

Page 251: That Gladstone delivered his speech in an extemporised hall in the old cloth-yard in Leeds was noted in *The Times*, 8.10. 1881.

Page 252: Gladstone's saying that Parnell appeared to wish to stand as Moses stood, but not as Moses stood to arrest the plague, *ibid.*

Page 252: His historic remark about the resources of civilisation not yet being exhausted, *ibid.*

Page 252: Parnell's Wexford speech in which he accused Gladstone of being a masquerading knight-errant is quoted from the *Freeman's Journal*, 10.10.1881.

Page 252: (footnote) Gladstone wrote to Lord Granville on 21.10.1881, saying he believed his cold was due to the excessive exertions in the Cloth Hall. The letter is quoted from *The Political Correspondence of Gladstone to Lord Granville*, (ed. Agatha Ram).

Page 253: Forster's opinion that Parnell had been moved by his tail was made in a letter to Gladstone, 26.1.1881. It is quoted from T. Wemyss Reid's *The Life of W. E. Forster*.

Page 253: His belief that boycotting must be beaten otherwise Parnell would beat the government, and that arresting the leaders was the only solution, was conveyed to Gladstone on 2.10.1881, and is quoted as above.

Page 253: Parnell's letter to Katharine O'Shea was written from Morrison's Hotel in Dublin as he was being arrested on 13.10.1881. It is quoted from her book *Charles Stewart Parnell, his love story and political life.*

Page 253: (footnote) The No-Rent manifesto issued from Kilmainham jail is quoted from Davitt's *The Fall of Feudalism.*

Page 255: Both Fanny Parnell's poems, on the Land Act of 1881 and 'Hold the Rent', were reprinted in the *Lays of the Land League*.

Page 256: The regimental orders of one of the secret societies were printed in H. O. Arnold Forster's *The Truth about the Land League, its Leaders and its Teachings*. Arnold Forster was W. E. Forster's adopted son, and sprang to his father's defence in this pamphlet, which had a great success.

Page 257: Mrs McDougall's article 'At Lough Mask House' appeared in the *Irish World*, 8.10.1881.

Page 257: That the people did not hold Boycott in much reverence on Achill island, *ibid.*

Page 258: That Boycott was the height of a great tyrant, *ibid.*

Page 258: Mrs McDougall's query about whether Boycott would have changed his views if put in the position of a serf, *ibid.*

Page 259: The agreement reached after Kilmainham that the nationalists would co-operate cordially with the Liberals is quoted from Conor Cruise O'Brien's *Parnell and his Party.*

Page 259: Queen Victoria's telegram asking whether it was possible that Davitt was being released is quoted from Gardiner's *The Life of Sir William Harcourt.*

Page 260: Davitt described Parnell's one man new departure in *The Fall of Feudalism.* It was a view shared by many on the Fenian side.

Page 260: Gladstone said in the House of Commons that the government had to deal with a different state of things in Ireland, that the social revolution was to be looked for in the foundation of the Land League. The date was 4.4.1882. (Hansard, vol. 268.)

Page 260: He said it was his firm opinion that the 1881 Land Act would not have become law without the Land League agitation during a debate on the Parnell Special Commission's report in the House of Commons, 3.3.1890. (Hansard, vol: 341.)

Page 261: John Dillon defended boycotting as a practice whereby the people of Ireland could defend themselves effectually and less violently than the previous methods of murder and incendiarism, in the House of Commons debate on the Prevention of Crime (Ireland) Bill, 24.5.1882. (Hansard, vol. 269.)

Page 261: Gladstone's reply in which he said that that which stood behind boycotting was the murder which was not to be denounced, *ibid.*

Page 261: William O'Brien said there was nothing like boycotting in a country like Ireland for keeping down outrages, that it was indubitably the peacemaker of Ireland, during his evidence to the Special Commission, 22.5.1889.

Page 262: He said that obstruction and boycotting were the two master keys to Parnell's success in his book *The Parnell of Real Life.*

Chapter 20: 'THE DEATH OF THE GENTLEMAN WITH WHOM THE NEVER-TO-BE-FORGOTTEN TERM "BOYCOTTED" ORIGINATED'

The chapter heading is taken from the *Norfolk News*, 26.6.1897: 'The death occurred on Saturday night of Captain Charles Cunningham Boycott at his residence, the Hollows, Flixton, near Bungay, at the age of 66 years. Captain Boycott, it will be remembered, was the gentleman with whom the never-to-be-forgotten term "boycotted" originated'.

Page 264: The first article on 'Parnellism and Crime' in which the Irish leaders were accused of being in intimate relations with avowed murderers, appeared in *The Times*, 7.3.1887. This article was written by Sir Robert Anderson, the former Assistant Police Commissioner who had ordered Davitt's arrest in 1870.

Page 264: That the Land League was a movement based on a scheme of assassination, *ibid.*

Page 264: The *Times* leader in which the English people were urged to shake off their flabby tolerance of evil and to realise that attacks upon the State by a contemptible minority of a minority could no longer be tolerated appeared on the same day, 7.3.1887.

Page 265: Parnell made his brief comments on *The Times* allegations, saying he had suffered more than any man from the terrible deed in Phoenix Park, and the Irish nation more than any nation, in the House of Commons, 18.4.1887. The remark is quoted from *Pleadings in O'Donnell v. Walter and Another and The Times.*

Page 269: It was John Macdonald who wrote of Boycott's name being as widely known as that of Homer, Moses, Dickens or Parnell in his *Daily News Diary of the Parnell Commission.*

Page 269: The description of Boycott with his rim of white hair and flowing beard, *ibid.*

Page 272: Parnell's comments on the findings of the Special Commission are quoted from F. S. Lyon's *Ireland Since the Famine.*

Page 272: Parnell's reference to Gladstone as 'the grand old spider' is quoted from Katharine O'Shea's book *Charles Stewart Parnell, his love story and political life.*

Page 273: Gladstone's comment on Parnell's death and fall was made personally to Barry O'Brien and is quoted from his *The Life of Charles Stewart Parnell.*

Page 275: Boycott's obituary, in which it was noted that he was stern and brusque of manner, appeared in the *Norfolk News*, 26.6.1897.

Page 275: The obituary in which it was noted that he was as popular as it was possible to be in his position as land agent appeared in the *Norfolk Chronicle* on the same date, 26.6.1897.

Page 275: The information about the creditor's suit against Annie Boycott on Monday 29 Day of November 1897 before Mr Justice Byrne at Chambers is contained in Chancery D. & O. 2288 J. 15 5001/5200. (Public Records Office, London.)

Page 275: The information about the further legal proceedings in Dublin is contained in M6 123 LA 23 and 29. (Public Records Office, Dublin.)

THE LIST OF ULSTERMEN INVOLVED IN THE RELIEF
EXPEDITION, TAKEN FROM THE BELFAST NEWS
LETTER, 15.11.1880

The Monaghan Contingent
James Carson, Monaghan
Joseph Porter, Monaghan
Robert Stewart, Monaghan
John Stewart Jun., Monaghan
Thomas Kerr, Monaghan
Joseph Wilson, Monaghan
William Wade, Monaghan
William Gillanders, Monaghan
Richard Tweedy, Monaghan
James Mills, Milltown
William Wilson, Milltown
Isaac Nesbitt, Milltown
Thomas Moorhead, Milltown
Jas Jeffers, Rossmore
William Madden, Rossmore
Samuel Gordon, Rossmore
Robert McBride, Tullyherim
Andrew McWilliams, Emyvale
David Boyd, Crosses
Thomas Graham, Crosses
William Smith, Ballinagall
John A. Hazlett, Anvagola
Joseph Miller, Killygavna
William McCoy, Carragh
Joseph McCormick, Aghaboy
Samuel Bateson, Strahan
Samuel Adams, Corlatt
Robert Hanna, Killydonnelly
Robert Thomas Hanna, Mullihara
John Thompson, Tirnaneill
Thomas McBirney, Knockacony
John Monaghan, Faulkland

The Cavan Contingent
George Smith
John Mullen
John Woods
Robert Gordon
William Hanna
William Stevens
G. Rodgers
George Montgomery
George Monaghan
Andrew Pollock
Samuel Wilson
Martin Beatty
William Moore
William Trevor
William Humphreys
John Smith
Samuel Dancy
John McClelland
John Ludlow
Thomas Byers
Moses Hyslop
Alexander Cox
John Carquedale
Robert Connolly
John Holyday

Bibliography

MANUSCRIPT MATERIAL

Gladstone Papers, British Museum.
Chancery Paper, Public Records Offices, London and Dublin.
Chief Secretary's Office correspondence, State Paper Office, Dublin Castle.

STATE PAPERS AND OFFICIAL PUBLICATIONS

Report of Her Majesty's Commissioners appointed to enquire into the workings of the Penal Servitude Acts, 1878–79. Vols. I, II and III.
Report of Her Majesty's Commissioners of Inquiry into the working of the Landlord and Tenant (Ireland) Act, 1870, and the Act amending the same, 1881. Vols XVIII and XIX. (The Bessborough Commission.)
Preliminary Report of Her Majesty's Commissioners on Agriculture, 1881. Vols XV and XVI.
The Special Commission Act 1888. Report of the proceedings before the Commissioners appointed by the Act (reprinted from *The Times*, London 1890).
Pleadings in O'Donnell v. Walter and Another and *The Times*. Articles . . . alluded to . . . in the same action. (H.M.S.O., 1888.)
Hansard's Parliamentary Debates, Third Series (1830–1891), vols 191, 220, 223, 247, 253, 255, 268, 269 and 341.

NEWSPAPERS AND JOURNALS

English:
Annual Register   *Norfolk News*
Daily News   *Penny Illustrated Paper*
Daily Telegraph   *Penny Pictorial News*
Graphic   *Standard*
Illustrated London News *The Times*
Norfolk Chronicle   *Vanity Fair*

Irish:

Ballinrobe Chronicle
Belfast News-Letter
Connaught Telegraph
Daily Express (Dublin)
Evening Mail (Dublin)
Freeman's Journal

Irish Felon
Irish Times
Mayo Constitution
Mayo Examiner
The Nation

Overseas:

Le Figaro
Gaelic–American
Irish World

New York Daily Tribune
New York Herald

CONTEMPORARY PAMPHLETS

Anon., *Ireland under the Land League*, Dublin, 1887.

Anon., *Parnellism and Crime*, London, 1887.

Anon., *What Science is Saying about Ireland*, Kingston-upon-Hull, 1881.

Audi Alteram Partem., *Irish Land as Viewed from British Shores*, London, 1880.

Bagenal, P. H., *The Irish Agitation in Parliament and on the Platform*, Dublin, 1881.

Blacker, Rev. R. S. C. MA, JP, *Erin, Her sister, her nurse and her doctor*, London, 1881.

Erck, Wentworth, *The Land Question*, Dublin, 1883.

Forster, H. O. Arnold, *The Truth about the Land League, its Leaders and its Teachings*, London, 1883 (third edition).

Fitzpatrick, Bernard, *A.B.C. of the Irish Land Question*, London, 1881.

George, Henry *The Irish Land Question*, New York, 1881.

Grant, Daniel, *Land Tenure in Ireland*, London, 1881.

Kinnear, John Boyd, *Ireland*, London, 1880.

Lord Erne and his Lough Mask Tenantry. Correspondence in Reference to the Agency of Captain Boycott, Dublin, 1880.

Nulty, Doctor Thomas (Bishop of Meath), *Letter to Joseph Cowen, M.P., on the State of Public Affairs in Ireland*, Dublin, 1881.

—— *The Land Agitation in Ireland*, Manchester, 1881.

Pim, Joseph T., *Ireland in 1880*, London, 1880.

Sinclair, W. J., *Irish Peasant Proprietors – a Reply to the Statement of Mr Tuke*, Edinburgh and London, 1880.

Tuke, James H., *A Visit to Donegal and Connaught in the Spring of 1880*, London, 1880.

Walters, John T., MA, *Ireland's Wrongs and How to Mend Them*, London, 1881.
Webb, T. E., *Confiscation or Contract?* Dublin, 1880.

N.B. Prior to 1900 places of publication only are given, post 1900 both publishers and place.

BOOKS

Abels, Jules, *The Parnell Tragedy*, London: Bodley Head, 1966.
Anderson, Sir Robert, *Sidelights on the Home Rule Movement*, London: Murray, 1906.
Barton, Sir Dunbar Plunket, *Timothy Healy: Memories and Anecdotes*, Dublin: Talbot Press, 1933.
Battiscombe, Georgina, *Mrs Gladstone: The Portrait of a Marriage*, London: Constable, 1956.
Becker, Bernard, *Disturbed Ireland*, London, 1881.
Blunt: Wilfred Scawen, *The Land War in Ireland*, London: Stephen, Swift, 1912.
Fashman, D. B., *The Life of Michael Davitt*, London: Washbourne, 1923. (Reprinted from an earlier edition.)
Chamberlain, Joseph C., *A Political Memoir 1880–1892* (edited from the original manuscript by C. H. D. Howard), London: Batchworth, 1953.
Clancy, James J., *The Land League Movement*, New York, 1881.
Churchill, Winston, *Lord Randolph Churchill*, London: Macmillan, 1906.
Corfe, Tom, *The Phoenix Park Murders*, London: Hodder & Stoughton, 1968.
Curtis, Edmund, *History of Ireland*, London: Methuen, 1936.
Davitt, Michael, *The Fall of Feudalism in Ireland, or the story of the Land League Revolution*, New York: Harper, 1904.
—— *Leaves from a Prison Diary: or lectures to a 'solitary' audience*, London, 1885.
—— *The Land League Proposal*, Glasgow, 1882.
—— *The Prison Life of Michael Davitt: related by himself*, Dublin, 1886.
Devoy, John, *The Land of Eire: the Irish Land League*, New York, 1882.
—— *Recollections of an Irish Rebel*, New York, 1929 (reprinted I.U.P., 1969).
—— *Post Bag 1871–1928*, (edited William O'Brien and Desmond Ryan). Dublin: Fallon, 1948 and 1953.
Dickinson, Emily, *A Patriot's Mistake: being personal recollections of the Parnell Family*, Dublin: Hodges, Figgis, 1905.
Dun, Finlay, *Landlords and Tenants in Ireland*, London, 1881.
Ervine, J. G. St John, *Parnell*, London: Ernest Benn, 1925.

Flatley, P. J., *Ireland and the Land League: the Key to the Irish Question*, Boston, 1881.

Gardiner, A. G., *The Life of Sir William Harcourt*, London: Constable, 1923.

Garvin, J. L., *The Life of Joseph Chamberlain*, vols. 1, 2 and 3. London: Macmillan, 1932, 1933 and 1934.

Gladstone, Mary, *Her Diaries & Letters* (edited Lucy Masterman). London: Methuen, 1930.

Gladstone, Viscount, *After Thirty Years*, London: Macmillan, 1928.

Good, J. W., *Michael Davitt*, Dublin: Cumann Leigheacht an Phobail, 1921.

Hammond, J. L., *Gladstone and the Irish Nation*, London: Longmans, 1938. (Reprinted by Frank Cass, 1964.)

Haslip, Joan, *Parnell*, London: Cobden-Sanderson, 1936.

Harrison, Henry, OBE, MC, *Parnell Vindicated*, London: Constable, 1931.

—— *Parnell, Joseph Chamberlain and 'The Times'*, Dublin: Browne & Nolan, 1953.

—— *Parnell, Joseph Chamberlain and Mr Garvin*, London: Robert Hale, 1938.

Healy, T. M., *Letters and Leaders of my Day*, London: Thornton Butterworth, 1928.

—— *Why there is an Irish Land Question and an Irish Land League*, Dublin, 1881.

—— *A Word for Ireland*, Dublin, 1886.

Hill, F. H., *Political Portraits*, London, 1873.

Horner, Charles F., *The Life of James Redpath*, New York: Baise & Hopkins, 1926.

Hurst, Michael, *Parnell and Irish Nationalism*, London: Routledge, 1968.

James, Robert Rhodes, *Lord Randolph Churchill*, London: Weidenfeld, 1959.

Jones, W. Bence, *The Life's Work in Ireland of a Landlord who tried to do his Duty*, London, 1880.

Lalor, James Fintan, *Collected Writings*, Dublin; Talbot Press, 1918.

Leslie, Sir Shane, *Studies in Sublime Failure*, London: Ernest Benn, 1932.

Lloyd, Clifford, *Ireland under the Land League*, London, 1892.

Locker Lampson, Godfrey, *A Consideration of the State of Ireland in the 19th Century*, London: Constable, 1907.

Lucy, Henry W., *The Diary of Two Parliaments 1874–1880 and 1880–1885*, London, 1885 and 1886.

—— *Sixty Years in the Wilderness*, London: Smith Elder, 1909.

Lynch, Arthur, MP, *Ireland: Vital Hour*, London: Stanley Paul, 1915.

Lyons, F. S. L., *The Fall of Parnell 1890–1891*, London: Routledge, 1960.

—— *Ireland Since the Famine: 1850 to the present*, London: Weidenfeld, 1971.

McCarthy, Justin, *Reminiscences*, London: 1899.

—— *The Story of an Irishman*, London: Chatto & Windus, 1904.

—— *Irish Recollections*, London: Hodder & Stoughton, 1911.

—— *Our Book of Memories – Letters of Justin McCarthy to Mrs Campbell Praed*, London: Chatto & Windus, 1912.

McCarthy, Michael J. F., *The Irish Revolution*, London: Blackwood, 1912.

Macdonald, John, *Daily News Diary of the Parnell Commission*, London, 1889.

MacDonagh, Michael, *The Life of William O'Brien*, London: Ernest Benn, 1928.

—— *The Home Rule Movement*, London: Fisher Unwin, 1920.

Magnus, Philip: *Gladstone*, London: Murray, 1954.

Mansergh, Nicholas, *The Irish Question: 1840–1921*, London: Allen & Unwin, 1965 (revised edition of *Ireland in the Age of Reform & Revolution*, 1940).

—— *Britain and Ireland*, London: Longmans, 1946.

Moody, T. W., *Essays in British and Irish History in Honour of James Edie Todd*, (*editor*), London: Muller, 1949.

—— *Michael Davitt and the British Labour Movement 1882–1906*, Transactions of the Royal Historical Society, 5th series, vol. 3, 1953.

Moore, George, *Parnell and his Island*, London, 1887.

Morley, John, *The Life of William Ewart Gladstone*, London: Macmillan, 1903.

—— *Recollections*, London: Macmillan, 1921.

O'Brien, Conor Cruise, *Parnell & His Party, 1880–1890*, O.U.P., 1957.

—— (editor) *The Shaping of Modern Ireland*, London: Routledge, 1960.

O'Brien, R. Barry, *The Life of Charles Stewart Parnell*, London, 1898.

O'Brien, William, *Recollections*, London: Macmillan, 1905.

—— *Evening Memories*, Dublin: Maunsel, 1920.

—— *The Parnell of Real Life*, London: Fisher Unwin, 1926.

O'Donnell, Frank Hugh, *A History of the Irish Parliamentary Party*, London: Longmans, 1910.

O'Connor, T. P., *The Parnell Movement*, London, 1889.

—— *Gladstone, Parnell and the Great Irish Struggle*, New York, 1887.

—— *Charles Stewart Parnell: A Memory*, London, 1891.

—— *Memoirs of an Old Parliamentarian*, London: Ernest Benn, 1929.

O'Flaherty, Liam, *The Life of Tim Healy*, London: Cape, 1927.

O'Hara, M. M., *Chief and Tribune: Parnell and Davitt*, Dublin: Maunsel, 1919.

O'Hegarty, P. S., *A History of Ireland Under the Union 1801–1922*, London: Methuen, 1952.

O'Neill, Brian, *The War for the Land in Ireland*, London: Martin Lawrence, 1933.

O'Shea, Katharine, *Charles Stewart Parnell – his Love Story and Political Life*, London: Cassell, 1914.

Palmer, N. D., *The Irish Land League Crisis*, Yale U.P., 1940.

Parnell, John Howard, *Charles Stewart Parnell*, London: Constable, 1916.

Pigott, Richard, *Personal Recollections of an Irish Journalist*, Dublin, 1882.

Pomfret, John E., *The Struggle for the Land in Ireland*, Princeton U.P., 1930.

Ramm, Agatha (editor), *The Political Correspondence of Mr Gladstone and Lord Granville 1876–1886*, O.U.P., 1962.

Redpath, James, *Talks about Ireland*, New York, 1881.

Reid, T. Wemyss, *The Life of the Rt. Hon. William Edward Forster*, London, 1888.

—— (editor), *The Life of William Ewart Gladstone*, London, 1899.

Russell, Charles, QC, MP, *New Views on Irish Land Grievances: Remedies*, London, 1880.

Russell, G. W. E., *Portraits of the Seventies*, London: Fisher Unwin, 1916.

—— *One Look Back*, London: Wells, Gardner, Darton, 1912.

Ryan, Desmond, *The Phoenix Flame: A Study of Fenianism and John Devoy*, London: Arthur Baker, 1937.

Shaw Lefevre, J. G., *English and Irish Land Questions*, London, 1881.

—— (Lord Eversley), *Gladstone and Ireland*, London: Methuen, 1912.

Sherlock, Thomas, *The Life of Charles Stewart Parnell*, Dublin, 1882 (reprinted Parkside Press, 1945).

Skeffington, F. Sheehy, *Michael Davitt: Revolutionary, Agitator and Labour Leader*, London: Fisher Unwin, 1908.

Strauss, E., *Irish Nationalism and British Democracy*, London: Methuen, 1951.

Sullivan, A. M., *Speeches and Addresses 1859 to 1881*, Dublin, 1886.

Sullivan, T. D., *Songs and Poems*, Dublin, 1899.

—— *Recollections of Troubled Times in Irish Politics*, Dublin: Gill, 1905.

—— *Lays of the Land League*, Dublin, 1887.

Sullivan, Maev, *No Man's Man*, Dublin: Browne & Nolan, 1943.

Thornley, David, *Isaac Butt and Home Rule*, London: MacGibbon & Kee, 1964.

Tynan, Katharine, *Memories*, London: Everleigh Nash, 1924.

—— *Twenty-five Years*, London: Smith Elder, 1913.

White, Terence de Vere, *The Road of Excess*, Dublin: Browne & Nolan, 1946.

Index

Index

Cavendish, Lord Frederick, 264, 265

The Celt, 49n

Central Land League of the Ladies of Ireland, 254-5, 260

Chamberlain, Joseph, 128, 129, 223, 239

Chester Castle, failure of arms raid on, 38-9, 73

Church Act (1869), 40-1, 42, 45, 46

Churchill, Lord Randolph, 127, 129-30, 223

Cincinnati (USA), Parnell's speech in (1880), 114-15

Clan na Gael, 111n, 116; creation of, 66; Davitt's US tour sponsored by, 78-9; dominated by middle-class, 79-80 &n; views on Irish land question, 80; support for Parnell by, 92-3, 113, 230

Claremorris (Mayo), 215, 248, 256; army reinforcements sent to, 161-2, 167, 168, 178-9; Ulster Relief Expedition, 169, 170, 175, 177, 178-82; and Boycott family's departure, 216-17

Clarke, Thomas, 30, 34

Clerkenwell prison, 39

Cockcroft, Mr (of Haslingden Post Office), 72, 73

Coercion Act (1881), 239-43, 250, 255

Coercion Bill (1886), 263-4

Coghill, Major, 167, 178, 179, 181, 200, 215, 222

Common Law rights, 24

Compensation for Disturbance Bill (1880), rejected, 127-9, 130-1

Connaught Telegraph, 33-4, 91, 92, 94, 98, 108, 129, 137, 144, 167-8, 179, 184, 189-90, 248

Connor, David, 146

Convention Act, 100

Crawford, Mr (leader of Boycott Relief Expedition), 175

Crom Castle, Fermanagh, 60, 146, 193, 194, 195, 196

cruelty to animals, 226

Curragh (Mayo), 101, 157

Daily Express (Dublin), 151, 152, 163, 164-6, 170, 176, 177, 178, 183, 185, 186, 190, 191, 192, 196, 197, 199, 200, 204, 206, 207, 208, 211, 230, 270

Daily News (London), 113-14; 'The Isolation of Captain Boycott' in, 148-51

Daily Telegraph (London), 200

Daly, James, 19, 108, 179, 180, 188

Dartmoor prison, 74, 75

Davitt, Michael, 55, 70, 104, 111, 118, 123, 125, 128, 144, 154, 189, 207, 214, 224, 231, 254 & n, 256, 266, 270; formative years in Lancashire, 71-2; right arm amputated, 72; joins Fenians, 72-3; sentenced to 15 years penal servitude, 73-4; appearance, 75; favours Fenian-Home Rule merger, 76, 77, 78, 80; meetings with Parnell, 76, 78; returns to Ireland, 76-7; American lecture tour of, 78-9, 82, 84, 203-4; Ford's support for, 79-80; attitude to New Departure, 82-3; attends IRS meeting in Paris, 83-4; land reform agitation of, 84, 85, 87-92; 1879 Dublin meeting with Parnell and Devoy, 92-4; and Westport meeting, 94-8; Mayo Land League inaugurated by, 99-101; his resentment of Parnell, 105-6; National Land League formed, 104, 106-7; arrested on seditious language charge, 108-9; Knockaroo speech initiates boycott campaign, 119-20, 135, 139, 269; against physical violence, 227; arrest of, 240-2; and released, 259; his role in Land League movement, 260-1; Parnell Special Commission and, 269, 271, 272; last years and death, 275-6

Day, Mr, 236

Devon Commission, 23, 24